W9-BLF-401

Please remember that this is a library book,
and that it belongs only temporarily to each
person who uses it. Be considerate. Do
not write in this, or any, library book.

TOBACCO AND AMERICANS

ROBERT K. HEIMANN

Tobacco and

Americans

NEW YORK : TORONTO : LONDON

McGraw-Hill Book Company, Inc.

ACKNOWLEDGMENTS

Any book which aims to be definitive owes much to writers and
record-keepers of past generations, many of them unknown. However, the author wishes to name and thank these contemporary
authorities for their valued aid and encouragement:

Charles E. Gage, pioneer in the field of U.S. Government tobacco
statistics, who gave the manuscript a painstaking scrutiny and made
many constructive suggestions.

Jerome E. Brooks, renowned tobacco scholar and annotator of the
Arents Collection, who read the text critically from the standpoint
of his specialty.

Sarah A. Dickson, Curator of the Arents Collection of the New
York Public Library, and Bella Landauer of the New York Historical Society, who opened their rich files of pictorial material for use
in this book.

R.K.H.

TOBACCO AND AMERICANS

What shapes the pattern of a society's growth?

This is a perennial question among social scientists and historians. Those who favor the Great Man Theory of history answer it in terms of political leaders. Others offer the economic formula, supply and demand. Anthropologists point to the "cake of custom"—the day-to-day mores and living habits of people in groups—as the basic heritage from which all civilization is compounded. Climate, war, geography, the diffusion of inventions and ideas from culture to culture are other explanations advanced from time to time as the emphasis of the social studies shifts.

After pursuing each of these theories in its turn, the student concludes that a nation's growth can hardly be explained in terms of any single factor. Custom cannot be explained apart from climate; supply and demand, war, great men and geography are all part of a mixture that makes men what they are, and at the same time provides the impetus for them to change.

These many influences show up clearly in a socio-economic cross-section, such as this account of Americans and tobacco. In some ways, a close look at a single facet of society can be more revealing than an attempt to encompass all facets at once.

The evolution of the tobacco business, linked closely with the growth of America itself, has been affected by all the factors with which the various schools of history deal. Climate regulated the growth of tobacco in the first place. The American Indian made it part of his "cake of custom." The various forms of taking tobacco were diffused, like inventions, to the Old World and back to the New by the mariners of Portugal, Spain, Holland and Great Britain. Its usefulness as a creature comfort has been dramatized in a series of wars. The demand for it in Europe was the economic base on which the Virginia and Maryland colonies were established. Sir Walter Raleigh, who planted the first English-speaking colony in this country, is thought of as the first English promoter of the "bewitching vegetable." Tobacco was the reason for Maryland's settlement by George Calvert and

his sons. A famous Colonial general, Israel Putnam, introduced the Cuban cigar to New England and another general, Ulysses S. Grant, became its living testimonial. And great men like Washington and Jefferson—both warriors and heads of state—played as prominent a role in tobacco as they did in statecraft itself. The story of Americans and tobacco contains grist for the mill of the sociologist as well as the economist and for that of the historian as well as the agriculturalist.

A casual look at the tobacco industry, which spends $150 million a year to advertise, might suggest that smoking — like foam rubber sofas and V-8 engines — owes its vogue to promotion. During the last century virtually every significant change in smoking habits has been heralded in a massive way by brand advertising.

But a closer examination shows that tobacco itself (as distinct from competing brands) requires less promotion than almost any other commodity except, perhaps, for food. Unlike the glittering new conveniences of the Machine Age, tobacco is a traditional pleasure. Through the centuries, ordinary men have prized the pleasure of smoking with no prompting whatsoever. The Spanish sailors in Columbus' little fleet adopted tobacco from the West Indians before their commanders understood the reason for its cultivation. London dandies sought it in the seventeenth century when it was worth its weight in silver, and their descendants cheerfully pay the British equivalent of 50c for twenty twentieth-century cigarettes. Americans drew their first livelihood from tobacco, used it as currency, grew it in their gardens for home use, chewed it on the open plains, puffed it in cabin or in camp, and carried it for barter. The doughboys of War I, the G. I. Joes of War II, and the drafted citizen-soldiers of the Korean War smoked under any and all circumstances.

Tobacco originated in America; it was this nation's first business; Americans brought it to its present stage of development. The story of tobacco is somewhat more than a business history. It is, in many ways, the story of America itself.

Searching for mineral wealth, the first explorers of the New World ignored the aromatic vegetable smoked and chewed by the North American natives. Europeans saw tobacco as savage incense or salve.

CERTAIN DRIED LEAVES

THE written history of Americans and of tobacco begins on October 12, 1492, when Christopher Columbus reached the beaches of San Salvador in the West Indies. According to the Admiral's journal, published some years afterward, the natives brought fruit, wooden spears, and "certain dried leaves" which gave off a distinct fragrance. The Spanish sailors in Columbus' command welcomed the fruit; the dried leaves they threw away.

Three days later, while cruising among the islands, the Admiral found a solitary Indian in a canoe. In addition to bread and water, he carried the same kind of dried leaves and made a great show of offering them to the white strangers in the white-winged vessels. No doubt the Spaniards wondered why the strange leaves were so highly valued.

The following month they found out why. Two sailors, Rodrigo de Jerez and Luis de Torres, were dispatched on a three days' reconnaissance across

Cuba, bearing letters of introduction to the Khan of Cathay. The Indians, they reported, wrapped the dried leaves in palm or maize "in the manner of a musket formed of paper," and after lighting one end inhaled the smoke through the other. To keep them glowing the Indians blew on the lighted ends between puffs, a gesture still common to cigar connoisseurs the world around. One of the two scouts, de Jerez, became a confirmed tobacco smoker, probably the first European to do so.

Smoke-filled hemisphere

As later voyagers were to discover, the New World was full of confirmed smokers, and had been for hundreds of years. What is more, every form of tobacco consumption—pipe, cigar, cigarette, snuff, chew—had become accepted custom long before the first Spaniards landed. The Caribs of the West Indies inhaled or snuffed a mixture that may have

included tobacco through a hollow Y-shaped tube called a *taboca* or *tobago*. This word was applied as "tabaco" to the leaf itself by the Spanish, and was later used to describe the *mousqueton* or roll fancied by the Cuban natives. To this day, a cigar in Cuba is "un tabaco." Cortez found Mexican Indians devoted to tobacco; in the well-developed civilization of the Aztecs, he observed an established use of flavored reed cigarettes. Countless tribes in what are now the United States and Canada smoked their tobacco in straight pipes — war pipes, peace pipes, and simple pleasure pipes—called "calumets" by the French explorers. The Quiché Mayans, like their Cuban contemporaries, were fond of cigars and may have originated the "smoke-filled room" of politics, since their councils were illuminated by fat-pine torches and accompanied by fat cigars. According to some etymologists their word for tobacco was "ziq" and their word for smoking

"zikar" — which may have prompted the Spanish word "cigarro." Even the use of plug tobacco was observed at the end of the sixteenth century — in Santo Domingo, by the famous Samuel de Champlain who was later to found Quebec.

In almost every region of the New World, the natives had a word for tobacco. In Brazil, it was *petum;* in Aztec Mexico, *picietl;* in Virginia, *uppowoc;* along the St. Lawrence, *quiecta;* in Peru, *sayri;* in Colombia, *yuri;* in Trinidad, *vreit.* What was the basic attraction that led the original American tribes to cultivate and cherish, each in its own way, the unique plant known to the English as the "Soverane Herb"? Oddly enough, the question cannot be answered in precise scientific terms even now.

Still, the widespread popularity of tobacco in pre-Columbian years is strikingly evident from its prominence in the reports of the first white explor-

7

Americans of the fifteenth century used tobacco in all forms known today. The taboca or Y-shaped snuffing-stick of Haiti may have named "tobacco."

Amerigo Vespucci saw Venezuelans with a green herb —"which they chewed like cattle to such an extent that they could scarcely talk . . . to allay thirst."

ers. Each thought he was chronicling something unique. In a sense this was true, for each saw the use of tobacco through his own haze of prejudice and preconception. Some saw it as religious ritual, some as medicine, some as a thirst-quencher, some as a vile heathen intoxicant, some as a primitive balm. Nevertheless it is illuminating to "discover" tobacco again through the eyes of the first white men to see it in the hemisphere of its origin.

Venezuela quid

Amerigo Vespucci reached Margarita Island off the coast of Venezuela in 1499, and there saw the natives chewing a "green herb which they chewed like cattle to such an extent that they could scarcely talk." The reason for this excessive use of "chaw" may well have been the lack of water on Margarita, whose sole supply of fresh water is its rainfall. As every chewer of tobacco knows, plug or twist induces salivation, so it is not surprising that each of Vespucci's Indians carried his supply of "green herb" in a gourd around his neck — the original tobacco pouch.

A similar observation was made in a life of Columbus which appeared in 1571, supposedly written by his son Ferdinand. In exploring Veragua (Costa Rica), the Admiral's brother met a cacique or chieftain and a score of men "putting a dry herb in their mouths and chewing it, and sometimes they put a certain powder that they carried together with that herb."

In their westward search for the East Indies, the Spaniards were everywhere greeted with tobacco. Cortez landed in Tabasco in 1519 and was immediately offered the leaf as a gesture of good will by the natives. He was, however, no more interested in tobacco than in peace. Not long after Cortez and company plundered the Aztec capitol at Mexico City, Fernando de Alarcón pushed farther west, reaching the mouth of the Colorado River on the Gulf of California in 1540. The Indians there, he reported, "carry their pipes with which to perfume themselves like the Tavagi people (Tobago inhabitants) of New Spain."

Cabral's cure-all

With the credulous enthusiasm characteristic of explorer nations, the Spanish, Portuguese and British pounced on tobacco as a miraculous panacea.

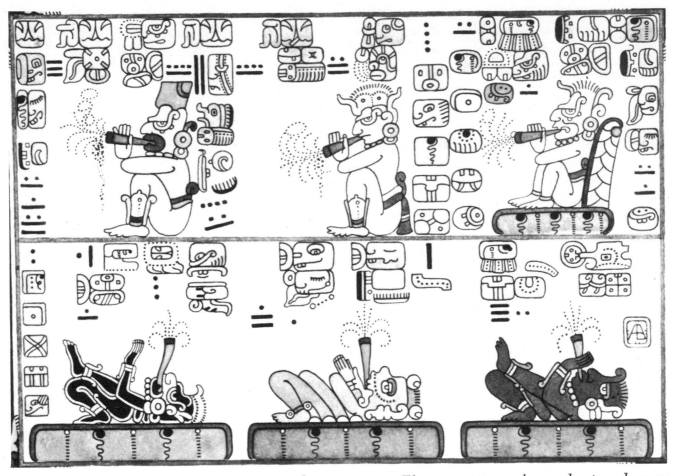

In Brazil, Central America and the West Indies—the tropical belt—cigar smoking was a prominent custom. These squatting and recumbent smokers are Aztecs, who seem very earnest about their puffing.

Dozens of scholars listed it as a cure for almost every known disease (later, skeptics listed it as a cause of almost every known disease). But neither the fanciful notions of the early herbalists nor the vigorous objections they prompted were greatly to influence the spread of the "witching weed" as an item of commerce.

In 1500, only eight years after Columbus' landfall, Pedro Alvarez Cabral and his Portuguese fleet veered off course and accidentally discovered Brazil. His description of tobacco did not see print until the Lisbon historian Damiâo de Goes published a 1571 work on the people of Sancta Cruz, of Brazil:

> They have many odoriferous and medicinal herbs different from ours; among them is one we call fumo (smoke, i.e., tobacco) which some call Betum and I will call the holy herb, because of its powerful virtue in wonderful ways, of which I have had experience, principally in desperate cases: for ulcerated abscesses, fistulas, sores, inveterate polyps and many other ailments.

The Portuguese were then at their peak as a great seafaring people, which is reflected by the fact that one of the most popular designations of tobacco in 16th-century Europe was their term, "herba sancta." This name is made even more logical by the nature of the tobacco rites among the Tupinambas of Brazil, as observed by Cabral:

> They carry a calabash made like the head of a man, with mouth, nostrils, eyes and hair, placed on the top of an arrow, within which they make smoke with dried leaves of the plant betum, and the smoke which is in the head they inhale to such an extent that they are drunk.

The "they" refers to the shamans or sorcerers: their prophecies uttered during the tobacco ritual were believed to be inspired by the gods.

Open eyes, closed minds

The reactions of the first *discubridores* and *conquistadores* like Columbus, Vespucci, Cabral, Cortez and Alarcón present an odd paradox. In spite

9

of the fact that they were innovators in a geographical sense, their values were those of a set social system. They would endure excruciating torture to seek out stores of existing wealth, but they lacked any notions of developing demand, of mass marketing, of capitalistic enterprise. So rigid was their concept of wealth that they were unable to see, for a time, the new wealth they had sailed so far to find.

The economic values of those early Spaniards and Portuguese were no more rigid than their social and religious beliefs. Automatically, as a matter of course, their physical conquests were accompanied by attempts to conquer the heathen spiritually, by force if need be. This contempt for savage beliefs blinded them to the nature of tobacco usage. Because the leaf was associated with heathen worship, they saw, or fancied, only the religious or medicoreligious significance of the leaf. So they described it as a curiosity, or at most as a curative. Their eyes were open, but their minds were not: they were incapable of understanding any religious or economic values that were not their own.

To the native Americans, on the other hand, wealth was not something to be hoarded but something to be used. Their gold took the form of plates, utensils, ornaments — not money. The Aztecs, for example, used the cacao bean as a medium of exchange, an item of everyday use which was too perishable to hoard. The economy of Mexican tribes and those to the north were fluid, dynamic, oriented to consumption. Where the Spanish suffered and thirsted and died in the deserts for their gold standard, the original Americans existed by and large for their standard of living.

So with the appeal of tobacco staring them in the face, the military captains and learned scholars missed its social and economic significance completely. Only after they actually lived among the savages did they realize that the leaf was an everyday custom as well as a pagan incense.

One of the most revealing, and amusing, statements by a "conscientious objector" to tobacco is that of Manoel de Nóbrega, who journeyed to Brazil in 1549 for the purpose of converting the heathen Indians:

> No one of our brothers uses it, nor does any other of the Christians, in order not to imitate the unbelievers who like it very much. I need it because of the dampness and my catarrh, but I

In Mexico, eastern U.S. and Canada, farming tribes cultivated Nicotiana rustica — a small-leaved type so bitter it was generally smoked through a pipe.

abstain — not what is useful for myself but what is good for many that they may be saved.

Nóbrega clearly expresses the germ of the opposition tobacco was to meet through the centuries.

Creature comfort

Nóbrega's solemn attitude was not shared by Gabriel de Sousa, who followed him to Bahio. "Certain of the chiefs, who are in council," he wrote, "take rolls of tobacco which they drink . . . all take it in turn." This referred neither to medical practise nor to religious ritual, but rather to communal custom like the "smoke-filled room" of the Mayans and the pipe-passing traditions of the Indians of the United States. De Sousa also noted that the most important aspect of all — the use of tobacco as a creature comfort — was, even in 1567, quite common among the whites and halfbreeds, who walked about with rolls of tobacco in their mouths, puffing constantly.

Across the Andes, Miguel Balboa made similar

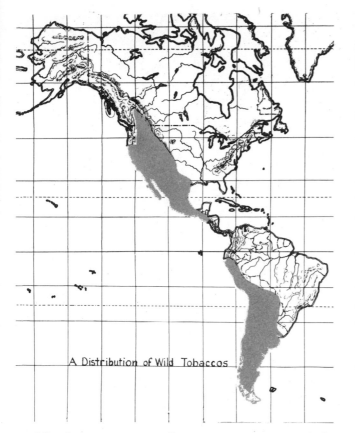

Wild tobaccos of several species grew west of the cordillera, mainly in temperate zones. It too was harsh and small-leaved—yet the natives smoked it.

Tall, broad-leaved tobacco—Nicotiana tabacum, the commercial species—originated in Brazil or Central America. It was mild enough to smoke in cigar form.

observations among the Incas of Peru late in the sixteenth century. Not only tobacco but also coca was involved in the rites of the priests. In their long second-hand descriptions of tobacco, several European "herbalists" described the milder variety of tobacco as "henbane of Peru" and other explorers wrote of its magical effects — as, for instance, in curing wounds made by poisoned arrows (!) It is clear enough that *Nicotiana tabacum,* soon to be a prime luxury throughout the world, was extensively grown and used across the upper half of South America and in Central America. At the same time the use of "yellow henbane," as the coarse *Nicotiana rustica* was first called, had long been cultivated by most of the tribes between Mexico City and the St. Lawrence, from the Mississippi-Missouri basin east to the Atlantic.

The origin of "tall tobacco," the commercial species, was in northern South America and Central America — in general, the tropical and subtropical belt of the hemisphere. This fits in not only with

botanical evidence, but also with the immediate appeal the species held for Portuguese sailors who carried it from Brazil. Since the first Spanish missionaries observed "two kinds" of tobacco in Mexico, it is apparent that the mild species was widely grown in at least the southern half of that country. The prominence of cigar smoking in the Mayan culture — whose relics include the oldest known records of tobacco use—suggests that the luxuriant jungles of Chiapas (Mexico's southernmost province) and adjacent Guatemala may have cradled the first *Nicotiana tabacum.* Human "relics"—primitive Lacandon tribes who may be descendants of the Maya — were found by American explorers in 1951 growing the plant in patches of cleared jungle, along with corn and beans. Like the ancients of their region, they chain-smoke cigars of their own making. It may be only a coincidence that these shy, savage people, virtually buried alive in matted greenery, pursue their tobacco custom within a hundred miles of Palenque, where the first sculp-

In Brazil, André Thevet in 1555 noted that petun (tobacco) was believed to be "wonderfully useful for several things." One use was medicinal: here a sick man is being "fumigated" with smoke from a large cigar. Another shakes a tammaraka or rattle —now a musical rather than a medical instrument.

tured picturization of a smoker was found.

The native tobacco of the temperate zone east of the Rockies (northern Mexico through Southern Canada) was *Nicotiana rustica*. It was not, strictly speaking, a wild plant but required cultivation. Small-leaved, it was at first confused with yellow henbane (while the tall, broad-leaved plant was dubbed "henbane of Peru"). Because of its strength and bitterness, it was generally smoked in a pipe, often blended with milder leaves of various plants. There is no question about its use on the mainland from the latitude of Mexico City to that of the St. Lawrence. Because Yucatan tobacco was brought to Cuba and Haiti around 1534 by the Spanish, it is thought that the bitter, biting *rustica* was exclu-

sively cultivated in those islands before the white discoverers arrived. On the other hand, the West Indies were closer to Central America, Venezuela and Brazil than to mainland North America — in climate, race, and cultural contact via Arawaks and Caribs, as well as geographically. Perhaps both kinds of tobacco were grown by the pre-Columbian Antilleans.

So far as is known, the truly wild tobaccos — *Nicotiana petunoides* according to one classifier — flourish only in the temperate zones of both North and South America west of the continental divide. Diaries of the explorers and fur traders who pierced the American Northwest refer to a strange type of tobacco smoked by Indian tribes. The presumption

Thevet also noted the use of tobacco for pleasure, as shown in this woodcut from his book, published in 1557. "The Christians there today," he wrote, "have become very attached to this plant." Thevet introduced tobacco in France, although Jean Nicot, for whom Nicotiana is named, was given the credit.

is that this native leaf was wild *petunoides* rather than cultivated *rustica;* but it was so quickly supplanted for Indian use by Virginia leaf (then entering its third century of white cultivation) that its exact nature is unknown. What is known is that *N. tabacum,* aboriginal product of Brazil and Yucatan, is the leaf that supplanted all others — first for personal use, then for trading.

The power of petun

Brazil, of course, was closest to seafarers of the Latin countries and was the hub of the tobacco world for a time. There is a suspicion that the plant received one of its names, "Herba Santa Croce," from the earliest name of Brazil, Sancta Cruz,

rather than from the Cardinal Prospero di Santa Croce who is said to have brought tobacco from Portugal into Italy. However that may be, virtually all the earliest writings on Brazil take ample note of the region's tobacco culture. Three members of de Villegagnon's colonizing expedition of 1555 gave their impressions of the leaf, each coloring his account according to his own personality. Nicolas Barré wrote simply:

> I have seen a plant that they call Petun, the size of large confrey; they suck the juice and inhale the smoke of this. With this plant they can endure hunger eight or nine days.

Jean de Léry recalled that

> the priests of the Tupinamba tribe often taking a wooden cane, four or five feet long, at the end of

which there is some of the plant *petun* ... dried and lighted, turning to all sides and blowing the smoke on the other savages, they said: 'Receive the spirit of power, that you may conquer your enemies.'

And,

You will never see the Brazilians when they do not each have a tube of this plant hung around their necks. All the time and even in talking to you it helps keep them in countenance ... I will say that, having myself tried the smoke of *petun,* I have found that it refreshes and keeps one from feeling hungry.

André Thevet, third of Villegagnon's chroniclers, also observed that the Brazilians believed tobacco to be "wonderfully useful for several things." His account was more descriptive and also more enthusiastic:

They carefully gather this herb and dry it in the shade of their little cabins. When it is dry they enclose a quantity of it in a palm leaf which is rather large, and roll it up about the length of a candle. They light it at one end and·take in the smoke by the nose and the mouth ... Even when they are taking counsel they inhale this smoke and then speak ... The Christians there today have become very attached to this plant and perfume ...

Thevet's reference to shade suggests the modern practise of raising shade-grown tobacco for rolling mild cigar leaf. His word "candle" is apt, since the cigar shape called "corona" was later patterned by the Cubans after a candle. But the most interesting aspect of all is the indication that others among the 600 Frenchmen who accompanied Villegagnon took to tobacco. The attraction must have been immediate, for the colony lasted only a few years, the last survivors being wiped out by antagonistic Portuguese a dozen years after the ambitious French founded their "permanent" settlement.

Thevet brought the first tobacco to France in 1556 or 1557; the leaf he introduced was the mild Brazilian *Nicotiana tabacum* which is now smoked everywhere for pleasure. It is interesting that Thevet resisted the temptation to tell tall tobacco tales, and explicitly disavowed any value of the leaf as a wonder drug. Ironically, Thevet is virtually unknown except to scholars while Jean Nicot, who sent tobacco to the French court several years afterward in the guise of a panacea, thereby gave his name to the plant. No doubt ambassador Nicot's "diplomacy" in naming tobacco the Queen's Herb

As a curious herb of a strange new world, tobacco inspired tall tales among the scholars of Europe. This version of homo Americanus, with claws and almond eyes, is purely imaginary. His long cigar, however, probably resembled the real native thing.

in honor of Catherine de Medici had something to do with this. And the fact that he sent the pungent, small-leaved *rustica* — hardly fit for human consumption except in powdered pinches — had something to do with the vogue for snuff which pervaded French court society for two hundred fifty years.

A general human need

Thevet's observations on the use of tobacco as a creature comfort were echoed later by one Juan de Cárdenas, who wrote that the smoking of cigarettes, cigars and pipes was common among the white men in Mexico by the late sixteenth century. Like Thevet before him, Cárdenas was enthusiastic about tobacco — "this precious herb is so general a human need not only for the sick but for the healthy." As a practising physician, he could be more specific in his "prescriptions" for its use than Thevet the adventurer. Nevertheless he was not so narrow in his concept of tobacco's usefulness as his medical colleagues nor, in fact, as most of the first explorers. "Soldiers," he wrote, "subject to privations, keep off cold, hunger and thirst by smoking; all the inhabitants of the hot countries of the Indies alleviate their discomforts by the smoke of this blessed and medicinal plant." Perhaps, as a learned citizen of Mexico, Cárdenas could afford to be more searching and more philosophical than the visiting explorers whose tales of tobacco as a sorcerer's aid were intended to produce a dramatic effect. At any rate, he took the trouble to set down his observations in some detail:

> . . . some are accustomed to take it in small clay or silver pipes or those of hard wood. Others wrap the tobacco in a corn husk or in paper or in a tube of cane . . . The smoke which is taken in clay, silver or wood pipes is stronger, because only the plant is smoked and no other thing outside of it; whereas smoked in a leaf, in paper or in a reed the smoke is weaker, since it is not only the tobacco which is smoked but also the leaf or the reed in which it is contained . . .

Typically sensational was the account written by Girolamo Benzoni, an Italian who came to Central America in 1541. He noted that the certain dried leaves were

> very much prized by the slaves which the Spaniards brought from Ethiopia . . . And when they wish to use them they take a leaf of the husk of their grain, and putting one of the others in it, they roll them tight together, then they set fire

Tall tobacco, about man's height, was illustrated with greater accuracy since the plant itself was brought to Europe only a generation or two after the discovery of the New World. It was raised at first not as a creature comfort but as a cure-all.

to one end and, putting one end into their mouth, they draw their breath through it. Then the smoke goes into the mouth, the throat and the head, and they retain it as long as they can, because they feel a pleasure in it.

He then adds,

And there are some who take so much of it that they fall down as if they were dead and remain the greater part of the day or night unconscious . . . See what a pestiferous and wicked poison from the devil it is. It has happened several times to me only to smell it while going along the road, in the provinces of Guatemala and Nicaragua, or entering into the house of some Indian who had taken the smoke, which in the Mexican language is called tabacco, and suddenly smelling the violent stench, I was forced to leave with speed.

Elsewhere north of Mexico explorers recorded tobacco in use both as a medicine and as a pleasurable custom. Giovanni de Verrazano explored the Atlantic Coast from North Carolina to New England in 1524 for Francis I of France, remaining 15 days in the Narragansett Bay area. "If afflicted with a wound," he related of the Indians, "they heal themselves with fire (tobacco smoke) without outcry." So another term for tobacco was coined: "heathen wound plant." Better known and more factual was the observation of Jacques Cartier, who voyaged the St. Lawrence River in 1534 and 1535.

They also have a plant of which they gather a great supply in the summer to last during the winter. This they prize very much, and only men use it, in the following manner. They dry it in the sun and carry it on their necks in a small animal skin, instead of a bag, with a pipe (cornet) of stone or wood . . . they never go anywhere without these things. We have tried this smoke; after taking some into our mouths it seemed like pepper it was so hot.

This, to be sure, was *Nicotiana rustica,* the northern leaf. Cartier's seared taste buds were an adequate explanation why cigar smoking was not popular among the tribes having no access to the large-leaved *Nicotiana tabacum* of South and Cen-

Jacques Cartier, who voyaged the Saint Lawrence in 1534, described the tobacco smoked by the Indians in pipes: "it seemed like pepper it was so hot."

Earliest known drawing of the calumet, or straight pipe, was made by Father Hennepin, who explored the Great Lakes and upper Mississippi in 1679-80.

tral America. Pipe-smoking was then the most acceptable way to consume strong tobacco, and remains so to the present day.

The classic description of tobacco in North America was furnished by Jacques Le Moyne de Morgues, who accompanied René de Laudonnière's 1564 expedition to Florida. Le Moyne not only described the life of the natives but turned out forty-seven paintings of them. One of several which illustrated smoking was captioned:

> . . . They also have a plant which the Brazilians call *petum* and the Spaniards *tapaco*. After carefully drying its leaves, they put them in the bowl of a pipe. They light the pipe, and, holding the other end in their mouths, they inhale the smoke so deeply that it comes out through their mouths and noses . . .

Enter the English

The same year Sir John Hawkins landed at Laudonnière's Fort Caroline and carried back to England this description of pipe smoking:

Accuracy of Hennepin's sketch is shown by modern photograph of Indian with his calumet or "pipe of peace." Feathers were highly prized but optional.

Sir Francis Drake landed in California about 1579, afterwards wrote that "the people came every day, with feathers and small bags filled with Tabaco."

> The Floridians when they travel have a kind of herb dried, which with a cane, and an earthen cup at the end, with fire, and the dried herbs put together, do suck through the cane the smoke thereof, which smoke satisfieth their hunger, and therewith they live four or five days without meat or drink . . .

Appended to this description of native custom is a curious comment on the French settlers' attitude toward tobacco:

> . . . and this all the Frenchmen used for this purpose: yet do they hold opinion withal, that it causeth water and flame to void from their stomacks . . .

Thus among the Europeans the appetite for tobacco was at variance with their intellectual distrust of any native custom, including smoking. This puritanical contradiction was to reappear many times in the later history of Europeans, Americans and tobacco.

Hawkins and his men were said to have introduced tobacco into England, and this is likely in view of the many voyages he made to the New World. The other sea-adventurers of the Elizabethan age, including Sir Francis Drake, followed thick and fast. They searched for the Northwest Passage, traded in the West Indies, fought the Spaniards, rounded Cape Horn, and explored the Pacific. Drake touched at California in 1578 or 1579, and his chronicle says "The people came every day, with feathers and small bags filled with *Tabaco*."

17

Pipes were a nearly-universal form of smoking and probably the oldest. The highly-developed culture of the Mayas included both the tubular pipe (black figure, bottom) and elbow pipe with bowl (figure at top center). Cigarette wrapped in cane and cigar in tobacco wrapper were "self-burning" tube pipes.

Pipe's progress

Among the native tribes up and down the hemisphere, pipe-smoking was the universal form of consuming tobacco. Even the Tupinambas of Brazil and the Mayans of Yucatan, favored with gentle *Nicotiana tabacum*, smoked the weed in pipes as well as cigars. The Mayans knew both the tubular pipe or "cane" and the elbow pipe with its upright bowl. There was hardly a culture in North or South America that did not leave some kind of pipe among its silent relics.

Botanical evidence also suggests that the pipe came first. Wild *Nicotiana* species, which had the widest distribution, were all small-leaved and hence unsuitable for rolling into cigars. Such tobacco was crumbled or even powdered, then tamped into a tubular receptacle to be lighted. The first known picture of the tobacco plant printed in Europe (1570) was accompanied by a diagram of a smoking tube used by Indians and sailors. This was not the ordinary tube pipe of stone, wood or clay, since the spiral twists of a flexible wrapper appear quite plainly (page 40). It could be called a palm-wrapped cigar or cigarette or, more precisely, a transitional stage between the tube pipe made to take a filler of crushed *Nicotiana rustica* and the cigar, a roll of fragrant broadleaf filler wrapped in a smooth leaf of the same. The appearance of this *puro* — the leaf, the whole leaf, and nothing but the leaf — must have followed the appearance of the tube pipe or palm funnel just as *Nicotiana tabacum* followed its wild parent plant.

The tobacco tradition, like all mores, is evolutionary rather than revolutionary. The first use of

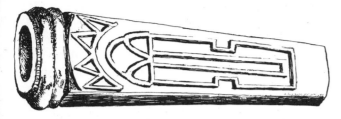

Tube pipe of San Juan Pueblo near Santa Fe. Used by priest in prayer for rain, it is called cloud-blower. Design signifies rain falling from clouds.

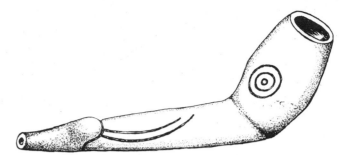

Elbow pipe of Aztec civilization, central Mexico. Logically, pipes appear among artifacts of ancient peoples simultaneously with origin of agriculture.

dark, rank tobacco — among Europeans just as among the Amerinds — required some dilution as a self-defense against tonguebite. Hence the pipe. Only the Spanish and Portuguese encountered growing broadleaf and were able to take over the advanced forms of smoking — cigars and cigarettes — from the savage Americans without repeating the evolutionary process themselves. Thus Seville smoked cigars and cigarettes for two centuries — roughly 1600 to 1800 — while the rest of Europe struggled with "nose warmers." Clay, a time-honored material for furnaces, was an obvious pipe material; the early pipes of Europe were stubby-stemmed "cutty pipes" or long-stemmed "church-wardens," both clay. In Turkey, the use of clay was varied with terracotta; in Alsace, with porcelain; and in Germany, with meerschaum, a light silicate. In the U. S. the classic variant was the "Missouri meerschaum" or corn-cob; in England a walnut

shell and straw likewise served the indigent.

Although it is their stone and pottery pipes which survive, the American Indians by and large smoked wooden pipes when the *conquistadores* and *discubridores* encountered them. Rosewood, cherrywood and Corsican briar root have evolved from the calumet.

The pipe was not the elementary form of tobacco consumption; no doubt chewing of tobacco came before it, as being not only possible but natural to the pre-cultural, or hunting-gathering stage. Pipes emerge as symbols of the transition to settled agriculture. It is yet another step before wild or semi-wild tobacco is replaced by the choice broadleaved species, and a quality of leaf good enough to smoke directly, in a self-consuming tube, is grown. But only sophisticated civilizations carry tobacco to the next phase, the "recipe" phase, where the already-delicate leaf is flavored and perfumed. At this stage

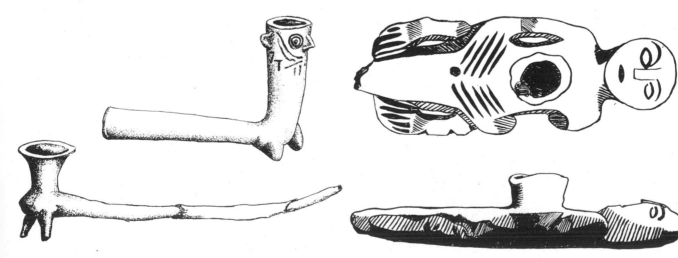

Upper pipe is from northern Chile, lower from the west coast of Mexico. Nicotiana rustica was grown along Pacific coast from Mexico to northern Chile.

Stone pipe with head-handle is from lower part of Chile. Pipes were smoked through North and South America a thousand years before Columbus landed.

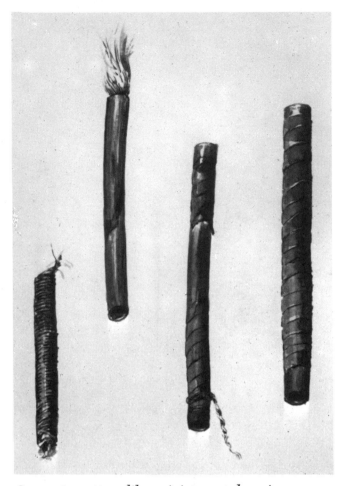

Cane cigarettes, like miniature tube pipes, were used by Pueblo Indians of New Mexico. Cigarettes are actual size; that on right is virtually the same size as 85-millimeter "king size" cigarettes.

Cigars were often tied with string, as in pottery picture of Maya. Posture of smoker, lack of ritual symbols show cigar's place in everyday activities.

the ritual of worship is one thing, the ritual of hedonistic living is another. For example, Bernal Diaz del Castillo recalled Montezuma's after-dinner custom:

> They also set upon the table three painted and gilded tubes containing liquidambar mixed with a certain plant they call *tobaco;* and when he finished eating, after they had sung and danced for him, and the table was cleared, he took the smoke of one of those tubes, and little by little with it he fell asleep.

The ambiguity of the word "civilization" can be realized from the fact that these same Aztecs also smoked ritual pipes on the sun-platforms where beating hearts were torn out of living humans as sacrifices to their deities. Be that as it may, the flavored reed-cigarette is not mentioned outside of Mexico and even there it was not a common article but a luxury. Cane cigarettes were used in what is now New Mexico by the settled but not sophisticated peoples of the desert pueblos; cane cigars by the Tupinambas of Brazil. These, however, were relatively crude forms of smoking — first cousins to the simple tube pipe.

The sociological aspects of tobacco use had little effect on the attitude of the discoverers toward it. They did not recognize the social systems of the American Indians as "cultures" at all. They could recognize worth in American products denied to Europe by nature and distance; they could not admit worth in the usages of naked people with dark skins. For this reason tobacco as a creature comfort first passed from the brown natives of the Caribbean to the black slaves of that region and of Seville. Only as a new therapeutic herb could the leaf command serious attention from the white Europeans; those who smoked for pleasure did so with a sense of sin.

The two-step nature of tobacco's passage from New World to Old is curiously reflected in the first "cigar-store Indians" to be set up in the shops of London. They were not American Indians at all, but blackamoors. As the Arawak and Carib natives of the Antilles died off under white rule, imported Africans took their place. In little gardens next to their huts these Negroes tilled tobacco for their own use, and for sale to mariners whose sensual curiosity was stronger than their sense of sin. It became usual in European ports to see sailors chewing, or puffing, or snuffing the strange, exotic leaf.

Virtuous vegetable

By the end of the New World's first century of recorded — or rather, semirecorded — history, the virtues of tobacco were not only well known, but generally exaggerated by those who wrote about it. Herbalists and learned physicians of Europe extolled its panacean qualities in great detail, many of them without having so much as seen a leaf of the plant.

Great names now enter the story of tobacco: Damião de Goes, archivist for the Portuguese king, who cultivated the amazing plant in the royal gardens and dubbed this (Portuguese) importation as the "holy herb" of miraculous power; Jean Nicot, French ambassador to Lisbon, who was given a plant by de Goes and in 1561 sent tobacco to the French court, a deed commemorated by the scientific name of the plant, *Nicotiana;* Cardinal Prospero di Santa Croce, credited with introducing the *herba panacea* into Italy the same year; and in England Sir Walter Raleigh who won Queen Elizabeth's approval of his pipe and so made the British Isles safe for tobacco fanciers. These are the names and dates given in most of the chronicles, each with a touch of dramatic spice; but the essential story of the tobacco is much simpler. It rests neither on powerful promoters nor on the prescriptions of learned medicine men, but on the trade in leaf begun well before they appeared on the scene. The story began with Rodrigo de Jerez who smoked, not to impress a court or to cure a wound, but because he liked it. And it continued with other sailors, Spanish and Portuguese, who found in tobacco the golden leaf of the New World while their captains were still dreaming of El Dorado, the golden king who did not exist.

Primitive Lacandons still grow tobacco for their cigars in thick jungles of Chiapas and Guatemala where Maya ruins are buried. These savages may be descendants of smoker on opposite page, and their cigars may be a continuation of the world's oldest tobacco tradition, going back perhaps 2,000 years.

Common seamen first took to tobacco as a creature comfort, generating a demand for it in the world's port cities. Portugal and Spain grew it for export in their new colonies, Brazil and the West Indies. The leaf left their tropical plantations in crude manufactured form, called "twist" or tobacco rope.

SPANISH GOLD

BECAUSE the educated Spaniard despised the brown unbaptised Americans, he was slow to understand their custom of smoking and chewing tobacco. And because of this, tobacco's potential value as an article of commerce did not occur to him at first. It is not surprising that, with gold on the brain, Columbus and his men threw away the "certain dried leaves" offered them by the Arawaks along with fruits and wooden spears.

But it is strange that, amidst all the "history" written down in the eventful century between Columbus' first voyage in 1492 and Drake's last trip to the West Indies in 1600, so little of the essential story of Americans and their tobacco was spelled out. To be sure, the navigators of that age were storytellers, not sociologists. Many used tobacco as "corroborative detail intended to lend artistic verisimilitude to an otherwise bald and unconvincing narrative." Anxious to amaze their countrymen, they chronicled it as a wonder of the new-found world. The renowned botanists of Europe seized on it as a new ingredient in their quest for the "wonder drug" that would cure everything. Though an ambassador, Jean Nicot seized his chance to play the discoverer and acted as a learned witch doctor to the French court (one of the early names for tobacco was *herbe de l'ambassadeur*). No doubt Sir Walter Raleigh also used the "witching weed" for dramatic effect, and created a sensation by parading his pipe before an enchanted Elizabeth. Certainly he was not the original British promoter of tobacco, which was smoked by goodly numbers of Englishmen thirty or forty years before he puffed his stuff at court.

Increasing familiarity with the Indians of the Americas soon made it clear that tobacco was not simply the ritualistic embroidery of a savage society. A few Europeans observed the part it played in the everyday life of ordinary natives. A few mentioned — with cultured disdain — the attraction

tobacco held for ordinary colonists. And a few referred, more or less in passing, to the tobacco trade between Indian tribes which had been going on for some hundreds of years. But it took about a century of observation before tobacco in European eyes ceased to be a kind of home-grown savage nostrum, before the white world realized that it had long been a kind of vegetable wampum.

Strong leaf, sweet leaf

Apparently the first white man to observe the American tobacco "industry" in its primeval state was Hernan Cortez, who conquered Mexico in 1519. In Tenochtitlan, now Mexico City, Indians sold "canes perfumed with liquidambar, filled with tobacco." Elaborate pipes as well as dried tobacco leaves were also sold in the market place by the naked Aztecs. As we have already noted, Bernal Diaz del Castillo described Montezuma smoking after dinner a tube holding liquidambar, "mixed

with a certain plant they call *tobaco*." The captains from Castille were much too preoccupied with blood and gold to bother about dried leaves. But a few years after the conquest, the priest Bernardino de Sahagún became missionary to the Mexican Indians and remained for 61 years. Sahagún, a most perceptive individual, wrote that "he who sells picietl crushes the leaves first, mixing them with lime, and he rubs the mixture well between his hands." The missionary was one of the first Europeans to discriminate between the two major varieties of tobacco, for picietl was a harsh, coarse species *(Nicotiana rustica)* growing in the colder latitudes, as distinct from yietl*(Nicotiana tabacum)*, a milder, sweeter sub-tropical species greatly improved by careful cultivation. The distinction is important to the history of tobacco, for the worldwide commerce that soon developed was based on *Nicotiana tabacum*. The crude *Nicotiana rustica* was a "poor man's tobacco" hardly worth exporting;

23

First white man to notice commercial distinction between the two major tobacco species was priest, Sahagún. He lived with Mexicans from 1529 to 1590.

Picture illustrating Sahagún's manuscript shows a native herald with trumpet and lighted cigarette. Latter was commercial item among Mexican Indians.

even savage palates required it to be mixed with lime or red willow bark before it could be smoked.

Of picietl Sahagún wrote: "Placed in the mouth it produces dizziness and stupefies." (Perhaps it did!) But to yietl, the smooth leaf, he attributed not only sweet-smoking qualities as a kind of ceremonial incense, but also a wide range of healing powers as a medicine for abscesses, sores, cold, snakebite, chills, convulsions, skin eruptions and internal disorders.

Demand on the prairie

About 1528, as Sahagún was taking up his long residence in Mexico, Cabeza de Vaca with 400 men took ship for Florida in search of the fabled seven cities of Cibola (which eventually turned out to be seven Indian pueblos along the upper Rio Grande river in what is now the state of New Mexico). Shipwreck and suffering shrunk de Vaca's force to four men in a few years. They were found in Texas, and de Vaca lived to write about his adventure and about the Indians of "Malhado" island: "Throughout this country they intoxicate themselves with a smoke, and they give whatever they possess for it." This early observation foreshadows the use of tobacco as a prime article of exchange in the 19th century commerce of the prairies — a barter economy between Indians and whites.

The first chronicler of the "rites of the islanders" was a monk, Romano Pane, who saw smoking only as a priestly function, a ritual which endowed the priests with gifts of prophecy. Fernández de Oviedo, who went to the Antilles in 1514 to smelt gold, did notice that ordinary men found pleasure in tobacco. Some of the Negro slaves brought by the Spaniards "grow the plant on their owners' farms and inhale its smoke, for they say that if they take tobacco when their day's work is over they forget their fatigue." Yet in spite of this observation Oviedo apparently never tried tobacco himself. Like nonsmokers of the centuries to follow he "could not imagine what pleasure they derive from this practice."

Neither could the first of the great missionary-historians, Bartolomé de las Casas. But he too noted that the Spaniards, like their black slaves, tried tobacco in Cuba and found it good, "The herb," he wrote, "is rolled up like a sort of bundle in a dried leaf. . . . They then light one end of it and

24

draw in the smoke at the other." But las Casas was preoccupied with the powers of darkness, and believed the devil was involved in the sniffing of cohobba and in the inspirations that followed.

Oviedo was published in 1535, las Casas in 1527. But even while they were seeing demons and devils, a global industry was springing to life under their uptilted noses. This development, hardly mentioned in print, was accomplished by men whose names (outside of Rodrigo de Jerez) are not even known: the sailors.

Portuguese and pigs' bladders

Sailors have always been the world's natural traders, quick to stir up a want, able to give "place utility" to the satisfaction of that want. It did not take them long to observe the pleasure-giving qualities of tobacco among the "Spice Islanders," to acquire the habit of its use themselves, and then to carry it from port to port in pigs' bladders — just as the merchant seamen of World War II quickly set up a flourishing business in captured Luger pistols after June 6, 1944. The speed and scope of their success is amazing. In Portugal proper, they spread the consumption of tobacco very soon after Columbus' first voyage. There was believed to be a tobacco merchant in Lisbon in 1523, although it is not clear whether he was "Antonio, tobacco mercador" or "Antonioto Baco, mercador." During the first thirty years following Columbus' discovery they not only introduced tobacco into India but established a regular leaf trade with that country: East Indiamen bound home were carrying it among their cargoes. *Fumo* (tobacco) was cultivated in the Portuguese colony of Sao Vicente, Brazil, in 1534. The Yucatan variety was transplanted about the same time to Santo Domingo and Cuba (whose natives had previously cultivated *Nicotiana rustica*); a market had obviously developed among the European settlers. And by 1548 some sixteen Portuguese settlements along the Brazilian coast were exporting tobacco to Lisbon.

In mid-sixteenth century the port of Lisbon was the crossroads of the seven seas. Before the century was out, Portuguese tobacco was being sold in Japan and China and had been introduced to the islands of the Malay Archipelago as well. (The rival Spanish were first with tobacco in the Philippines.) Early in the seventeenth century, Arabia and

Cabeza de Vaca was shipwrecked in 1528, wandered lost through Texas deserts for several years. He described Indians who "intoxicate themselves with smoke, and they give whatever they possess for it."

Abyssinia were added to Portugal's list.

After Bartolomo Diaz, Vasco de Gama and Cabral opened the sea-lane around the Cape of Good Hope, Portugal enjoyed a monopoly on trade along the east and west coasts of Africa. The word "fumu" (based on the Portuguese *fumo*) was used in the Congo for tobacco, suggesting its introduction from Portugal's plantations in Brazil. On the other side of the dark continent, the Arabs called tobacco "Bortugal." It is a tribute to the wide-ranging Portuguese sailors that both central Africa and Arabia took up smoking even before nearby Italy adopted the custom.

There is, to be sure, one logical reason why this commercial ten-strike, this golden trade, was slighted by the scholarly writers of the time. To-

Tobacco's place in mystical nature-worship of the American Indian is expressed in woodcut, "The Great Spirit," published in nineteenth-century New York.

The association of smoking with heathen rites made it unacceptable to Europeans who first encountered the custom; its part in daily life was overlooked.

bacco was associated with heathen ritual, and in the sight of God-fearing Christians was therefore wholly evil. This attitude was first applied to Rodrigo de Jerez, who smoked as he strolled the streets of his native Ayamonte, was suspected of harboring a devil, and was promptly clapped into prison by the Inquisition. (When he emerged, most of his countrymen had taken up smoking!)

Whiffing around the world

A similar reception awaited the first smokers of tobacco in England, Switzerland, Greece, and Italy, while the death penalty was imposed in Russia, Turkey, Persia and India. Most violent of the anti-tobacco monarchs was Murad IV of Turkey who forbad his subjects to smoke in 1633 and thereafter executed smokers regularly — as many as eighteen in a day. Nevertheless, the trade prospered. Tobacco

penetrated Africa along with, and as barter for, the slave-traders. Magellan brought it around Cape Horn to the Philippines. In faraway Japan 150 persons were apprehended for buying and selling tobacco contrary to the Shogun's command and were in jeopardy of their lives, according to an Englishman's letter dated 1614. By 1644 tobacco had taken a strong enough hold on the Chinese to warrant similar attention by their emperor. Great stores of tobacco were burned. Still, the golden trade grew.

History was to repeat itself many times in the years to follow, and tobacco's continuing spread was to be punctuated by violent controversies about its use. But the growth phase initiated by the Portuguese mariners was itself a repetition of previous history—the spread of tobacco through North, Central and South America.

Maya

This "prehistoric history" begins with the Mayan civilization of Yucatan and Central America, which antedates the birth of Christ. The priest-dominated Mayans left stone carvings of priests smoking as a part of sun-worship. *Nicotiana tabacum* is a subtropical plant in origin, and its special taste and aroma have been known in Central America for perhaps two thousand years — certainly for the last fifteen hundred. The first picture of tobacco-smoking is thought to be the Old Man of Palenque, carved in stone by the Mayans in what is now Chiapas, Mexico. The old man is clearly a priest, the pipe is a straight tubular or "cane" pipe, and the temple in which the carving was found dates from about 400 A.D. It is significant that tobacco consumption in its most advanced form — the flavored cigarette — was in everyday use less than a hundred miles from Palenque in the year 1519, when Cortez landed in nearby Tabasco. The year before Juan de Grijalva had seen cigarette smokers when he landed a little farther to the northeast at Yucatan. (Both tobago, the Caribbean word for snuff-pipe, and tabaco, the European word for the leaf, may be derived from Tabasco.) The early Mayan use of tobacco as an incense accompanying worship had its Old World analogue in the religious smoke rituals of the Greeks and Romans. And the Old World smoking of hempseed after meals by Scythians and Babylonians, as related by Herodotus, suggests the modern (and Mayan) after-dinner cigar. At any rate, the common man of Central America did not leave the leaf to his priests but used it himself as an everyday pleasure.

It is thought that migrating Mayans brought pipe and plant to the more northerly Toltec and Aztec tribes. This is suggested by the circumstance, noted by Sahagún, that the Aztecs knew both the small-leaved northern species, *Nicotiana rustica*, and the large-leaved subtropical plant, *Nicotiana tabacum*. The Aztecs enjoyed a culture parallel to that of the Mayans, and were sufficiently advanced and pleasure-loving to have adopted the more palatable plant as a result of cultural and agricultural diffusion from the south. Tobacco smoke accompanied human Aztec sacrifices on the sun-platforms; and as a great metropolis, with a population thrice that of Lisbon in 1519, Tenochtitlan knew the after-dinner smoke as well.

Indian transplant

In eastern North America generally, and in the Mississippi basin particularly, pipe-smoking began around the year 500. Archeologists have traced a a great change in Indian life occurring about that time, a change from the very primitive hunting-gathering stage to a new way of life based on settled villages, agriculture, pottery-making and

Oldest known representation of smoker is Old Man of Palenque (southern Mexico). Stone carving from Maya temple shows priest puffing on tubular pipe.

27

"Smoke-filled room" of U.S. politics derives from ancient Mayan and Aztec use of cigars or pipes in council chambers. The custom spread northward to U.S. and Canadian tribes, persists to present day.

pipe-smoking. Some attribute this change to an "invasion" by the Mayans, whose square pyramids suggest the structures left by the North American "Mound Builders." While archeologists can establish the time when pipes appeared among these mound-building tribes, their science cannot specifically identify tobacco as the vegetable smoked. However, the long-standing use of tobacco in Central America and the spread of corn, beans and squash from that region to the northern tribes makes it almost certain that tobacco, either alone or in combination with some other leaf, was used to fill the stone pipes found in the mounds.

The Mandan Indians of Dacotah Territory, first seen by white men in 1738, are believed to have been closest culturally to the Mound Builders of a thousand years before. They were sedentary dwellers, clustering in stout lodges of timber roofed with earth, seeking safety in numbers as well as in walls. They stood in the same antagonistic relationship to the marauding nomads of other Sioux nations as

did the Mound Builders to the primitive hunters surrounding them. Most important, the Mandans grew their own food, a step which other tribes in and around the buffalo country found hard to take. Along with corn and beans the Mandans raised tobacco for use in their pipes and, possibly, for trading.

Still farther north, in the Great Lakes region of the U. S. and Canada, tobacco was not only grown for tribal use but also for inter-tribal trading when the white explorers—Frenchmen in this area—first appeared. Samuel de Champlain was the great name here. One reason he noticed the savage commerce in tobacco was, perhaps, the fact that he had witnessed the flourishing Spanish trade in the West Indies around 1600 before mounting his expedition to Canada eight years later. As an adventurer on a Spanish ship, Champlain noted tobacco production on Puerto Rico and described the manufacture of plug or twist tobacco on Santo Domingo. There tobacco "dried and then made into little cakes" had

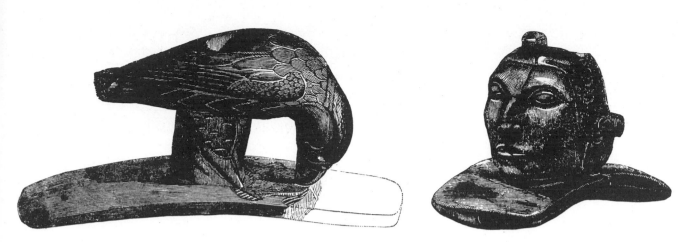

Carved pipes left by Mound Builders (left, from Grave Creek, Virginia; right, from Chillicothe, Ohio) date from about 500 A.D. Around that time the Mayan and Toltec civilizations were diffused along Mississippi Valley. Their sedentary way of life included cultivation of corn, beans, tobacco.

already became an article of trade called "casse-tabac" from the wicker baskets in which it was shipped.

In 1615 Champlain was exploring Quebec, mak- ing friends of some tribes and enemies of others and trying to chart the country around the "Sweet-water Sea" — Lake Huron. One tribe of Indians was so conspicuously devoted to *Nicotiana rustica*

Mandan Indians of North Dakota, as seen by white man in 1738, had culture resembling that of early Mound Builders. They clustered in towns to protect against raiders, and lived by farming rather than animal-like hunting and gathering. They too grew tobacco and smoked pipes in their timbered lodges.

that they became known as the Tobacco Nation, or Petuns. Like most other farmers whose land can produce the leaf, these Tobacco Hurons or Wyandots used their crops in trade; each year they traveled to Quebec with corn and tobacco to exchange for moose skins. Details of their leaf cultivation were not recorded, except that the men cared for the tobacco crop while the women grew corn, beans, squash, peas and melons. Jean de Brebeuf in 1636 wrote this description of tobacco consumption by the Hurons:

> They believe that there is nothing so suitable as Tobacco to appease the passions; that is why they never attend a council without a pipe or calumet in their mouths. The smoke, they say, gives them intelligence, and enables them to see clearly through the most intricate matters.

It appears that the Hurons carried their tobacco in a crude manufactured form, for there are references to "tobacco cakes." Its value as an article of trade did not depend only on its use as a creature comfort, for it was used in rituals by most of the Northeastern tribes. Before a hunt, for example, tobacco and skins were fastened to the end of a pole and offered to Oussakita, the manito of all the animals that move on the earth or in the air; the same offering was made to Michibichi, the manito of waters and fishes, except that it was thrown into the water rather than raised in the air. Bits of tobacco were thrown into ceremonial fires, or even into stormy waters, to appease the gods.

Tribes of the Great Lakes country suffered frequent epidemics in their raw climate. Among their cures was the "sweat bath": a sweat house was made of stakes and beaver robes, and vapor created inside by throwing water or tobacco on red hot stones. In times of illness or other trouble, it

Habit du Commandant & de sa Femme de Cabo verde

Portuguese were first to plant tobacco for export in their new possessions. These included Brazil, the Cape Verde Islands, and coastal Africa. This old print of a plantation scene in the Cape Verdes shows a common native (E) with an exaggerated pipe and a slave (F) with tusk, presumably from Africa.

Spain followed Portugal in building a leaf trade, but did business with Europe while the Portuguese were preoccupied with Africa and Asia. So tobacco became "Spanish gold." Most Spanish leaf was from West Indies although some was raised and cured in Paraguay, where this picture was drawn from life.

was almost automatic among the Lakes tribes to throw tobacco into the family fire as an appeal to the gods. It is strikingly evident that, in one way or another, the tobacco tradition had been implanted among virtually all the Indian peoples from Paraguay to Quebec by the time the whites crossed the Atlantic. From Mexico northward, tobacco moved largely by land; to the south, where the matted jungle limited overland travel, it moved by water.

Brown sailors and white

As the seagoing Phoenicians were to the urban Babylonians, so the Carib Indians of the Caribbean islands were to the urban Aztecs. Caribs ranged the Antilles, found *Nicotiana tabacum*, and probably spread it through much of South America as well as some West Indian islands. Tobacco was "launched"—geographically, socially and even economically — by brown sailors in the Americas long before the white sailors came from Europe.

The Spanish sailors were almost as alert to ex-

ploit tobacco as were the Portuguese, and had the advantage of controlling the West Indies and Central America, convenient sources of supply for the European trade.

Nicotiana tabacum, the commercial leaf, was transplanted from Yucatan to Cuba and to Haiti during the 1530s. The tobacco seen by Columbus and smoked by Rodrigo de Jerez may have been not the prized "henbane of Peru" but the powerful "yellow henbane" or *rustica* which at the time of the transplant was being tried and rejected as hot and peppery by Cartier on the St. Lawrence River.

This white transplant of the mild, sweet species into the West Indies was more for the convenience of Spanish slaves and sailors than for serious commercial exploitation. But trade in tobacco was self-generating: from Indian to slave, from slave to sailor, from sailor to anybody in any port. The new leaf was first recognized by Spanish officialdom in 1557, when slaves were barred from keeping taverns for sailors and from selling tobacco. Traffic in

31

First picture of a New World tobacco factory was published in 1667, probably depicts an establishment somewhere in the West Indies. Under the shed at right (1) leaf is being air-cured under shelter as much of today's harvested tobacco is cured. The stripper (2) removes the stem or midrib from each leaf, still a hand operation in many factories of today. The workers at (3) and (4) are twisting the tobacco leaves into a kind of cable and rolling it into tight coils on a wheel, a form of preparation

which is now obsolete. "Tobacco roll," also called "twist" or "rope" was the universal form of tobacco product for nearly three centuries. Made of tough, dark tobacco which is now valueless except as chew, it could be sliced into a pipe, chewed, or ground into snuff. Under the shed at left men are scraping and grinding roots of cassava or manioc, a tropical plant native to America which yields tapioca. The house of the colonial master is at the rear, with its occupant casting a supervisory eye on the work.

33

tobacco by then was heavy enough, and profitable enough, for white Spaniards to take over. Europe at the same time was responding en masse to the "Spanish" leaf brought from Iberian colonies, by initiating tobacco culture of its own. First plantings are dated in 1554 for Belgium, 1556 for France, 1559 for Germany, 1561 for Holland, and 1570 for England. It required only a demonstration of smokability for the leaf to create a demand in strength. The universality of its spread in Africa was strikingly summarized some centuries later by the British sociologist Lord Raglan:

> There is not a single cultural element common to all the territories and peoples of black Africa with the single exception of tobacco.

The same may be said for green America: not one native culture in temperate and tropical North, Central and South America was found to lack some form of tobacco usage. (Some scholars, reasoning backwards from Raglan's observation, advanced the theory that tobacco originated in the dark continent, a theory since disproved.)

As a Spanish possession before 1590, Holland took to tobacco before the British did. Netherlanders have been inveterate pipe-smokers for 375 years.

So Columbus' search for the Spice Islands of the East ended in the finding of an herb that replaced spice as the "wealth of the Indies." The Age of Exploration introduced four exotic stimulants: tobacco from Brazil, tea from China, coffee from Africa, and chocolate from Mexico. All were denounced as wicked owing to their heathen origin; but while the tobacco ritual was not acceptable to Christian clerics as black magic, tobacco medicine was acceptable to Christian apothecaries as brown magic. This was the wedge by which the savage custom pried open the Old World market; for a while virtually all the shops which dispensed tobacco were those of apothecaries. Holland especially, a Spanish possession until 1590, took eagerly to the "bewitching vegetable," which had been brought to the Low Countries as early as 1550. A brisk traffic between the Antilles and the English Channel sprang up. Nearby England was just as logical a market as the Netherlands, and the Spanish sailors proceeded to tap it, despite and during the bitter sea war between the two nations that raged until 1604. Cornwall, the westernmost jut of land in southern England, was the point of entry in the 1590s, when Spanish leaf was regularly smuggled ashore along the south coast to avoid the Queen's penny-a-pound duty. It is perhaps a measure of the strength of demand that the Cornishmen refused to countenance an import duty on tobacco and fixed the royal tax collector at sword's point to keep him from the performance of his duties.

Dutch seamen added pull to the market by smuggling tobacco from the West Indies to Europe — mainly to England—beginning about the year 1575. By the end of the century tobacco completely dominated the Spanish West Indies; as Philip III recognized officially, "it is the principal crop the natives possess" and "was highly esteemed and sought after." Mainly to injure the Dutch, whose smuggling activities he could not put down, the Spanish king decreed in 1606 that all tobacco planting in Santo Domingo, Cuba, Margarita, Venezuela, Puerto Rico, and other islands should cease for ten years. But Philip's attempt at remote control of his colonies was no more effective than his attempt to sweep the Dutchmen from the Spanish Main.

Meanwhile the seafarers of England, intent on beating Spain at her own game — piracy — could not fail to notice the brown leaf which was being

Sir John Hawkins preyed on Portugese Africa and on the Spanish West Indies between 1562 and 1565. He and his crew probably brought smoking to England.

Sir Francis Drake also specialized in plundering the Spanish Main. In 1600 he recorded the trading of iron tools for tobacco on the island of Haiti.

converted into Spanish gold. Sir John Hawkins attacked Portuguese West Africa in 1562 and the Spanish Antilles two years later. Returning by way of the Florida coast and the French colony at Fort Caroline, he had a third opportunity to see and try smoking. On the basis of probabilities, Hawkins is assumed to have begun the tobacco vogue in Britain. In 1585 Drake blazed through the Spanish Main, burning, boarding, plundering. When he reached the island of Dominica (Haiti) the natives, by then no lovers of Spaniards and their works, were said to have brought large quantities of tobacco to the English from their houses. Whether tobacco was proferred to the Englishmen as fancied liberators, or whether the English demanded the local stores in the best traditions of sixteenth-century piracy, Drake does not state.

On his return voyage to Britain, Drake put in at Roanoke Island, North Carolina, and picked up the survivors of an English settlement established there in 1584. Among the refugees from hunger and Indian hostilities was the surveyor-historian Thomas Hariot. In his "briefe and true report of the new found land of Virginia: of the commodities there found and to be raised, as well marchantable, as others for victuall, etc." Hariot included tobacco:

> There is an herb called uppowoc, which sows itself. In the West Indies it has several names, according to the different places where it grows and is used, but the Spaniards generally call it tobacco. Its leaves are dried, made into powder, and then smoked by being sucked through clay pipes into the stomach and head . . .
> While we were there we used to suck in the smoke as they did, and now that we are back in England we still do. We have found many rare and wonderful proofs of the uppowoc's virtues, which would themselves require a volume to relate. There is sufficient evidence in the fact that it is used by so many men and women of great calling, as well as by some learned physicians.

If Hawkins and his crew had not been the first to puff pipes in England, Hariot and his fellow-adventurers certainly would have been. But the evidence points to Hawkins. A book published in England in 1570 declared that

> You see many sailors, and all those who come back from America, carrying little funnels made from a palm leaf or a reed in the extreme end of which they insert the rolled and powdered leaves of this plant.

This was the herbal written by Matthias de L'Obel, a citizen of the Low Countries who encouraged high consumption of "Nicosiana Sanasancta." First published in English, de L'Obel's work included the first accurate picture of the tobacco plant. However, the illustration — widely used by other scholarly writers — also showed a savage smoking what seems to be a three-foot cornucopia. This picture (page 40) is somewhat less than accurate; judging by the text, de L'Obel was attempting to describe the rolled cigar and the tube pipe as a single form. Be that as it may, de L'Obel confirmed the fact that tobacco smoking had come to be practised in England by "many sailors."

Well before Drake's 1585 sally to the West Indies, tobacco had come to be valued by the English for personal use if not for resale in Britain. But Hariot, or Roanoke's governor Ralph Lane, or one of the Roanoke explorers — Captain Philip Amadas and Captain Arthur Barlowe — certainly brought Carolina seed to their sponsor, Sir Walter Raleigh. These were planted by Raleigh on his Ireland estate, but in spite of his efforts Sir Walter was unable to convert the English tabackians to the rank *Nicotiana rustica* when Spanish leaf was available.

Drake returned to Dominica some years later, and the log of his 1600 voyage describes his dealings with the natives:

After defeating the Spanish Armada, Britain sent her privateers to burn and pillage Spain's ports of trade in the New World. Sir Walter Raleigh made a triumphal attack on Guiana in 1595 and observed the traffic in Trinidad tobacco. But the English wanted to seize gold, not to enter the leaf trade.

Sir Walter Raleigh popularized pipe-smoking at the English court. "Tobagies" multiplied, and demand for Spanish leaf soon exceeded the limited supply.

By 1611, when this title-page for a play pictured a smoker, tobacco was a prominent feature of life in England, which had become a major leaf market.

Then we stood for Dominica, an Island full of inhabitants of the race of the Canibals. . . . in it groweth great store of Tabacco: where most of our English and French men barter knives, hatchets, sawes, and such like iron tools in truck of Tabacco.

After the Spanish Armada was defeated, English captains penetrated Spanish waters almost at will. Sir Robert Dudley landed in Trinidad, Venezuela, Puerto Rico and Bermuda in the course of his 1594-95 expedition, and his written account shows that he was quite tobacco-conscious. He traded for tobacco in Trinidad, referred to the coast of Caracas as "one of the fruitfullest places in the world for excellent good tobacco," and added that "in the high land of Paria I was informed by divers of these Indians, that there was . . . great store of most excellent Cane-tobacco." Sir Walter Raleigh made a triumphant journey to Guiana in 1595 and described the Tiuitiuas at the mouth of the river Orinoco:

They make the most and fairest houses, and sell them into Guiana for golde, and into Treinedado for Tobacco, in the excessive taking wereof, they exceed all nations . . .

Despite this direct allusion to the worth of tobacco in terms of gold, Raleigh and the English generally were still content to buy their leaf at home from the Spaniards. Their hearts were then set, not on building up a lucrative commodity trade, but on finding El Dorado and his golden treasure before the Spanish did. In this respect the English of the 1590s were in the same state of mind as the Spanish of the 1520s — they saw tobacco as a picturesque custom, a native oddity. Raleigh's Guiana voyage was followed up the very next year by his lieutenant, Lawrence Keymis, who described a parley with some Orinoco chiefs in these words:

> Thus they sit talking, and taking Tobacco some two hours, and until their pipes be all spent (for by them they measure the time of this their solemn conference) no man must interrupt... for this is their religion...

Keymis was still engaged in the wild gold chase for El Dorado, and the emergence of England as the dominant tobacco trader had to wait for that fever to cool.

Eager Europe

The potential of tobacco as a consumer's good was appreciated by the trade-conscious Dutch very soon after the Portuguese and Spanish staked out

In 1642 Pope Urban VIII prohibited the taking of tobacco in churches, the custom having gained so strong a hold, "yea; even on priests and clerics."

their plantations in the New World. Educated in France and writing in Antwerp, Matthias de L'Obel observed in 1571 that the mariners in the West Indies trade smoked enthusiastically "since they attribute to it the power of allaying hunger and thirst, exhilirating the spirits and renovating the animal powers." Perhaps de L'Obel read too much into the simple fact that sailors smoked for pleasure, but he had the wit to grasp the leaf's non-medicinal significance and to encourage its cultivation in the Low Countries. The Dutch took to the leaf more quickly than the English, despite the straw-like character of the tobacco grown in their own fields. For centuries they consumed more leaf per head than either England or Germany, although they constituted a smaller market. "The pipe," wrote Washington Irving, "is never out of the mouth of the true-born Nederlander."

Wrote a German ambassador to the Hague in 1627:

> I cannot refrain from a few words of protest against the astounding fashion lately introduced from America — a sort of smoke-tippling, one might call it, which enslaves its victims more completely than any other form of intoxication, old or new. These madmen will swallow and inhale with incredible eagerness the smoke of a plant they call Herba Nicotiana, or tobacco.

Even as this was written, tobacco cultivation had crossed the Rhine, and smoking was spreading through Germany, Switzerland and Austria, Hungary, Sweden, Poland, Russia and Turkey. Princes and pontiffs, alarmed respectively by fires resulting from careless smoking and by the origin of tobacco among heathen savages, laid down prohibitions. But both royalty and clergy soon grew to enjoy the bewitching vegetable. In 1642 a Papal Bull issued by Urban VIII noted that "the use of the herb commonly called tobacco has gained so strong a hold on persons of both sexes, yea, even priests and clerics" that it behooved the Pope to prohibit its use in churches. During the next 20 years or so, most of the princes gave the new custom their approval. Like James I of England, they became aware of the revenues to be had from taxes on consumption and from the sale of growing, manufacturing, and trading rights. The rapid expansion of this European market was to prove crucial to the survival of the first American colonies.

There was one interesting difference between

tobacco's introduction on the continent and its rise in England. Nicot had sent the plant to the French court as a specific; it was adopted by Europe doubtless because of its pleasurable utility, but under the guise of medicine and with the endorsement of the physicians. There was no such endorsement of any consequence in England. Raleigh, and the sailors who preceded him, puffed their pipes for personal solace. This was a result of the late arrival of Britons generally in the New World; by the time Spain's dominion over the western seas was broken tobacco was no longer a barbarous custom of the naked heathen, but a going commodity among the white settlers of America.

From palm leaf to pipe

Out of the early seaborne traffic in leaf emerges a curious but distinctive fact about tobacco: the taste for it is not invariably "ritualistic" nor con-

fined to a particular form of use. Rather, the mode of consumption is flexible and influenced by culture and environment, which are themselves always changing. But shifting fashions in smoking do not seem to affect the essential object of the taste, the tobacco. In the Spanish West Indies the cigar or the palm-wrapped cigarette was the preferred form of consumption, not only among the Indians but among the whites and Negroes who took to smoking. Outside Cuba, however, the cigar was retarded by the lack of skilled rollers and by the fact that it was unsuitable for smoking outdoors in raw weather. This last affected most of all the habits of the Spanish sailors, who took up chewing with equal relish. Yet their principal customers in England, Holland and Germany were almost exclusively pipe smokers. Perhaps the North Europeans were initially conditioned to the pipe by the harshness of the leaf they grew at home; perhaps the leaf

During the early 1600s tobacco was being grown in the Rhine valley, although its hay-like character required that it be blended with American tobacco.

Germany, Switzerland, Austria, Hungary, Sweden and Russia took up smoking; this European market enabled the Chesapeake settlements to survive.

Botanical sketch of tobacco appeared in many herbals of Europe from 1570 on. Smoking apparatus at right confused the spiral-wrapped cigar with the funnel-like tubular pipe. But the print confirmed role of sailors in spreading leaf. Caption read: "Nicotiana is packed into a fundibulum, a sort of tube used by Indians and by sailors when smoking."

that reached them from the Spanish Main — often transshipped in French or Flemish bottoms — was only relatively milder than their own, but not the choice tobacco that the directness of cigar smoking requires. Though both factors may have operated, it is certain that climate also played an important part. A given smoker can enjoy many more cigars per day in Havana than he can in wintertime New York or London. The southern smoker tends to like his roll sweet, the northern smoker straight or lightly flavored. The difference is obvious today to a student of brand preferences in cigarettes — in Cuba, they are heavy with molasses; in the American South, the sweetest, most heavily "cased" brands are best liked; in the temperate latitudes, moderately flavored or lightly flavored blends are most popular; and in the British Isles, straight Virginia with no sweetening at all is the ideal.

Shillings for Spanish

By sixteenth century standards, the British market for tobacco was an eager and growing one. Both Spencer and Ben Jonson mentioned the custom of smoking in their works before the century was out,

and visitors to Britain wrote that the English were constantly smoking at bull-baiting, at bear-whipping, in the courtroom, and everywhere else. Some taverns were called "tobagies," as others were called alehouses or coffeehouses. In 1599 a pound of Cuban tobacco was said to have sold for $125 in London. Violent price fluctuations around the turn of the century — a pound of leaf ranging from 2 shillings to 90 shillings over a 22-year span — evidenced the inability of supply to keep up with demand. Wrote Thomas Platter in 1605:

> In the taverns tobacco or heathen wound plant is provided, which everyone gets for a penny . . . at plays, inns or at any place they light up and drink. . . . The plant is brought in great quantities from the Indies and one kind is stronger than the other, as one can tell by the tongue.

That same year a pamphleteer advised that tobacco be grown at home so that England would not have to pay 200,000 pounds sterling a year to the rival Spanish colonists. (At an average of 30 shillings per pound, this suggests a consumption of 130,000 pounds of leaf.) However the English soil and climate proved more suitable for raising *Nicotiana rustica* than *Nicotiana tabacum,* and the Spanish continued to sell thousands of pounds of the preferred kind to Britain — with and without benefit of duty — until the middle of the seventeenth century. Owing to the undependable supply and to mounting taxes, counterfeit and adulterated tobacco became common in England, which made "Spanish tobacco" all the more highly prized. In fact, the adjective "Spanish" denoted tobacco of the highest quality in Britain and the U. S. until about 1860.

Foundation: "Smoak"

In the last analysis, the survival of the first English Colonies stemmed from the early trading zest of the Spaniards. Despite the vicious sea war with the English that raged from 1558 to 1604, the Spanish sailors bearded the lion in his den by pressing their tobacco trade through the South Coast ports and smugglers' coves. Thereby, they opened up the world's greatest market for imported tobacco (which Britain remains to this day), and it was this market, along with its European offshoots, that was to sustain the economy of the American Colonies during their first two centuries of existence.

For Britain to shake off Spain as her tobacconist and put down her own tobacco roots in the New World, required the fierce economic imperialism generated under the Virgin Queen for whom Virginia is named. How this imperialism was to operate for three full centuries is illustrated by the episode of Drake standing for Dominica to barter hatchets and saws "in trucke of Tabacco." His exchange — manufactured goods for raw stuffs not available at home — was to be the formula and foundation of the British Empire, as it was to be the formula for the Chesapeake colonies "founded upon smoak."

Then as now the best Spanish American tobacco was grown in Cuba's western tip. Except for telephone poles and wires at left, the lush vegas of Cuba's Vuelta Abajo today look much the same as in 1600.

Although Englishmen bitterly fought Spaniards on the high seas, they continued to pay high prices for Spanish tobacco at home, smuggling the leaf into the coves of Cornwall to evade the duties.

Desperate for the means to trade for supplies in England, Jamestowners tried tobacco. Virginia and Maryland leaf soon passed Spanish in the European markets and supported the Chesapeake colonies for nearly two centuries. The tidewater planters were, in effect, field hands to His Majesty; there was no improvement in the leaf, no local manufacture.

THE TIDEWATER PLANTERS

IN recent years the intensity of competition among manufacturers has overshadowed competition among growers. But competition for leaf markets was the dominant aspect of the tobacco industry throughout the sixteenth, seventeenth and eighteenth centuries. It was a knowledge of this, and an awareness of the "two kinds" of tobacco, that prompted the desperate John Rolfe to grow a new strain in the Virginia tidewater in 1612. As often happens in and out of the tobacco industry, desperation may succeed when nothing else can.

Rolfe and his wife had left England for the Jamestown colony in 1609. They were shipwrecked on Bermuda, where their first child was born and died. In the spring of 1610 they reached Jamestown to find only a few dozen gaunt survivors of a harrowing winter that became known as the "Starving Time." During the next two years Rolfe, a man of twenty-five sobered by tragedy, tried to grow a smokable leaf from the strain cultivated by the Virginia Indians, the small-leaved *Nicotiana rustica*. But the native tobacco could be appreciated only by the natives; the settlers found it "poor and weak and of a biting taste." In the midst of his experiments, his wife also died.

It is not recorded how Rolfe came by seed of the large-leaved Spanish tobacco (*Nicotiana tabacum*), but he had the enterprise to plant a crop in 1612 and ship a small quantity to England in 1613. This may have been his last cast of the dice, but it was a natural. Two years later, Virginia was supplying to London one pound of tobacco for every twenty supplied by the Spanish; by 1619, the Virginia staple exceeded the Spanish product on the London market; and in 1620 Virginia exports exactly doubled the 1619 quantity.

James Towne

Rolfe's contribution is best appreciated against the background of the Jamestown settlement. In its first decade, this was no tidy transplant of the English countryside to sunny, green glades and abundant harvests. Jamestown was a pestiferous mantrap on a swampy island, comparable in bodily misery to the Black Hole of Calcutta and the concentration camps of Nazi Germany. Of 1,000 souls poured into the colony in its first four years, 800 died. Starvation went so far that one settler killed, salted and ate his wife. Until Rolfe's crop found its market, human folly ran wild. Two thirds of the

early arrivals were persons of "qualitie," who expected the other third to provide for their wants. The first leaders were a succession of incompetents who never managed to get a food crop planted, stole from and murdered the friendly Indians who were almost their sole supply of food, roamed the tidewater tributaries looking for the "Back Sea" that washed the East Indies, and filled the holds of their tiny supply ships with yellow earth—"fool's gold"—to be assayed for gold content in Britain. Several of the early commanders deserted the dying colonists, taking needed ships with them.

Amidst all the suffering there was no thought of emulating the Spanish colonies and turning the rich earth to a profit. The adventurers who first crossed on the 100-ton Susan Constant, the 40-ton Goodspeed and the 20-ton Discovery—105 reckless souls—were certainly aware of the tobacco trade. Their little fleet had made its landfall in the West Indies near Dominica, "a very faire Iland full of sweet and good smells" including, at that time, the scent of tobacco. Furthermore, survivors of the "Lost Colony" of Roanoke Island had indicated in words and pictures how the native Indians of that region grew tobacco.

Like the early Spaniards, however, the first Jamestowners came to the New World not to make a living but to make a killing. They envisioned the natives as Aztecs ripe for plucking, and looked forward to looting jewel-encrusted chamber pots made of solid gold. Thus, two-thirds of them saw no reason why they should not continue to write "Gent" after their names, signifying that they were above manual labor. They were, after all, investors in the Virginia Company to the extent of twelve and a half pounds sterling apiece.

Unfortunately the other third—who crossed the Atlantic on credit and worked off their passage by five or six years of indentured labor—had even less incentive for hard work. The terms of their indentures kept them in a kind of communistic slavery. For their labor they were to receive only sustenance from the common harvest; what they produced they had to share on an equal basis with everyone else. It was no wonder that Marshall Thomas Dale found no corn crop planted when he arrived in May of 1611.

It required the no-nonsense hand of Dale, a veteran mercenary soldier, to break up this fool's paradise. He organized work gangs to till the soil, build

Financed by the Virginia Company of London, with New World gold the objective, the Susan Constant and two smaller ships reached the James River in 1607 after a six-month trip. In the three vessels were 105 adventurers; 66 died within five months. By 1611 1,000 settlers had come and 800 had died. This 1957 replica of the Constant was built for the celebration of Jamestown's 350th anniversary.

barns and a wharf, and dig new wells. With a keen awareness of human nature, he granted a hundred acres of land to each man after he worked out of bondage. Toughened by the European wars, Dale played his role of soldier to the hilt. He not only took the law into his own hands, but declared it to be martial law. Commandeering a visiting British warship of fourteen guns, he sailed it up the James to "requisition" corn from the Indians and on the same expedition kidnapped Powhatan's 18-year-old daughter Pocahontas.

One thing Dale could not order was the shipment of supplies and reinforcements from England. Organized with the expectation of immediate wealth, the Virginia Company was growing more and more reluctant to throw good money after bad. While the Jamestowners were shriveling from starvation and dying of malaria on their dank island, shipments of supplies were delayed for weeks and months in England. And even under military rule, it would take time to convert Jamestown from a crazy communism of lazy desperadoes and sullen serfs to a self-supporting colony of energetic farmers. It would take time for John Rolfe to recover from his personal losses and develop the merchantable commodity England expected.

Powhatan

This time was granted by Powhatan, a 70-year-old chief of chiefs who comes closest to the roman-

Powhatan's lodge was the "long house" typical of many eastern forest tribes. These Algonquin people had progressed beyond the hunting-gathering stage, lived in more or less permanent villages forming a well-ordered society. They cultivated corn, beans and tobacco and maintained community storehouses. This modern replica was also built to mark the 350th anniversary of the founding of Jamestown.

tic notion of the American Indian as a "noble savage."

Secure in the esteem of his own people, aware of the perfidiousness of the desperate English (John Smith plotted to murder him and make off with his corn store), Powhatan not only refrained from wiping out the Jamestowners but supplied them with venison, fowl, squirrels, fish and corn. When the English kidnapped his daughter Pocahontas, he sent the demanded ransom but wisely decided not to enter Jamestown himself. True to form, the English then increased the ransom. Meanwhile Sir Thomas Dale persuaded the captive Pocahontas to renounce her heathen faith and accept Christian baptism, along with the name Rebecca, and took her upriver in an attempt to worm another shipload of corn out of Powhatan.

Pocahontas

Perhaps Rolfe sensed that something had to be done to end such comic-opera intrigues before the Indians ended the whole show. At any event, he asked Dale for permission to marry Pocahontas "for the good of this Plantation." It seems doubtful that Rolfe's was a grand passion, for Pocahontas— called "Little Wanton" by her own people—was not unknown to the Englishmen, having once cartwheeled through their little settlement in a spirit of youthful play. Furthermore, Little Wanton had married a young brave of her own tribe four years

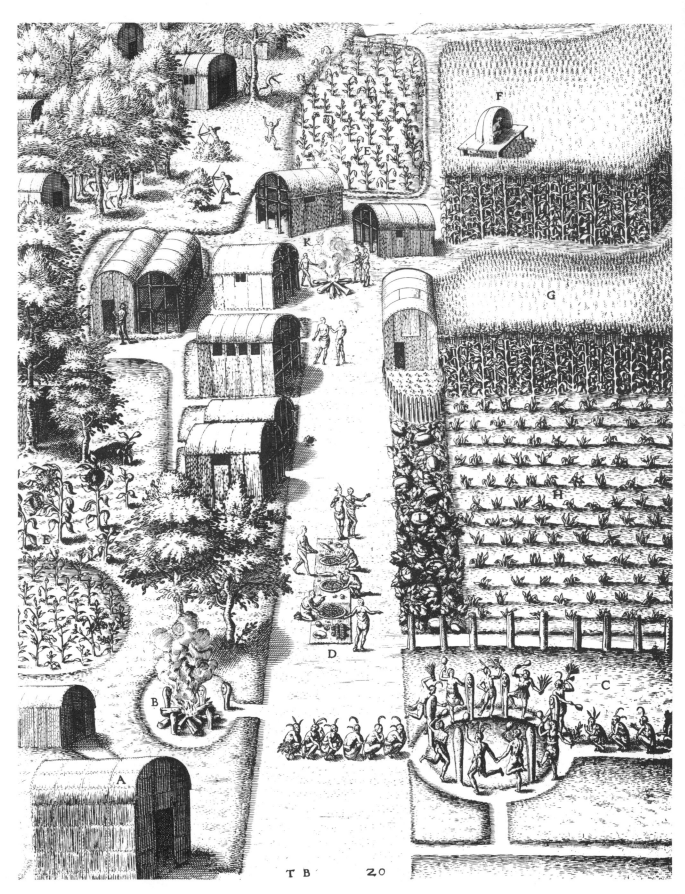

First picture of American tobacco farming resulted from Walter Raleigh's unsuccessful effort to settle Roanoke Island in 1585. It depicts the village of Secota in the North Carolina tidewater. (E) marks a tobacco field. The other crops were pumpkins (I) and corn (H,G). Shed at (F) holds a field sentinel.

earlier. But Rolfe's request led Dale to withdraw the troops and give over the savage pawn to be his bride in April, 1614.

So Rolfe crowned his economic success with a diplomatic one by marrying Pocahontas, daughter of the chief of chiefs, Powhatan. Peace with the Virginia Indians was assured for a time, as were continued payments on Little Wanton's dowry—foodstuffs for the still famished English. In 1616 he took his bride in triumph to London—was this a promotional stunt for tobacco?—where she died. When Rolfe returned to Jamestown, tobacco was literally growing in the streets.

The deare bought kind

Rolfe's switch to Latin American seed was not a lucky accident, for he knew of the "two kinds" of tobacco, and described the kind "known to be verie vendible in England," i.e., the large-leaved Spanish. He was, before going to Jamestown, a confirmed pipe smoker. The 1597 herbal of John Gerard has a section on "yellow Henbane, or English tobacco . . . brought from Trinidada, as also from Virginia." Gerard thought Indian tobacco was best for Indians and that "being now planted in the gardens of England . . . better for the constitution of our bodies." It is quite possible that Rolfe's fruitless experimentation with *Nicotiana rustica* was based on some such notion, along with the practical consideration that the coarser plant was then being grown in England. On the other hand, Gerard himself recognized that "our Taback-ians" preferred the "far fetch't and deare bought" kind to the *rustica*.

The new strain, as the reaction of the London market showed, was infinitely superior to the native North American tobacco. In the trade it was described as "Trynidado" or "Oronoko" leaf—the kind Englishmen meant when they referred to Spanish tobacco. Yet Rolfe's crop was a far cry from the leaf we know today. Planted on the rich, moist bottom lands of the tidewater, it was heavy and strong: today it would be classed as "shipping leaf" —this being a euphemism for tobacco not suitable for U. S. forms of consumption. Rolfe's dark air-cured product, in the years before blending, before flue-curing, before slow aging and humidity control, would resemble the coarsest, darkest type of chewing tobacco seen today.

Powhatan was the most powerful Indian chieftain in the Chesapeake area. Despite settlers' efforts to murder him, he kept them alive with corn and meat.

The wisest fool in Christendom

Nevertheless, it found acceptance in an England accustomed to the best that the Spanish possessions —Santo Domingo, Venezuela, Puerto Rico, Cuba— could ship. And it won this acceptance in the midst of the first great tobacco controversy. In 1604 the king himself, James I, issued a "Counterblaste to Tobacco" in which he characterized whiffing as a "vile and stinking custome" and discouraged his subjects from imitating the "barbarous and beastly manners of the wild, Godless and slavish Indians." At the same time the dour Scotch Monarch imposed a duty of six shillings eight pence over and above the two-penny tax then existing—from two to two-and-eighty pence in one swoop, an increase of 4,000%. Later he restricted tobacco-selling to persons holding royal warrants (which were rented for a yearly stipend). He also sold concessions for pipe making and pipe selling, fully justifying his reputation as "the wisest fool in Christendom."

Iron-handed Thomas Dale, Jamestown's Marshal, had Pocahontas kidnapped and held for ransom. With the colony's secretary, Ralph Hamor, Dale voyaged up the York to demand corn from Opechan- *cano, uncle of Pocahontas (above). War was averted when Pocahontas married John Rolfe, but ten years later, after both she and her father Powhatan were dead, Opechancano massacred 349 of 1,200 colonists.*

Almost from the first, leaf quality was a prime objective (apart from the intrinsic superiority of "Spanish" seeded tobacco over the indigenous North American variety). One reason was the swindling and adulteration that characterized the earliest years in England when tobacco commanded its weight in silver. Before the sixteenth century was over, protests were voiced in London against the apothecaries who mixed genuine leaf with worthless vegetable stuffs. The Spanish, too, were accused of "sophisticating" their leaf with the filth of sugar (molasses), pepper, wine lees, honey, and berry juice and of secreting rotten and withered leaf under good. This last, not unknown even today, came to be described as "nesting." In 1619 James I decreed inspection of all leaf (and sold the

concessions), a decree to which no more attention was paid than to most of his ukases. British merchants awoke to the potential profits in re-exported leaf, and this gave further impetus to the practice of adulteration with starch, oil, coal dust or sweepings for the home market. As the Virginia planters extended their acreage, their English customers were becoming more and more guarded in their purchases, and a planter's reputation for quality was a valuable asset. A new curing method—hanging the leaves on sticks for an "air cure"—replaced fermentation in heaps, and this not only improved the final product but reduced spoilage. In 1619 — the sixth year of the Chesapeake trade — the Virginia House of Burgesses banned second-growth tobacco, ordered the trashy grades destroyed, and initiated an inspection system. There were, to be sure, numerous evasions. Not until a century later could the inspection system be described as generally effective. But the immediate effect was to bring American shipping leaf to a standard which was competitive with, if not equal to, the West Indian "Spanish." Ultimately—that is, after two and a half centuries — quality-consciousness was to create U. S. leaf grades superior to all others for the light smokes (pipe and cigarette); the old Spanish possessions still grow the best tobacco for the heavy smoke (cigar).

The Jamestowners were helped in the very first years of their leaf trade by a commercial mistake on the part of Spain. In 1614, just before Virginia tobacco became a factor in the world market, the Spanish king ordered that all export tobacco from his colonies was to be shipped to Seville under penalty of death. This drastic step was intended (1) to diversify the agriculture of Spain's possessions and (2) to protect the product against the market glut occasioned from time to time by overplanting. One result of this was to make Seville a repository for the choicest tobaccos grown in the New World, and thus a famous cigar manufacturing city. But it put a crimp in the Spaniards' freedom of trade (even though it did not stop global smuggling) just as a hungry rival was entering competition for the English and European trade.

Spark of freedom

Given the chance, the Virginia colonists might have achieved economic independence—and perhaps political independence — much sooner than they did. In 1621 they tried to take advantage of Spain's Seville bottleneck by entering the European market on their own. Even then, in the fourteenth year of the first permanent settlement, they struck off a fitful spark of freedom. Appropriately, it was John Rolfe who made the first of many protests against the Crown's ruthless colonial policy; in his petition for free trade appear the first stirrings of the drive for liberty that would create a new nation 160 years later. He requested that

> our ancient liberty be restored or otherwise to send for us all home and not suffer the heathen to triumph over us.

The moribund Virginia Company, a financial disappointment from its founding, was afraid to risk a head-on clash with the king and withheld Rolfe's petition. Instead it pursued a bypass policy as a last resort: all of the 1621 crop was sent to Holland and paid no British tariff.

But the British had no intention of letting their overseas offspring become a well-to-do orphan. After four years of proposals and debates in Parliament, the Crown declared tobacco a royal monopoly and clamped a tight hand on Virginia leaf. In order to maximize his revenue therefrom James decreed (1) an end to tobacco-growing in England proper, (2) an end to tobacco trading with Spain and (3) that all American tobacco be landed in the city of London. None of these rulings was wholly effective, but they provided an umbrella of protectionism under which the traffic in Virginia leaf continued to increase. They also rendered the Jamestowners completely dependent on the London leaf merchants: free enterprise was to be a long time in coming.

Powhatan's daughter Pocahontas was kidnapped and held for ransom by Jamestowners. She married John Rolfe, bringing about a temporary state of peace.

Tobacco five to one

The idea of diversified crops, which worried the Spanish into the fatal error of too much planning, was intermittently bothersome to the Virginia tobaccomen. In the early years of Jamestown Sir Thomas Dale required each tobacco farmer to raise corn as well. (Like most of the solemn prescriptions about tobacco laid down by captains, kings and savants, this decree was ignored.) The Virginia Company itself subsidized fishing, lumbering, shipbuilding, iron and glass manufacture from 1608 onward, but in 1621 the practice of raising funds by lottery was ended and the Company itself died from financial malnutrition, along with the ambitious enterprises it had encouraged. At that stage there was no economic advantage in diversifying away from tobacco cultivation. Captain John Smith estimated that a man's labor in raising tobacco was worth fifty pounds sterling a year, as against ten pounds in raising corn. Tobacco required less cleared ground, and less shipping space, than any other crop. These economic facts of life were recognized in England by the year 1624, when Virginia was given its monopoly on exports to the mother country and all foreign trade in tobacco prohibited. Tidewater tobacco burgeoned. In 1628, under Charles I, the planters shipped 500,000 pounds; in 1638, 1,400,000 pounds. This was a classic example of the system of colonial specialization which eventually made Britain the wealthiest nation in the world.

Calverts, cod and conscience

If tobacco was the saving of Virginia, it was no less the support of Maryland. A "great man" of the Elizabethan era, somewhat junior to Raleigh in age but an adventurer of equal vision, plays a large part here. After twenty years of high public office in England proper, George Calvert was made Lord Baltimore by a grateful James I in 1625 (his barony of Baltimore was in Ireland). Five years before, Calvert had bought part of Newfoundland Island and established a settlement there, but by 1629 he decided that—notwithstanding the run of codfish in that part of the New World—the rigorous climate and the hostility of the French had rendered his colony of "Avalonia" a failure. Eschewing the cod, he asked a grant of land for himself and forty Avalonians on the Chesapeake so that he "might do the King and my Country more service there by.

When Rolfe returned to Jamestown, the tobacco crop he had started had spread even into the streets of that tiny island town. Leaf supported the colony.

This was not the native Indian tobacco, which did not sell in England, but a mild strain grown from Latin American seed that produced Spanish tobacco.

planting of Tobacco." By 1632, when the Maryland charter was passed, the first Lord Baltimore was dead. His eldest son, Cecil, became the second Lord Baltimore and another son, Leonard, became the first Governor of Maryland. Actual colonization of what is now the Old Line State began in 1634, and George Calvert's vision of tobacco fields was soon realized by his sons. From the first, Maryland showed an independence of thought and act that went beyond anything seen in the other settlements. (Maryland was not technically a Crown colony but a palatinate, the Calverts enjoying royal prerogatives of their own.) Unlike John Smith and Thomas Dale, the Calverts did not use strong-arm tactics in dealing with the Indians — they bought needed land from the natives instead of appropriating it. Unlike Virginia, Maryland completely divorced church and state and welcomed all faiths. This "security of conscience" principle extended to economics as well; time and again Maryland refused to follow Virginia's lead as to tobacco inspection, crop control, and hogshead size, even where it would have been in mutual interest to have done so. During the colonial period there was no appreciable difference between Maryland leaf and the Oronoko grown in Virginia: both were known in Europe as "Virginia tobacco," a term still used. During the last century, Maryland tobacco has emerged as a unique variety, soft brown in color, easily distinguished from the lemon-yellow Bright leaf which is the big tobacco crop of Virginia, the Carolinas, Georgia and Florida.

Clouds over Europe

British mercantilism was based on a rigid imperial monopoly of trade with the colonies, a monopoly which included the means of transport as well as the source of raw supplies. To protect the interests of the Virginia Company (and to check the drain on Britain's silver reserve caused by purchases of Spanish tobacco), Spain's leaf after 1631 paid a duty of two shillings (then worth about $5) per pound as against the ninepence ($1.90) paid by Virginia leaf. Thirty years later the differential was ten shillings against one shilling eightpence.

The Spanish trade had no sooner been doomed to extinction than the doughty Hollanders had to be put down. The Dutch fleet rivaled the English during most of the seventeenth century, and secured a

George Calvert, Lord Baltimore, could not make a success of his Newfoundland settlement, asked for Maryland grant so that he "might do the King and my country more service there by planting Tabacco."

good share of the Virginia-Maryland carrying trade in its early phase. The British acted quite directly, commandeering Dutch merchantmen laden

Unlike Virginians, Marylanders avoided strong-arm tactics, bought the land they needed from Indians instead of appropriating it in the name of James.

51

Chesapeake waters had 4,600 miles of shoreline, a great advantage. Deep-water ships could be moored at plantation landings; leaf raised on tidewater *bottomland was cured near water's edge and rolled only a short distance to the docks. Cutting roads through virgin forests was thus held to a minimum.*

with British colonial produce and, after the rivalry had burst into open warfare, seizing New Amsterdam to plug an important leak in the American leaf traffic.

Great Water

This trade, as yet, was very little influenced by manufacturing reputation. Neither "Havana cigars" nor "American cigarettes" had established their ascendancy. The trade was almost exclusively a leaf trade conducted, as originally, by sailors; hence convenient access by merchantmen was the most important asset of an agricultural area in that virtually roadless wilderness. The Chesapeake tidewater lapped at 4,600 miles of shoreline, including 150 rivers and inlets which a deepwater bottom could navigate for distances up to 100 miles. (The Indian word, k'tchisipik, meant "Great Water.") Thousands of ocean vessels could find safe harbor in the 3000 square miles of sheltered Chesapeake

Bay waters—more, certainly, than could be berthed in all the developed harbors of the Spanish West Indies.

The flat coastal country surrounding the Chesapeake was well laced with rivers and creeks suitable for small "flats" and canoes. This was important; the number of plantations which could wharf ocean-going bottoms was necessarily limited, and overland transport was rough on tobacco. The stoutest hogshead could not take many miles along the rolling roads without losing some leaf and gaining some mud. Even the shallowest streams were made navigable for tobacco by the use of a catamaran—two canoes in parallel supporting a platform between them on which were lashed half a dozen hogsheads. When the hogsheads were floated downriver to the ship landing, the platform could be dismantled and the canoes paddled back upriver singly.

The risk of "ducked tobacco" on the rivers was no

greater at first than the risk of piracy or spoilage on the high seas, and probably a good deal smaller: during the first fifty years of the American tobacco trade many a shipload was captured by flying Dutchmen. Some of the Dutch privateers actually entered the Chesapeake estuary to take or sink leaf-laden Virginiamen. Around 1690 the Crown awoke to the economic losses implicit in the sink-or-swim system and arranged for the tobacco ships to move in massed fleets convoyed by warships. During most of the eighteenth century this protection was given almost exclusively to the Chesapeake-England trade route, commerce with other British colonies being left pretty much to run its own gauntlet of Spanish and Dutch raiders. For the most part, it was effective.

This special Crown protection meant that the potentialities of the tobacco trade were limited only by the extent of demand, and demand seemed limitless during the first two centuries of Virginia and Maryland settlement. Exports increased steadily from 1,400,000 pounds a year during the 1630s to 23,300,000 pounds in 1698. The latter amount included 1,300,000 pounds shipped to, of all places, Spain and Portugal. (To add salt to the wound, the Virginians also carried on a profitable, though small, trade in tobacco with the Spanish West Indies, without benefit of legal sanction.) In the same year, 1698, the Spanish trade with England was just 27,000 pounds!

As the seventeenth century drew to its close, the demand for tobacco in England was, if not stable, a regular and accepted part of British life. In 1665 William Kemp blandly wrote

> The American silver-weed, or tobacco is . . . an excellent defence against bad air, being smoked in a pipe, either by itself or with nutmeg shred . . . it is good to warm one being cold, and will cool one being hot.

The crop itself had not changed since Rolfe described it as "strong, sweet, and pleasant as any under the sun"—a slight exaggeration except for the first adjective. An acre of Virginia bottomland yielded about 500 pounds, about enough to fill a single hogshead. The London merchants received something like five shillings a pound for it; the New World planters received about an eighth of that amount. For the small Virginia planter, tobacco was perforce a peripatetic occupation: after three

Virginia tobacco did not equal Spanish in quality, but was given customs preference by British king. "Best Virginia" became the English staple and was well-advertised by hundreds of London trade signs.

plantings the leaf yield visibly diminished, and fresh land was sought. This posed no particular problem for the "one-hogshead man"; tobacco culture spread first along the James, then along the York, the Rappahannock and the Potomac. The price of leaf went down gradually—from five shillings to four shillings, one shilling, sixpence and, in the eighteenth century, to a penny or two a pound. Quantity being the only answer to depressed prices, tobacco leapfrogged up the rivers toward the fall line—the first "westward expansion." The fall line was, in fact, the first "frontier" of fur trading and cattle grazing; Colonel William Byrd owned a fort near what is now Richmond during the seventeenth century.

The tidewater planters did not have to curb production to the needs of England itself; their leaf was transshipped to the European continent in

Tobacco catamaran—twin canoes with crossbeams—was devised to move hogsheads down the shallowest creeks. Once the leaf had been loaded onto ocean-

going ships, the platform between the two canoes was dismantled and they were paddled back up the river singly. "Ducked tobacco" was not uncommon.

ever-increasing volume—a practise encouraged by a "drawback" granted to English re-exporters of all but h'appeny of the import duty. The European market was sizable: in 1706, for example, Holland alone grew 20,000,000 pounds of leaf—almost as much as the colonial planters exported. However, the Netherlanders themselves described their leaf as having a "stinking, filthy" aroma. The sweet, bright Oronoco of the New World was needed to make the homegrown stuff palatable. Queen Anne's War (1702-13) cut off trade with France, Spain, Flanders and the Baltic. With ships by the score ferrying leaf from the tidewater, England was overwhelmed with it while Netherland and German farmers struggled to increase their output. Despite

this long break the European market was not lost; demand for the mild "Oronoko" of Virginia and Maryland survived hostilities. In 1750 the tidewater planters shipped 72,000,000 pounds, of which 54,000,000 were re-exported to European nations; in 1775 of a total shipment of 100,000,000 pounds, 90,000,000 was ultimately consumed on the continent. Now and again, this burgeoning trade received a setback—as when war closed the European ports to British merchantmen. However, so important had tobacco become to both France and Britain that the trade was carried on by mutual consent during the Anglo-French war of the 1740s, British ships landing leaf at the French ports under a flag of truce.

Extensive network of rivers and inlets throughout the Chesapeake tidewater enabled tobacco planting to spread inland. Where depth of stream permitted,

heavy riverboats like the above were used. Limits of leaf cultivation were determined almost wholly by access to water, roads being few and primitive.

The re-export of leaf tobacco from London to the continent was not entirely a boon to the Chesapeake plantations. Spanish tobacco remained a competitive factor in the European trade, and the extra freight, handling, insurance and commission borne by Virginia leaf reduced by so much the price received by growers. A Maryland man calculated that the loss to colonists on every hogshead resold in Europe was three pounds sterling.

There were other disappointments. In 1698 British diplomacy tried to open the Russian market to colonial leaf by setting up a factory with the understanding that Virginia tobacco would be processed therein. However, the arrangement fizzled and later backfired. When the factory was built and operative, the Czar approved the use of Russian leaf, violating the agreement. And a few years later, the use of "English tobacco"—meaning Virginia—was prohibited outright in Russia. With Portugal and Spain supplying southern Europe, the tobacco grown in the tidewater, which under the Navigation Acts of 1651 and 1660 could be shipped only in English vessels, was restricted to the countries of northern Europe: England, Holland, Germany, Scandinavia and France.

Gray-land grades

One of the most striking characteristics of *Nicotiana tabacum* is that it is more true to the earth in which it grows than to the seed from which it springs. Seed tobacco from North Carolina, now the center of Bright tobacco, has been transplanted into Cuba in an effort to grow American cigarette grades on that island; in two seasons, the Carolina seed generates Cuban cigar leaf. Despite the development of new curing processes and new hybrid strains, the primary influence on the characteristics of the leaf is the soil and climate in which it matures.

This fact was demonstrated, and its significance largely overlooked, by the tidewater planters. Their trade with the Old World was built on "dark air-cured," a strong heavy leaf of the kind that rich bottom land produces. This was the type called "Oronoko" by the London merchants from its resemblance to the rich product of the Orinoco River region. But very early in the development of the tidewater plantations – about 1650 – one Edward Digges cultivated a tract of land on the York River.

Earliest English symbol of American tobacco was a black "Indian" with pipe and bunch of leaves. It appeared both as a three-dimensional show figure and on two-dimensional trade signs like this one.

Digges Neck yielded a leaf much milder and more aromatic than the Oronoko, so much so that it was given its own name, "sweet-scented." This light leaf commanded a premium in England almost from its first appearance, and for more than a century hogsheads labeled E. D. were highly prized. "E. Dees," in fact, came to be a synonym for the choicest grades of leaf, and "sweet-scented parishes" came to mean the wealthiest. The reason for the development of "sweet-scented"—the earliest form of Bright tobacco—was not some unique cure or hybridization but the soil of Digges Neck itself—sandy, light-colored loam visibly different from the dark bottomlands nearby. When the prosperous Digges extended his plantation beyond the gray granitic belt, he applied the famous "E.D." mark to the new land's leaf and was reproved by his London agent, who advised him it was inferior and would ruin the "E. Dees" reputation.

Oronoko wins

The small proportion of sandy land in the tidewater kept sweet-scented to a small portion of the crop. Although British smokers favored the milder leaf, their tobacconists preferred to handle the common Oronoko—which came in at bargain prices during years of glut. Furthermore the continental markets, weaned on vile *Nicotiana rustica* of their own growing, were satisfied with the comparative pleasantness of Oronoko, and the overseas demand

First of the tidewater's "great houses" was Green
Springs, built by luxury-loving governor, William

Berkeley. By levying harsh taxes on the colonists,
collected in tobacco, Berkeley inspired rebellion.

for sweet-scented was not great enough to force its
development. This would have entailed the movement of tobacco culture away from the tidewater
and into the piedmont, and here a further obstacle
delayed such a movement for two centuries—the
fall line. The abrupt waterfalls on all the tidewater
tributaries, setting off the rocky foothills of the
piedmont from the flats of tidewater, marked the
upper limit of navigation. Since the tobacco trade
was based on direct access to ocean-going ships,
the fall line hemmed in the tobacco plantations
during the early colonial period.

However, this was no safeguard against overproduction. With much of the tidewater country given
over to closely-spaced tobacco stalks, it required
only forty years before the London warehouses
were choked with leaf. Prices dropped, planters
grew desperate. In 1639, half the crop was burned
in order to reduce the total to the 1630 level of
1,500,000 pounds. This gave only temporary relief.
As the surplus reappeared, individual planters
packed their hogsheads with trash tobacco in an

effort to increase volume and compensate for the
low prices. This was an outright abandonment of
any pretense to quality, and the planters paid heavily for it.

Bacon's rebellion

The glut became glaringly evident by 1660, and
set in motion the vicious cycle all too familiar to
those who live by tilling the soil. Hogsheads
weighted with dirt, straw, trash and scrap gave the
English and Europeans a good reason not merely
to pay less, but not to buy at all. Divested of livelihood, the smaller planters turned west, casting
about for new lands and possibly new crops, or with
an eye on the lucrative fur trade with the Indians.
Here they encountered Governor Berkeley's wall
of frontier forts, built to protect white from red
and, remembering the Powhatan days, vice versa.
Violations of Berkeley's "forest curtain" led to
squabbles not only with the Indians but with
Berkeley, who had imposed heavy taxes to build
the outposts. Taxes were paid in tobacco, and

Berkeley's useless forts were said to be "a design of the grandees to engross all of the tobacco into their own hands."

The result was a foretaste of the American Revolution. Colonists along the upper James River named a young planter of good family, Nathaniel Bacon, to form their own militia in defiance of Berkeley. General Bacon with his volunteers set off to find the Susquehannock Indians, and Berkeley with his troops marched up the James to find Bacon, whose farm was near the "Falls of the Farre West," now Richmond.

Both sides organized "navies" using merchant ships, and although the Governor's force of 80 men and four ships controlled the Chesapeake, Bacon controlled all but the coastal portion of Virginia. Believing themselves in the right, the rebels were eager for a showdown fight with Berkeley's diffident soldiers, but the climax battle was never fought. Bacon sickened in the fall of 1676 and died of a fever. His followers, still disdainful of the Gov-

ernor but unwilling to risk an eventual clash with British troops, lost heart. Many were tricked into giving up their arms by the vengeful Governor, who was said to have hanged more Virginians after Bacon's death than had been killed in the rebellion. He was recalled to England and discarded as "an old fool" by Charles II, but the bitter blood remained. Had Bacon lived, the War of Independence might have begun in 1676 instead of 1776.

Cutters and Pluckers

The end of Bacon and his rebellion did not solve the tobacco problem. At first, the colonial governments tried to limit the number of plants each worker might set out. In the sparsely settled tidewater, laced with creeks and rivers, this was unenforceable. Then Virginia tried a "stint" — complete suspension of all trade in tobacco — first in 1663, and again in 1666 and 1681. If enforced, the stint would have worked: in 1667 a severe August storm destroyed two-thirds of the crop, and prices

Bacon's Rebellion of 1676 expressed resentment of smaller planters toward Governor Berkeley and his heavy taxes. Berkeley and cronies were suspected of trying to "engross all the tobacco into their own hands." Nathaniel Bacon and central Virginia militia confronted Berkeley and his Burgesses at sword's point (above), later burned Jamestown to the ground. But Bacon died and so did the revolt.

57

advanced. But the colonists could not create such "luck" themselves. The first two times a stint was proposed, Maryland refused to go along with Virginia; the third time the royal Customs officers refused to permit it. Enraged planters instituted their own crop control the following year, 1682, rioting and destroying the better part of a million pounds of leaf. The plant-cutting riots were illegal but effective: prices rose the year afterward. Like Rolfe's unpresented petition for freedom of trade 60 years before, this revolt of the "Cutters and Pluckers" was another tug at the Crown's ruthless imperialism — a step in the gradual progression towards a tug of war.

Carolina competition

As production outran demand, Virginia also sought to bring the two into balance by closing Old Dominion ports to North Carolina tobacco. Later, when roads were built, the "importation" of North Carolina leaf into Virginia by either route was prohibited. Eventually, these actions were revoked by the mother country; but North Carolina's leaf culture was throttled for 60 years, since its colonial tobacco region was inaccessible to deepwater craft. The interstate tobacco rivalry brought into the open in 1679 by Virginia's first exclusion act was a long and bitter one, and had profound effects on both states two centuries later.

Actually, high feeling between Virginians and Carolinians had begun even before 1650. It grew from the economic enterprise of the New England traders, combined with the tricky shoals and shallow inlets of North Carolina's Outer Banks—insulating the coast from marine commerce, but made to order for piracy and smuggling. Ever alert to potential trading profits, New Englanders in vessels of light draft took out most of the Carolina leaf by sea, coastering it to their own ports and thence to the ports of Europe. Bypassing the King's customsmen, the New Englanders undercut British leaf merchants in the important continental market. Many Virginia planters did not take kindly to this arrangement, and for a while North Carolina was known as "Rogues Harbour." Parliament in 1673 tried to stop the practice by levying a penny-a-pound export duty on intercolonial leaf shipments. Faced with economic isolation, the Carolinians rebelled immediately, demanding the right to freedom of trade. Just as the Cornishmen brushed aside Queen Elizabeth's agents a century before to maintain duty-free trade in Spanish leaf, so the Carolinians set up a cry of "God Dame ye Collector" and elected their own governor, John Culpeper. Fearful that the disorder would lead to revocation of their charter, the Lords Proprietors covered up "Culpeper's Rebellion" and assured His Majesty that the plantation tax was being enforced. It was not; nor were Culpeper and his "rabble" punished. Another pull away from imperial servitude and

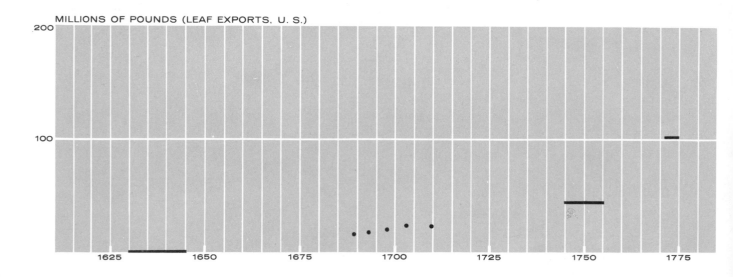

MILLIONS OF POUNDS (LEAF EXPORTS, U. S.)

Considering the limited area planted to tobacco, the expert volume reached by the planters of the tidewater was substantial. For a period of wooden, *wind-driven merchant ships, the 23,000,000 pounds of 1703 was no mean quantity. Huge, slave-manned plantations began to develop about the year 1690.*

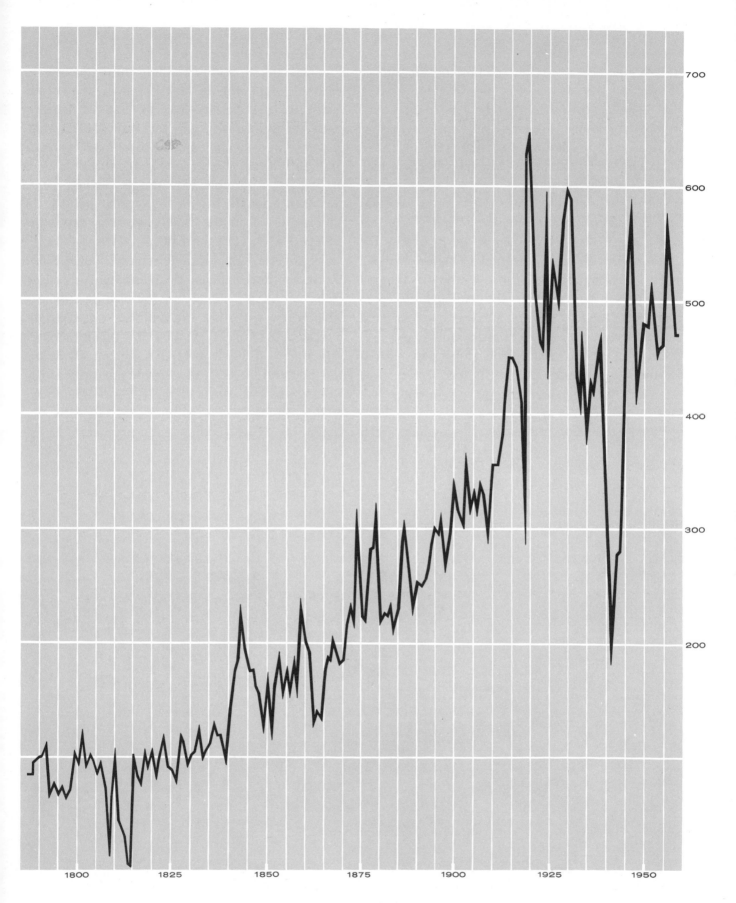

700

600

500

400

300

200

1800   1825   1850   1875   1900   1925   1950

*Sixfold increase from the tidewater export peak
to that of 1920 underestimates the actual growth
of the American tobacco crop. By 1860, the amount*
*of leaf manufactured for U.S. consumption equaled
the poundage shipped abroad. During colonial days
almost the entire tobacco crop was sold overseas.*

59

toward freedom had been, in its small way, successful.

It is significant, in view of the later emergence of the U.S. as the world's industrial pacesetter, that each major incident in the long pull toward independence was centered not on religious or political integrity but on economic freedom. In the nature of the colonial economy, most of these incidents involved tobacco.

Nor did they always take the form of petitions and rebellions. In the course of each year's leaf trade, there was a continual effort to bypass the grasping British crown. Around 1690, for example, a considerable part of the tobacco crop was shipped in bulk, not hogsheaded. This enabled a ship to carry more tobacco, making it easier to unload—and easier to smuggle ashore. English women and children came aboard before the cargo had cleared Customs to buy loose leaf "at the mast." Not to be done out of its royalties, the Crown prohibited all import of bulk leaf in 1698.

This kind of "honest smuggling" was, however, a drop in the hogshead compared to the Smuggler's Fleet, comprising ships of Scotland, Ireland, New England and Holland, all calling at the Chesapeake wharves quite openly to take off cargoes of tobacco. In 1692 the Collector of Customs there reported to his English chief that "in these three years last past there has not been above five ships trading legally in all those rivers and nigh thirty Sayle of Scotch, Irish and New Englandmen." There were not enough British bottoms to handle the Virginia trade at the time; and there were not enough warships in the British navy to police the many-fingered Chesapeake estuary. Futhermore, Scottish settlers came to the plantations in considerable numbers — many tobacco manufacturers of later years were their descendants — making enforcement of the Navigation Act against Scotch ships doubly difficult. Before the Union of Scotland and England in 1707, the former was regarded as a foreign nation, especially in the economic sense; in this situation the Scotch smuggled. After the Union, the Scottish ships had equal access to the

"Smugglers' Fleet" of ships from Holland, Ireland, New England and Scotland was as large as Britain's "Tobacco Fleet" of 300 ships. Scots were not only proficient tobacco runners but major manufacturers of snuff. Hogsheads unloaded at Broomidaw on Clyde in eighteenth century supplied Glasgow snuff works.

imperial colonies; in this situation the canny Scotch continued to evade the duty, for they managed to pay more for leaf in America and sell it for less in Bristol, London and Liverpool.

Strings across the sea

Contributing to the so-called economic yoke, which required the War of Independence to throw off, was the staggering growth of planters' debts to the British merchants receiving their goods on consignment. It was a long time between seeding plants and seeing payment, so the colonials generally drew credit from their British consignees for the purchase of furniture, clothing and other amenities which could not be grown on tidewater loam. All but the simplest manufactured objects — even clay pipes and factory-ground snuff — were imported from Britain. These long-range billings provided chances enough for cheating. But a more serious result was that the planter, once in debt to a given agent, lost his individual freedom of trade and had to accept whatever price that particular agent would pay for his leaf. In some cases the debt interest amounted almost to usury, and in most cases plantations were worked for generations without ever being out of debt. As the tobacco trade wore on into the eighteenth century, British buyers began to operate in the tidewater colonies. This did not relieve the debt problem, since they preferred to buy in quantity from the big planters for ease of loading and shipment, and since most planters, large and small, preferred to gamble for a possibly high price on the London market against the certainly low price at Chesapeake dockside. They were, after all, adventurers first and settlers afterward. They had to be, to build a civilization on a single cash crop, 3,000 miles from the source of most other supplies.

This situation was doubly frustrating because there was no possible remedy under the imperialist restraints. Virginia leaf was an important factor in the world market, but Virginia men were not. The lack of merchandising and manufacturing by settlers was almost complete: the only record of a tobacco factory before 1750 gives its leaf requirement as sixty hogsheads a year—30,000 pounds, or one-tenth of one per cent of the average crop. While the tidewater men worked only for quantity, the Spanish and Portuguese colonists were manufactur-

ers of quality products. Their Varinas tobacco rope and Canaster—twist in a basket—were acquiring a reputation and bringing good prices. The imperialism of the Iberian nations was, if anything, more naked in its cruelty than that of the British Crown. But the iron grip of Spain was accompanied by more enlightened economics than that of Britain: in the Antilles, there was no wild scramble to pack hogsheads with anything that grew green and dried brown—cultivation was controlled, and only the production of choice leaf encouraged.

There were two sides to the no-manufacturing coin: it appears that the tidewater people were more or less content to be field hands of His Majesty. Such local manufacture as there was revolved around the working of hides and wool to provide clothing. When the tobacco market was glutted and prices dropped, a spate of manufacturing began, particularly in cotton. The British would register official alarm, tobacco prices would rise, manufacturing would dwindle, and the colonists would resume planting and prizing. One of their gover-

Desire to imitate English manor life led Virginia planters to go into debt to their British tobacco agents. Debts mounted with succeeding generations.

Tomahawk pipe was invented by white man for trade with Indians during early 1700s. It was a highly successful item of barter, usually made of iron.

Indians carried pipe and skin tobacco pouch slung from neck or belt. Clay pipe was invented by red men but quickly imitated and mass-produced by the whites. Since Indians preferred white man's pipes and white man's tobacco, Virginia leaf and clays made in England were exchanged for furs and land.

nors, Gooch, declared the extremes of climate "indispose both whites and blacks to hard working . . . where the earth produces enough to purchase and supply all the necessitys of life without the drudgery of much toil, men are tempted to be lazy." This may not have been the whole story; certainly the original Jamestowners did not find the good earth very fruitful without "the drudgery of much toil." Nevertheless, Gooch's observation probably applied, or was intended to apply, to the small landholders who by nature kept their exertions to a minimum.

Common clay

As in the Spanish discovery days, only the rough-and-ready consumer around 1700 chewed any substantial amount of leaf, and that more from necessity than choice. Even he was likely to take up the pipe during moments of leisure. Between the two forms, per capita consumption was evidently quite considerable in those classes which had taken to tobacco at all. One such was the 40,000-man British Navy; at that time three-fourths of the King's tars were estimated to chew and/or smoke one pound of tobacco each month. This figures to a per capita usage of about nine pounds a year — not far below the twelve pounds a year now consumed by the average American.

The everyday use of tobacco was even less complicated than the rather elementary routine of harvesting and hogsheading. A likely-looking leaf or two was snatched from the nearest available source –usually a crack in a hogshead—and stuffed into mouth or pipe. Although active males were the chewers of cud, almost everyone smoked a clay pipe—men, women and Indians. The latter had invented pipes centuries before whites arrived and had made them in a wide range of materials—soapstone, bone, wood, clay and even porcelain. The Red Pipe-Stone Quarry of the northern plains, whose very location was secret, was a kind of hallowed shrine long before white men streamed into Dakotah territory. Since the Indians' primary food crop was corn, they are credited with originating the corncob pipe as well.

Of all these types the brittle clay was most common. It was quickly imitated and mass-produced by English pipemakers whose clays found a ready market in America, not only among the white set-

Clay pipe reached social heights in Prussia under Frederick William I, the "smoking king." Regular *gatherings of his intimates known as the "Tobacco Parliament" were dedicated to pipes and politics.*

tlers but among the red inhabitants as well. The typical Indian brave east of the Rockies carried his pipe and his animal-skin·tobacco pouch wherever he went. As the white settler developed a better-tasting crop, the Indian abandoned his own tobacco-growing to barter for white man's leaf. Similarly, the red men preferred English clays when they could trade for them (although the long, feathered wooden calumet, usually a sacred or ceremonial object, remained an Indian artifact).

Trade with the Indians was always a profitable undertaking, and the whites could afford to go to considerable trouble to give the red-skinned trappers what they wanted for their pelts. Some unknown merchandising genius, aware of the place of warrier prowess and tobacco in the Indian scheme of things, invented the tomahawk pipe early in the eighteenth century. This was usually an iron affair, and was apparently one of the most eagerly sought barter items during the pre-Revolutionary years. Aside from furs, the only worth-

while property the Indian could offer was land. This they would sell very cheaply: there is a seventeenth-century record of the purchase of land in New Jersey in which 125 pipes and 100 Jews harps constituted the sole consideration. Part of Pennsylvania was bought with pipes by William Penn, the colony's founder.

In Europe, tobacco in general and the pipe in particular were exalted to an incredible degree. The French playwright Moliere wrote of the leaf: "It is the passion of honest men and he who lives without tobacco is not worthy of living."(!) Frederick William I of Prussia (1688-1740) was known to Europe as "the smoking king"; his Tobacco Parliament was a regular gathering of intimates devoted to beer and pipe smoking with political overtones.

As a rule, pipes had small bowls; the dark air-cured leaf of the seventeenth century was a powerful shag, best smoked in small doses. For the same reason pipe stems were fairly long compared with

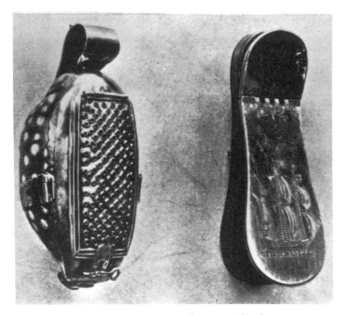

First snuff, like first pipe leaf and chew, was a "do-it-yourself" product. Tobacco rope was ground into coarse powder or "rapee" using pocket rasps.

The eighteenth century was the great age of snuff. Inlaid silver snuffboxes like these were displayed by upper classes and "worn" like personal jewelry.

today's; the luxury clay of the times had a curved stem so long it was known as a "yard of clay." The unblended strength of the rank shipping leaf, which required a robust palate to appreciate, also contributed to the vogue for snuff among the more delicately constituted upper classes.

Snuff

Most of the Indians encountered by the English colonists of North America were pipe smokers; the native snuff-takers lived in tropical America. Hence the initial spread of tobacco among Englishmen was in pipes. Snuff did not become an everyday commodity until late in the 1600s: thought to have antiseptic properties, it was prescribed for use against the Plague. It did not become fashionable until the turn of the eighteenth century. Under Queen Anne the snuff-box became indispensable to the well-turned-out gentleman, while the smoking of clay pipes was relegated to philosophers and the lower classes.

Among the first snuff-takers were members of the clergy, who found *tabacum pulveratum* an inconspicuous way to consume the leaf. In the *haute monde,* however, snuffing was a conspicuous form of consumption. Its origin with the naked Arawaks of Cuba and Hispaniola was overlooked by the French, who raised it to an elaborate social ritual

imitated by the upper classes of Britain. The high society of the colonies followed the British in adopting this flamboyant excuse for graceful finger-movements, ostentatious snuff-boxes, and the flourishing of silken handkerchiefs.

Although a fast fad for "sniveling and snorting" developed during the latter half of the seventeenth century, the courtly eighteenth century was the great age of snuff. Tobacco powder was sold by the ton, not only among the well-born and the clergy but also among the ordinary subjects of Portugal, Spain, Italy, France and, lastly, England. Pulverized and perfumed, tobacco was inserted up the nostrils in dainty pinches and the excess removed with a tiny snuffspoon. For those of lofty station, snuff had a dual advantage: not only was it a means by which soothing scents were introduced into the organ of smell, but it also blanketed the user's olfactory sensibilities against other strong odors. Among the lowly who were the source of some of these odors, snuff served an even more practical purpose: it induced sneezing, which was thought to have therapeutic value.

At first, snuffing was just as crude as the chewing or burning of whatever hank of leaf came to hand. The powder was not milled in factories but prepared from standard tobacco rope by the consumer on a "grate-your-own" basis. From the French word for rasp, used to grate the dried leaf, comes the term rapee, still used to designate coarse snuff. Factory mills could grind the tobacco much finer, and snuff-making became a thriving business in many cities of western Europe, most notably Glasgow. The Scotch were quick to import leaf from the Chesapeake colonies; their merchants even set up stores in the interior where they could barter merchandise for leaf before it got to the wharves. They were just as quick to manufacture and export snuff. During the first half of the eighteenth century Scotch snuff had its greatest sale in London, and that city's "overseas suburb," Virginia, also formed a good market. So assiduously did the colonists take to the snuffing custom that small mills were started in Virginia about 1730, in Rhode Island about 1750, and in New York City about the year 1760. Only the last-named enterprise, founded by Pierre Lorillard, has survived to the present day; thus the P. Lorillard Company is the nation's oldest tobacco manufacturer. During the 1800s, in England, the original tobacconist's signs of the black Virginia Indian gave way to that of a Scot, which eventually culminated in the cigar store Indian of the U.S.

Although the varieties of snuff were almost infinite, there were three basic types made in Europe from Virginia leaf. Scotch snuff was a dry, strong, virtually unflavored product which was finely ground. Maccaboy snuff was moist and heavily scented. Rapee snuff, also known as Swedish, was grated to a more coarse consistency. None of these could quite duplicate the distinctive flavor of Seville or Spanish snuff, ground from Havana leaf and known as "Musty." In almost any form, Virginia shipping leaf suffered by comparison with Spanish tobacco.

Tobacco roads

Much of the "adventure" or business risk of the tidewater tobacco trade revolved around the matter of shipping. In order to economize on shipping space, most leaf was prized (compressed) into hogsheads. At first these were 400 to 600 pounds in weight, the average growing to 1,200 pounds as hogshead dimensions increased. The crude coopering of the day, and the equally crude packing of the leaf for a 3,000-mile journey, were not calculated to preserve the finest leaf quality. Since not

Kilted Scot replaced black "Virginia boy" as the tobacconist's trade figure, reflecting Scotland's dominance in the business of snuff manufacturing.

Later advertisement for the leading English snuff ignored "sniff appeal" in favor of "snob appeal."

65

every plantation could touch water, many hogsheads had to be rolled to the nearest tobacco wharf over rough trails — "rolling roads" or "tobacco roads." Even a mile of this involved a certain amount of bruising, and ten or twenty miles could ruin a season's work. From wharves the hogsheads were loaded directly or lightered in flat scows to the ships, generally built to stow hogsheads seven deep. Should the hogs vary to any extent from the accepted size, the end cask would be cropped to fit it into the hold. Shipwreck or piracy meant a 100% loss, but the normal course of water transport usually reduced the value of the leaf to some degree: rotting in a leaky bottom, withering in hot climates, petty thievery through the loose staves everywhere. Crucial as these risks were to individual planters, a bigger menace to the leaf trade as a whole was the great fertility of the tidewater land and the consequent over-production.

The quest for quality

Eventually, Virginia came to grips with crop control by setting up inspection warehouses to cut off the export of trash, lugs, suckers, slips and sweepings at the source. These warehouses or "rolling houses" were located within one mile of deep water by law. After a false start in 1713, an inspection act with teeth was passed in 1730. "Tobacco

Planters who owned deep-water wharves made money by assembling small farmers' crops into a single large shipment, imported goods to trade for leaf. Illustration is part of an eighteenth-century map.

"Rolling road" or "tobacco road" was crude trail over which hogsheads were bumped to water's edge. Rolling hogs over rough roads usually resulted in bruised, dirty tobacco; for this reason, the law specified that inspection warehouses be within a mile of deep water. One hogshead held 400 or 500 pounds of leaf, representing a whole year's cash crop for small farmers called "one-hogshead men."

notes" certifying leaf for export were issued by the public inspectors; leaf not qualifying was burned: this included bruised, worm-eaten, barn-burned or smoked tobacco and all ground leaves. Almost immediately, the international reputation of Virginia leaf was restored. Maryland held aloof as its leaf sank into comparative disrepute, but she too had suffered from overproduction and had experienced a "cutters and pluckers" revolt in 1730. Maryland finally passed its own inspection act in 1747.

So effective was this quality control that "tobacco notes" or "crop notes" began to take the place of leaf itself as colonial currency. This did not mark any great change in the tobacco culture itself, but merely replaced the old leaf-barter system with a more stable currency, now based on a commodity of standardized quality. Taxes and other fees had long been paid in tobacco. The story is told that wives were "bought" for tobacco by the Jamestown colonists; actually, the passage fees of twelve English ladies who journeyed thither with matrimonial intent were paid in leaf. For more than a hundred years, clergymen's salaries were set by law in terms of leaf—16,000 pounds (tobacco, not sterling) per year. This made each minister his own leaf expert and, willy-nilly, a speculator in tobacco.

Mr. Patrick Henry

In 1758 the use of tobacco as money touched off the celebrated trial of the Parson's Cause, whose central issue was the right of Virginia to pass her own laws. The law in question was known as the Two Penny Act, and provided that debts payable in leaf could be discharged in currency instead; bad weather had led the legislature to anticipate a small crop. The clergymen resisted, since the small crop made for higher prices, and the following year obtained an Order of Council from the Crown declaring the Two Penny Act null and void. Some of the clergymen then brought suit against Virginia for their "losses"—the difference between two pence per pound and the higher market price. A 27-year-old lawyer named Patrick Henry pleaded the case for the taxpayers against one of these clergymen, basing his argument on the right of Virginia to manage its own affairs without arbitrary interference from a tyrannical king. Henry's unsuspected genius as an orator made the jury's "blood to run cold, and their hair to rise on end." No wonder: his words were nothing less than treason from the British point of view. But the verdict was another step on the road to independence: the plaintiff, Reverend James Maury, was awarded one

Patrick Henry won fame defending Virginia's right to pay clergy in cash instead of tobacco, a right not recognized by the British king. In 1775 Henry rallied the colonies to rebel against imperialist Britain: "I know not what course others may take, but as for me, give me liberty or give me death!"

penny in damages and the royal veto was flaunted. Henry, who had taken the case with tongue in cheek as a means to achieve notoriety, eventually succumbed to the force of his own reasoning. Seventeen years later, in St. John's Episcopal Church of Richmond, he was to voice for the Virginia Convention and the colonies the rallying cry of a new nation:

> Is life so dear, or peace so sweet, as to be purchased at the price of chains and slavery? Forbid it, Almighty God! I know not what course others may take, but as for me, give me liberty or give me death!

First families of Virginia

Primitive as the tobacco currency system sounds, the civilization that evolved with it was anything but primitive. Great plantations, great manor houses, great names grew up in the Chesapeake along with the six-foot stalks of *Nicotiana tabacum*.

Before 1700, estates of 5,000 acres or so were the rule; in the next century they ran as high as 300,000 acres.

Despite the Crown's ban on manufacture, estates of this size turned out shoes, cloth, hemp, bar iron, and nails in addition to tobacco. Inevitably, they also turned out men of ability.

The most famous concentration of tobacco plantations or "hundreds" was stretched along the James River between Jamestown Island and the falls at what is now Richmond. Westover, Berkeley Hundred, Shirley Hundred and Bermuda Hundred adjoined each other. Although these could trace their patents to the early years of settlement, none became great establishments until 1700 or thereabouts. Before that time, tobacco farming was largely a hundred-acre proposition; most of the work was done by free citizenry. The first slave ship arrived in 1619, but there was comparatively little importation of captured Africans for the next 50 years or so. It was not until the slave traffic became heavy and vast land-holdings were accumulated by wealthy proprietors that the sizable plantations evolved. When that happened, the small planter or "one-hogshead man" was squeezed into insignificance, or moved west.

Hundreds into thousands

But it was from small beginnings that the huge plantations — like Virginia itself — began. Berkeley Hundred, which grew into a 20,000-acre domain, was settled in 1619 as an independent colony or, more properly, as a colony within a colony. Thirty-eight men landed and declared a day of Thanksgiving on December 3, almost a year before the Pilgrims held a similar observance in Massachusetts. They included a cooper, carpenter, shoemaker, blacksmith, cook, gunsmith and other artisans; Richard Berkeley and the other absentee owners intended that the venture should be independent of relief ships, with its own supply facilities and a diversified crop.

For a while, everything went along swimmingly. A college was set up, Indians converted to Christianity, and some brick construction initiated. By 1622 there were 1,200 living colonists in the James area. But Powhatan had died in 1618 and his brother Opechancano, who succeeded him, was not so forbearing a king. The apparent permanence of the white settlements disturbed the Indians, but they were careful not to show it. On Good Friday of 1622 groups of the redmen wandered into the white homes and mess halls, many sitting down to breakfast with the English. As if by a signal they seized their hosts' knives and muskets, and in a trice 349 settlers were massacred. Only Jamestown, which had been warned of the plot, suffered no casualties. Again the little walled island became the lone outpost in a hostile forest; most of the survivors fled there, since the methodical Indians had destroyed their food barns. By 1632, Berkeley had reverted almost to a wilderness.

In time, settlement resumed. Most settlers were content merely to survive, but a few worked and fought their way into the big-planter class. One such was Benjamin Harrison II, son of a modest colonist who had acquired 200 acres across from Jamestown and increased it to 500 by his death

around 1650. The second Harrison became a sheriff, then a Burgess, and climaxed his career with the purchase of Berkeley Hundred in 1691. Under the third Benjamin Harrison the old place flowered into a mighty establishment of 20,000 acres with a fine brick manor house, slaves to grow the tobacco and tend the flocks, and a deep-water landing; it was known for a time as "Harrison's Landing." As the years revolved, tobacco increased and so did the Harrisons. The fourth Benjamin Harrison was a lord of the manor rather than a struggling planter-merchant; the fifth Benjamin Harrison had the wealth and leisure to devote his time to statecraft: he was a delegate to the Continental Congress, close friend of a wealthier planter, George Washington, and, later, the first governor of independent Virginia.

To an extent, these great plantations were accidents of geography; most of them were fortunate enough to embrace deep-water landings. Less fortunately-situated growers took to delivering

Tobacco spawned great Virginia plantations which set the pattern of life in the South. This was the Byrd manor house at Westover, on the James River.

Berkeley Hundred dates from 1619; a Thanksgiving Day was celebrated there almost a year before the Pilgrims landed at Plymouth Rock. The manor house *was built in 1726 by Benjamin Harrison, a tobacco planter whose grandson became the ninth President and whose great-great-grandson the twenty-third.*

their hogsheads to the waterside plantation for shipment in the next available bottom. Gradually the big plantation came to furnish cooperage and other services; from this developed the plantation store which took leaf in trade for imported goods. In time, the planter became an importer, a boat-builder, a storekeeper, or a cotton spinner—sometimes all of these in one. In addition to his leaf tobacco he might export sawed lumber, furs or hides. In some measure these establishments were independent of the violent price fluctuations of to-bacco: they could "wait out" the market and ship in vast quantities when the price was right. So evolved the Berkeley Hundreds, the Westovers, the Carters Groves.

Leaf men into leaders

The successful managers of these plantations were not transplanted English aristocrats, but rather energetic members of the lower and middle classes who generated their own aristocracy in the New World by dint of their own labor. Among them were William Fitzhugh of Bedford, whose income in 1686 ran to 60,000 pounds sterling and who left a plantation of 54,000 acres on his death in 1701. William Byrd II of Westover was the son of the Colonel Byrd who traded with Indians from his fort on the fall-line frontier. Like Fitzhugh, he became a member of the House of Burgesses, was educated in England, amassed one of the largest libraries in the Colonies, and held 179,000 acres by

The most impressive plantations were those along the broad James between Richmond and the island of Jamestown. Westover, Berkeley Hundred, and Shir- *ley Hundred were contiguous. The brick barn at Shirley (above) was put up in the early 1700s and is still used; the plantation was worked as early as 1613.*

1744. Not surprisingly, Byrd was moved to write that tobacco's uses went far beyond smoking: "We should wear it about our clothes, and about our coaches. We should hang bundles of it round our beds, and in the apartments wherein we most converse." The most powerful of the planters was Robert Carter (1663-1732), better known as King Carter. His holdings exceeded 300,000 acres and he dominated not only the Virginia political scene, holding virtually every leading office at one time or another, but also ruled his local parish in spiritual matters, the minister being, in effect, his assistant. Services did not begin—in fact, the congregation did not enter church—until Carter arrived.

Carter and his counterparts were to Virginia what the cattle barons would be to the early West and the oil millionnaires to Texas. Vast holdings like Carter's 333,000 acres were not all worked by one owner's slaves. Some were worked by tenant farmers who paid rent in produce. Some were held as "reserve land" to replace the acreage constantly being worn out by mass tobacco cultivation. Plantation life was an alternation between the monotonous, seasonal sequence of seeding-priming-curing and the occasional bursts of social excitement that befit the lives of "landed gentry." Their pattern became the pattern of the whole South through the ascendancy of cotton, for as time went on the tobacco cash crop was supplemented on the large plantations by the raising of fruit, cattle and grain,

The great men of colonial Virginia originated not from the English aristocracy but from middle-class settlers who developed ability managing their own

estates. George Washington, for example, was born in this modest homestead on Bridges Creek, within sight of the Potomac. Ground floor had four rooms.

making each estate essentially sufficient unto itself. The storybook land of cavaliers and cotton fields swept away by the War Between the States took its shape from the little knot of successful tobacco growers clustered around the Chesapeake. With their success, which was the success of business acumen, grew political vision. Trained in the management of self-sufficient plantations supporting up to 1,000 souls apiece, they passed easily into the management of whole colonies and the conduct of international affairs—first under, then against, the haughty kings of England.

As it is usually expounded, the "great man theory of history" is somewhat one-sided. It cites the acts of great men as determining the course of events, and often ignores the events which shaped the great men. The experience of the Virginia colony — thrown on its own, forced to produce or starve, buffeted in its trade growth by the international

winds of war and politics—was a crucible all in itself, trying and testing and turning out men of ability. This unique and demanding situation bred the men it needed: Fitzhughs, Byrds, Carters, Digges, Lees, Randolphs,. Nelsons, Harrisons. And in its fullest flower the tobacco culture also bred George Washington, Thomas Jefferson, James Madison.

Washington

George Washington knew his tobacco. In 1760 he wrote that "Rain for near four weeks has given a sad turn to our expectations . . . a great deal of Tobacco being Drownd, and the rest spotting very fast, which is always a consequence of so much Wet Weather." Too much rain is still a major hazard to the South's big cash crop—apart from the unsightly spots, it "washes out" the leaves and renders them weak in flavor. Too little rain, of course, carries drastic results of its own.

As Commander in Chief of the Revolutionary armies Washington asked his fellow-Americans to help his soldiers: "If you can't send money, send tobacco."

But even more, Washington knew men. While one of the large tobacco planters of his day, he could see better than most what was happening to the Colonies' No. 1 cash crop under the London-consignment system. In four years out of five, he estimated, tobacco shipped on consignment to England actually returned lower prices than those obtainable at home. If the results of his career as a planter are any measure, Washington must be accounted as a self-made success. His landholdings west of the Appalachians alone exceeded 45,000 acres; when the Declaration of Independence was written, he was reputed to have been the wealthiest man in Virginia, possibly the wealthiest in the colonies. It was this, more than his limited military experience on the frontier, that led to his appointment as commander-in-chief of the Continental armies. Washington's sagacity was not confined to a business knowledge of his fellow man; he was a

natural leader as well as a natural gentleman. In 1776, year of his most serious Revolutionary reverse, loss of New York to the British, he appealed to his countrymen for aid to the army: "I say, if you can't send money, send tobacco." After he had ceased to grow tobacco for the market, he permitted his tenant to grow tobacco on his estate so as to provide leaf for family chewing and smoking.

Tobacco in Revolution

During the Revolutionary campaigns tobacco played its part as a sustainer of morale, much as it has in all wars since. In 1777 the British Colonel St. Leger and his Indian ally, Joseph Brant, found their drive across New York State blocked at Oriskany. General Nicholas Herkimer with 800 militiamen moved to strengthen that strongpoint and were ambushed by St. Leger and his Indians. Although a ball had shattered his leg and killed his horse, Herkimer continued to command his troops while smoking his pipe. The engagement was broken off by the British, who were unable to reduce the fort at Oriskany and retreated to Oswego.

The immediate importance of tobacco to the success of the Revolution went beyond twist for the troops. The Chesapeake colonies continued to export leaf during the war years; the Continental Congress used it to build up credits aboard. In 1777 Benjamin Franklin in Paris drew 2,000,000 livres against a contract to deliver 5,000 hogsheads of Virginia leaf. Of all people, the British were in a position to appreciate the value of leaf tobacco as currency reserve. British men-of-war, alerted to intercept America's chief source of foreign exchange, seized an estimated 34,000,000 pounds; but an additional 53,000,000 pounds—slightly more than half a normal year's export—reached the overseas markets during the war years. England used her ground troops as well as her ships to stopper this funnel of American strength. In 1780 and 1781 Cornwallis and his armies made the destruction of tobacco in Virginia a primary mission. Ten thousand hogsheads are supposed to have been burned in the course of the "Tobacco War," among them the leaf stores on Thomas Jefferson's plantation at Elk Island. Although the "useless and barbarous injury" done to his property by Cornwallis would have more than paid his debt to British creditors, Jefferson did not claim immunity on that account. Nor did he seek refuge in the "sequestration" laws passed by Virginia to wipe out private debts to the English. His personal declaration of dependence in this matter was quite as admirable as the more famous Declaration of Independence he had penned in Philadelphia seven years before. "Substantial justice is my object, as decided by reason, and not by authority or compulsion." This was one of the proudest moments in the long history of Americans and tobacco.

Tidewater's ebb

The fight for independence was led and financed by aristocrats like Washington and Jefferson and Benjamin Harrison V. But in the process of displacing the British aristocrats, they displaced themselves too. Not only tobacco and barns but slaves were lost during the "Tobacco War" of 1780 and 1781. The debts to British merchants remained an obstacle to resumption of the trade in Virginia leaf. Cash was low. So was the raw energy which

had built up the plantations in the first place. Men looked to a new frontier and a new life across the Appalachians, among them the youngest son of the fifth Benjamin Harrison, William Henry Harrison. President George Washington, young William's guardian after his father died in 1791, got the restless youngster an ensign's commission, and the new ensign joined his regiment in Cincinnati. In effect, he rejected his aristocratic tidewater background; in 1811 he defeated Tecumseh at Tippecanoe and in 1840 ran for President as "Old Tippecanoe." By then his personality was of the "log-cabin" cast; but as a token of respect to the great days of the tidewater, "just plain Bill" Harrison stopped at Berkeley Hundred on the way to the White House to write his inaugural speech in the room where he was born.

Old Tippecanoe died a month after taking office as the ninth President. His grandson, Benjamin Harrison VIII, was to be the twenty-third President. But neither belonged to the world of the tide-

Washington was one of the large tobacco planters of his day, shipped considerable leaf to England. An acute businessman, he warned that leaf shipped to Britain on consignment brought less money than that sold on domestic market, in four years out of five. Mount Vernon crop was therefore diversified.

water tobacco. Berkeley Hundred, topheavy with debt, was sold to the Carters of next-door Shirley only a year or two after William Henry Harrison paid the place his last visit. Most of the other large plantations, and the aristocrats who went with them, were to fade out of the tobacco story in a similar way. Independence and democracy brought in a new kind of economy to replace the static master-and-slave arrangement of a colonial possession.

Independence

Not a few of the Virginia gentlemen supported the Revolution in the belief that victory would automatically discharge them of their hereditary debts to English factors. But the Treaty of Paris (1783) did not cancel out the tobacco debts. Some of the tidewater planters set about settling them. Others pleaded "sequestration" and were sued in the courts by their British creditors, who generally collected. The controversy dragged on for twenty years and was finally solved by Congressional action, the Federal Government paying £600,000 to Britain in full settlement of all the outstanding claims.

If the revolutionaries had wondered why they fought, as many of them doubtless did, the post-war resurgence of their tobacco trade formed part of the answer. At the recommendation of Lafayette, France opened her ports to Virginia leaf in 1784, granting Americans the right of deposit at Lorient. The French government went so far as to urge the Farmers-General (France's monopoly) to forego its accustomed practise of *prélation*—lowering the purchase price of leaf after it was contracted for. This drastic suggestion was made because the British, also keenly interested in American tobacco, were offering every inducement to the new United States in an effort to restore commercial ties with its offspring.

It has been said that the failure of Congress to settle the planters' debts immediately after the Revolution was responsible for the passing of the aristocratic tobacco culture of Old Virginia, since debt settlement proved the financial ruin of some of its finest families. But the prosperity of the tobacco trade does not bear this out. In 1783, leaf exports from Virginia alone jumped to more than 86,000,000 pounds, as against the average of

Pipe-smoking hero was General Nicholas Herkimer. His leg shattered when troops were ambushed near Oriskany, New York by British, Herkimer puffed on his pipe, directed skirmish until enemy withdrew.

12,000,000 during the war years of 1776-1782. And in 1791, leaf exports constituted fully a fifth of all U. S. exports in point of dollar value. With no more than the ordinary year-to-year variations, the lucrative leaf business continued at a high level right up to the export embargo of 1808. There was, to be sure, a decided movement of tobacco cultivation out of the Virginia tidewater (it began as early as 1700 when English settlers crossed the Cumberland Gap and planted tobacco in Kentucky). But the westering was prompted not by the impoverishment of a few individual planters, but by the impoverishment of the tidewater soil itself.

Thomas Jefferson, planter

Jefferson's major influence on the history of the United States—and on the tobacco industry — was exerted during the early 1800s, and was felt in the West rather than in the tidewater country. But as a tobacco planter himself, familiar with the cross-currents of supply and demand that made leaf prices so unstable, he worried about Virginia's concentration on the one crop. At the outbreak of the Revolution he, along with two out of three tobacco planters, was a financial prisoner of his British agents, and owed nearly 10,000 pounds sterling to

75

Monticello, designed by Thomas Jefferson, is now monument to his memory. Bricks, timber and nails to build it were made on the property. Like many tobacco planters, Jefferson owed large amounts to British merchants. Although redcoats had destroyed his leaf stores during 1780-81, Jefferson insisted on paying off his tobacco debts in full. "Justice is my object," said he, "as decided by reason and not by authority or compulsion." Monticello manor house was begun in 1769, not completed until 1809.

Glasgow and London firms. Jefferson deeply resented the debts peculiar to the tobacco trade which "had become hereditary from father to son, for many generations, so that the planters were a species of property, annexed to certain merchants in London." In 1781 he wrote that leaf culture

> was fast declining at the commencement of this war, and that of wheat taking its place: and it must continue to decline on the return of peace. I suspect that the change in the temperature of our climate has become sensible to that plant, which, to be good, requires an extraordinary degree of heat. But it requires still more indispensably an uncommon fertility of soil: and the price which it commands at market will not enable the planter to produce this by manure. Was the supply still to depend on Virginia and

Maryland alone, as its culture becomes more difficult, the price would rise, so as to enable the planter to surmount those difficulties and to live. But the western country on the Mississippi, and the midlands of Georgia, having fresh and fertile lands in abundance, and a hotter sun, will be able to undersell these two states, and will oblige them to abandon the raising tobacco altogether.

These remarks imply that exhaustion of the tidewater soil and lack of crop rotation were having some effect on the quality of leaf. Jefferson's prophecies of the spread of tobacco cultivation and the replacement of tidewater tobacco by wheat were correct, although his notions on temperature change and "hotter suns" were not. Later he echoed Washington's shrewd observation on the transoceanic tobacco trade: "Tobacco always sells better in Virginia than in the hands of a London merchant ... submit to anything rather than to an obligation to ship your tobacco."

The Morris business

The precept of business management spelled out by Jefferson, the farmer-philosopher, was vividly underlined by a great transaction between the French tobacco monopoly and Robert Morris, a Philadelphian who had helped finance the American Revolution. The terms provided for the delivery of 60,000 hogsheads of tobacco to the French Farmers-General in 1785-87. In return for the exclusive agency as supplier to France, Morris agreed to supply the leaf at 22½ Virginia shillings per hundredweight (the "normal" price at the time was 40 shillings).

Reaction to this in the Chesapeake area was mildly typified by a letter written by William Hemsley of Queen Anne County to his leaf dealer in Baltimore, which related in part:

> ... In a letter Mr. Morris wrote me by the post on Saturday he says by Way of postscript that I must get Tobacco down to 25/per 100 ct. as soon as possible. I flatter myself you will not try the experiment, because I do not think it will succeed. The planters will send their Tobacco to Baltimore and barter it away in any shape before they will take that price ...

Morris was branded a traitor, a profiteer and a blackguard. The planters depended on the French market to take about a fourth of their crops. Morris' "package deal" may have been good business—an attempt to secure a wholesale discount on a bulk lot—but Jefferson wrote that it "had thrown the commerce of that article in agonies." Washington was torn between sympathy for his fellow-planters and obligation to Morris, who had furnished funds in the nation's dark hours. Morris himself did not make out well on the deal, for part of the shipment was lost at sea and the hard-bargaining French quibbled about the quality of the delivered portion.

In the end, the invidious arrangement all but severed Franco-American trade. Extensive diplomatic exchanges between Thomas Jefferson and the French minister Vergennes were intended, first, to abrogate the Morris contract and, second, to eliminate the French tobacco monopoly, the Farmers-General. Neither was accomplished. Owing to the sharp policy and transparent chicanery of the French monopoly, the American leaf trade, greatest commercial prize of the era, was not won by France even though she was at the time the largest consumer in Europe. Resentment among French businessmen, whose commerce with the U. S. hinged on tobacco imports, was among the factors leading to the fall of the French monarchy in the bloody revolution of 1789.

A hundred years later, in 1880, the U. S. Department of Agriculture was to report that

> Tobacco is, for several reasons, held longer in stock than the raw material of most manufacturers, its production fluctuating more than that of corn and wheat. Prices are therefore variable, stimulating heavy movement when low, and causing inequalities in the quantities held. The gov-

Robert Morris, a Philadelphian who helped finance the American Revolution, became agent for French tobacco monopoly in 1785, contracted to ship leaf 44% below normal price. He was branded a traitor.

James Madison in 1794 opposed a tax on tobacco as unequal. He felt it would deprive poorer people of innocent gratification. Congress compromised with a tax on snuff, did not tax chew and pipe tobacco.

ernment monopolies of several countries buy irregularly, in large quantities, as the required types are found in sufficient abundance and of desirable prices, and the trade is liable to sudden and marked disturbance by the meteoric incursions of these *regie* buyers. With a necessity for a much larger "visible supply," for these reasons, than the current requirement for the year's manufacture, the record of stocks and probable crop at the close of each year is examined with great care by dealers and manufacturers; and the subject is invested with additional interest from the mystery of the *regie* surplus, which it fails to penetrate. The probable crop is also a somewhat uncertain element, because the curing is not complete, and if the quantity could be precisely determined, the quality and available value could not be so early as the close of December . . .

This statement of the situation applied from the very beginning to Virginia's trade with the French monopoly and, to an extent, to the monopoly exercised by the London merchants.

Leaf and taxes

The momentum generated by the strong demand for tobacco had from the very first carried its own penalty: heavy taxes. British Crown revenue on the leaf amounted to the equivalent of $6,500,000 in 1689, $16,500,000 at the outbreak of the American Revolution. These amounts — enormous for that period, and probably equal to the levies from all the other British possessions combined — were raised on only a small fraction of the tidewater leaf traffic. In 1775 only ten per cent of the colonies' exports were taxed at the full rate of eightpence plus; the remainder, re-exported to Europe, yielded only halfpenny a pound. Tobacco consumed in Britain thus bore almost the entire tax burden. (This levy, once imposed successfully, set a precedent for other governments to follow. Today, American tobacco in the form of cigarettes is taxed at the rate of $1.43 per pound by the federal government alone, with state governments adding another $.60 per pound on the average, and many cities another 17c or more on top of that. A pound of tobacco selling for 60c in leaf form thus returns three to four times that amount to tax authorities by the time it reaches the smoker.)

Since tobacco traffic on this side of the Atlantic was in hogsheads rather than in pounds, the principal revenue to Virginia and Maryland came from an export duty of two shillings per hogshead. There was also the 1673 penny-a-pound "plantation tax" on tobacco shipped from colony to colony, but collecting it proved difficult. Perhaps for this reason the King in 1693 granted to the College of William and Mary all plantation taxes on tobacco in Virginia and Maryland.

Smoking vs. snuffing

Taxes are always controversial, and extra-heavy taxes are even more so. One of the first tax debates in the Congress of the infant United States had to do not with leaf tobacco but with manufactured tobacco and snuff. Alexander Hamilton, the first Secretary of the Treasury, discussed the imposition of excise taxes with tobacco makers of Philadelphia a few years after the Revolutionary War. After extensive argument, Congress took the position that snuff was a foppish fancy and should bear a tax, while ordinary citizens who smoked or chewed would not be injured by such a levy. During debate James Madison delivered this opinion:

As to the subject before the House, it was proper to choose taxes the *least unequal*. Tobacco excise was a burden the most *unequal*. It fell upon the poor, upon sailors, day laborers, and other people of these classes, while the rich will often escape it. Much has been said about the taxing of luxury. The pleasures of life consisted in a series of innocent gratifications, and he felt no satisfaction in the prospect of their being squeezed. Sumptuary laws had never, he believed, answered any good purpose.

The original bill provided for excises on refined sugar, tobacco and snuff. As passed in 1794, the word "tobacco" was taken out. The Philadelphia manufacturers, in pressing for this desirable result, presented a succinct description of the nascent American manufacturing industry:

> Before the revolution, the American consumption of manufactured tobacco was almost exclusively supplied by British manufacturers. In Pennsylvania there existed but one snuff-mill; and all the other colonies could reckon but one more. . . . Manufactured tobacco is of a late date in this country. Previous to the war, little or none was ever used, at least in New England; the inhabitants there were accustomed to use the leaf-tobacco, and that of their own raising. The manufacture was begun in the large seaport towns, for the accommodation of foreigners, and sailors, who wanted it for their sea stores, and to carry as *ventures* [smuggling] to those places, where tobacco was heavily dutied. By degrees the use of manufactured tobacco has extended into the country . . .

Freedom to manufacture

Between the lines of this short description can be sensed the great economic change that was to come over the United States with its release from vassalage to the King. In the tidewater, tobacco production was diminishing in the interest of greater self-sufficiency; in the west, tobacco culture would receive new impetus as the trading crop for pioneer settlers; and in the cities of the East coast manufacturing — not only of tobacco but of other goods — was already beginning a vigorous growth that hasn't stopped yet. As a consumer's good, tobacco was reaching new peaks; America was literally growing up in smoke.

Tightly bound to England by traditional ties as well as those of credit, their manufacturing enterprise squelched by imperial policy, the men of tidewater had been fleeced repeatedly by the economic bullies of Europe. Only where they had achieved a "balanced economy"—on the largest, self-sufficient plantations—did they enjoy any degree of economic independence. The Morris contract drove home to them their own shortcomings as businessmen, but it was a long time after the Revolution—three-quarters of a century—before the major industry of the Chesapeake region could be brought into a balance between export and manufacture.

Better as businessmen, and perhaps for that reason soonest aware of the need for independence of trade as a basis for political freedom, were their fellow-Americans of the North, the Yankees.

YANKEES AND LONG NINES

IF Virginia was the womb of the Colonies, New England was their sharp eye. In one, tobacco renewed the cornucopia with seasonal, sleepy regularity; in the other, rocky soil and biting frost compelled the Yankee to fight nature, to shift for himself, to adapt. Virginia showed the measured enterprise of a rich land mined for its treasures; New England the quick enterprise, the alertness, the trading instinct of an orphan forced to live by his wits.

The tobacco trade furnishes ample evidence of Yankee enterprise. Like the Jamestowners, the first colonists were quick to perceive the Indian culture of the leaf, and quick to plant it themselves. Connecticut was settled in 1633, and before 1640 tobacco crops were being raised at Windsor. The bitter taste of the *rustica* variety smoked in pipes by the Indians led the Connecticut growers to follow Rolfe's sequence in switching to the large-leaved "Spanish" plant: seed for this purpose was obtained from Virginia. The importance of tobacco during the very earliest years of New England is seen in the fact that protective legislation was enacted by Connecticut in 1640, and even earlier

by Massachusetts. Citizens were forbidden to consume any tobacco grown in other colonies, under a penalty of five shillings per pound. This set a pattern for New Englanders which lasted more than 150 years—they satisfied personal tobacco needs by growing their own and using it in unmanufactured, "home-made" form.

The native Indian habits of consumption, like native Indian farming methods, were taken over by the whites. As among most North American tribes, the pipe was most in evidence, but where the redmen mixed the coarse indigenous leaf with sumac or willow bark for smoking, the whites used straight "Virginia leaf" grown from Latin America seed. The Indians of that region also rolled their leaf into crude cigars, a practice which seems to have been imitated to some extent by the Yankees. Thus, from the start, Connecticut settlers were very much aware of the cigar, which was to dominate the later tobacco industry of their state. The special requirements of a marketable brown roll—Havana leaf for filler and smooth leaf for wrapper — were not available to Yankee hands for the better part of two centuries. Putting it another way, the leaf first

raised in the Connecticut River valley was not suitable for first-class cigar manufacture, although the thrifty New Englanders found it good enough for their own use.

Trick of the trade

The sharp commercial aptitude bred by a sparse environment showed itself in the Yankees' immediate invasion of the world tobacco trade. In 1650, still within the first generation of New England settlement, the British Parliament became alarmed at the amount of "New-England leaf" imported by Old England. A duty was imposed, matching that on tidewater leaf. But the Connecticut Valley product did not then (and does not now) resemble Virginia leaf, and commanded no market outside New England. Furthermore the total area suitable for tobacco, a maximum of 31,000 acres, was not cultivate until 1921, and as late as 1839 production figures indicate that less than 400 acres were planted to leaf. Even the latter figure represents a considerable post-Revolutionary expansion of leaf trade so it is certain that the few hogsheads Massachusetts and Connecticut could have grown in 1650 would

have been scarcely noticed in the massive flow of tidewater tobacco.

Yankee sailors, aware of the burgeoning demand for the "golden leaf," were simply buying tobacco in quantity from Virginia and Maryland planters, re-shipping it from Boston as New England leaf. Later they entered the North Carolina region, plying the shifting channels of the Outer Banks to take out leaf excluded from the Virginia ports. From the point of view of imperialist Britain, this was smuggling; in the eyes of the New England shipmasters, it was merely undeclared economic independence.

To the early Yankees smuggling was very nearly an article of faith. The original Pilgrimage from Britain was a flight from restraint — religious restraint, political restraint, economic restraint. The concepts of natural law and the rights of man applied as much to the coffee-house and the exchange as to the chapel. One Englishman observed that the New Englanders would

> complain and smuggle, and smuggle and complain, 'till all restraints are removed and 'till he can both buy and sell, whenever, and whereso-

ever, he pleases. Anything short of this, is still a Grievance, a Badge of Slavery.

In many ways the New England approach to business most closely resembled that of the dour, thrifty Scotch. Before they were united with the hated English in 1707, the practical Highlanders imposed a lower duty on colonial leaf and used the margin to undersell London tobaccomen in their own market.

After the England-Scotland "union," this trade advantage disappeared, so the Scotch set about intensifying their smuggling activity and continued to play profitable hob in the London leaf market. No self-respecting Yankee shipman could ignore so conspicuous an example of successful free enterprise.

In manufacturing also, the Scotch set an enviable example. Very early in the game they took to snuff manufacture, which could be a most economical process: in general "smutchin" could be adequately described as flour of tobacco stalk. It lent itself to the many variations demanded by ladies and gentlemen of fashion. There was colored snuff, bleached snuff, perfumed snuff, spiced snuff; morning snuff, afternoon snuff, evening snuff, snuff for pleasure, snuff for medicinal use. Snuff-boxes, like gentlemen's canes, were never "carried" but always "worn": a design suitable for summer might be utterly *de trop* during the winter season.

The Yankees, with a natural affinity for the practical Scotch, tried to emulate them in smutchin as well as in smuggling.

One of the first American snuff manufactories was built in Rhode Island around 1750 by a New England immigrant from Scotland named Gilbert Stuart (his son, born in the living quarters of the second story in 1755, was to become famous for his great portraits, particularly that of George Washington). It was Stuart's aim to use the nearby Connecticut Valley leaf as a source of supply, but although his snuff was up to snuff, he was hampered by the unavailability of glass bottles. Like the early Spanish sailors, Stuart tried to make do with dried animal bladders for containers, but this crude packing discouraged sales and the factory closed down. The story illustrates the obstacles in the way of even the simplest kind of manufacture before the War of Independence.

Although their manufacturing efforts were foredoomed to failure, the contraband leaf commerce carried on by daring, darting Yankee merchant sloops was one of many ventures that built the reputation of the New England traders. During the century preceding the Revolution, the austere colonies of New England supported an eightfold population increase; while the lush loam of the Chesapeake colonies supported a tenfold increase, nearly half of which was accounted for by the importation of slaves. These statistics alone tell the story of Yankee enterprise.

"No smoking"

Within New England itself, the use of tobacco passed through a controversial stage at the begin-

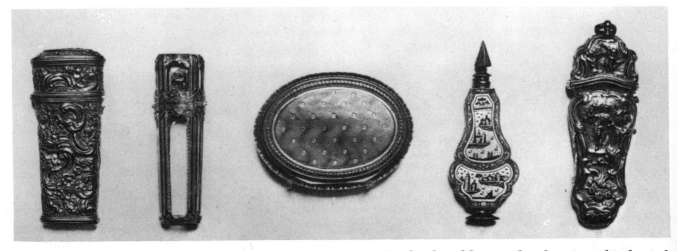

Snuff bottles of eighteenth-century Europe were as elaborate as today's perfume vials. Snuffmakers of

New England could get no bottles of any kind, tried animal bladders with no success, eventually gave up.

General Israel Putman brought three donkey-loads of Havana cigars to Connecticut in 1762, thereby starting New England's long cigar tradition. "Old Put" was a Yankee idol. He had out-dueled a British officer by sitting longest near a keg of "powder," calmly puffing his pipe (the keg contained onions). A "rough, fiery genius," Putnam was to win renown as a Yankee commander at the Battle of Bunker Hill.

ning. Like the dour James I, the dour Puritans looked at the Indians and their customs with particular disgust. To this was added a distinctly blue-nosed attitude toward creature comforts and sensual pleasures in general. In 1647 the Connecticut General Court ordered that no one

> under the age of 20 years, nor any other that hath not allreaddy accustomed himself to the use thereof

should take tobacco without a physician's certificate that it was "useful for him," plus a license from the Court. Furthermore, tobacco could not be taken in public, or even in the open fields or woods except on journeys of 10 miles or more. A citizen might smoke at "the ordinary tyme of repast comonly called dynner." But no more than two could enjoy their after-dinner pipe in the same house at the same time.

In New Haven a fine of sixpence was imposed in 1646 for smoking in public, and in 1655 it was ordered that

> no tobacco shall be taken in the streets, yards or aboute the howses in any plantation or farme in this jurisdiction without dores, neere or aboute the towne, or in the meeting howse, or body of the trayne Souldiors, or any other place where they may doe mischief thereby, under the penalty of 84 pence a pipe or a time, wch is to goe to him that informs and prosecuts.

Those lacking 84 pence would be given a sojourn in the stocks.

New England taverns like the Fountain House on the Boston-Salem road kept a cigar barrel, gave cigars *"free" to their patrons. Of scant commercial value, they were crude, homemade rolls of unblended leaf.*

Like the fulminations of James I in England, these statutes represented a minority viewpoint and did not stand up. Home cultivation of tobacco and its informal sale to neighbors continued to grow, along with maritime leaf commerce. While the colonial courts closed their eyes to the circumvention of His Majesty's duty on Virginia tobacco, they were keen to enforce the embargo on trade with the Dutch of Nieuw Amsterdam. One Captain John Manning was tried in 1654 on a charge of supplying the Dutch with provisions, having delivered at "Munnadoes" (Manhattan) "thirty-six hogsheads of tobacco the one time and thirty-five the other," having been "two time at Verginia since he came from Boston." And although the New England magistrates were in theory against tobacco consumption, they recognized its importance as a home industry needing protection. In 1662 the

Hartford court held "that whenever Tobacco is landed in this Colony" the master of the vessel or merchant importer should pay the custom master of the port twenty-five shillings per hogshead. In 1680 the Connecticut Governor reported: "We have no need of Virginia trade most people planting so much Tobacco as they spend."

Voyages from the valley

After 1700 the New England tobacco crop, concentrated in the Connecticut River valley around the original River Towns of Windsor, Hartford and Wethersfield, increased beyond home consumption needs. On a small scale, tobacco grown in New England began to appear in the cargoes of merchant ships built in New England. Tobacco was exported from Wethersfield to the West Indies as early as 1704. A brigantine built at Windsor in 1749 showed

10,296 pounds of tobacco in 27 casks on her bill of lading for a 1750 voyage to the West Indies. Thirty casks of tobacco weighing 12,664 pounds were shipped in the brigantine *Olive* to Barbados in 1751, and a similar amount to the same destination the following year. The Ellsworth family of Windsor sold 26,000 pounds of tobacco pressed into shipping casks to one Captain Ebenezer Grant in 1752. These amounts were piddling, and the brigantines and schooners insignificant when compared to the heavily-laden ships of the Virginia tobacco fleet. Selling Connecticut tobacco in the West Indies was like carrying coals to Newcastle, for the Spanish Empire, still a mighty maritime power, controlled almost every West Indian source of choice cigar leaf. From the rich *vegas* or bottomlands of Cuba, bathed all year in warm, moist air, they could take two plantings of aromatic leaf for every single crop of fiery shoestring grown in the short Connecticut summer; but the smallest chance for gain was worth a Yankee try.

To preserve even this modest trade the tobacco towns along the Connecticut River instituted a rigorous inspection procedure in 1753, only twenty-three years after the tidewater planters took the same step. Experts were designated as "surveyors and packers" of tobacco, with power to discard poor and damaged tobacco from all export shipments. (No planter was permitted to pack or press his own leaf.) Even in a commodity which reached a production peak of only 20,000 pounds in 1801, quality control was important to maintain demand abroad.

Apparently, Yankee specialization was successful even on this limited scale: in 1825 a warehouse was built expressly to handle tobacco exports, five miles north of Windsor on the Connecticut River at a spot still called Warehouse Point.

Havanas via donkeys

With its short growing season — 90 days in the year for tobacco—New England could not hope to

New England cigars, made from coarse "shoe-string" tobacco, were part of the Yankee pedlar's stock in trade. Farmers kept small tobacco patches, rolled cigars to smoke or exchange for store merchandise.

Shoe-string leaf was also grown in Pennsylvania's York and Lancaster counties, was rolled into long, sweetened cigars that teamsters could either smoke *or chew. These became known as "stogies" from the name of the town where covered wagons were made —Conestoga. Thus, stogie soon meant any cheap cigar.*

export agriculture produce in any quantity. Manufacturing, however, was something else again. And in 1762 an American army officer provided a new impetus. General Israel Putnam, who had served with the British forces in the capture of Cuba, brought three donkey-loads of Havana cigars with him on his return to Connecticut.

Putnam, a "rough, fiery genius" who was later to become the hero of the Battle of Bunker Hill, was perhaps the leading citizen of Connecticut before the Revolution. Typical was his response to a personal challenge sent him by a British officer during the French and Indian War. Bent on a duel, the Britisher found Old Put seated on a keg puffing away at his pipe. "I have never been good at firing pistols," said Putnam; "If we fight with them, you will have an unfair advantage. Here is a powder keg. I have bored a hole and inserted a small fuse

in it. So if you will be good enough to sit down, I will light the fuse, and he who dares sit the longest shall be called the bravest." When the flame was an inch from the keg, the Englishman retreated at full speed. Putnam's triumph was sweetened by the fact that the keg contained not powder, but onions. It is no wonder that the smoking habits of such a dyed-in-the-wool Yankee commanded attention.

However, the sudden interest in cigars which sprang up was not entirely due to "Old Put's" importation. Germany, inspired by the cigar products of Seville, generated a demand for the brown roll and during the American Revolution "tobacco sticks" were being made in Rome. As in previous centuries, the mariners who called at New England ports undoubtedly helped to popularize the revived cigar.

At any rate, the cigar gathered new converts in

Long nines and short sixes were terms for ordinary cigars of common leaf. Good cigars were those made at least partly from Havana leaf; these were sold as "Half Spanish." (Typical 10c cigar today still uses Havana in filler.) Clear Havanas, made wholly of Cuban leaf, were too expensive for mass market.

the homemade tobacco trade of New England. Farmers rolled their own, using the leaf they grew themselves. Unbranded and crudely put together, they nevertheless became part of the Yankee pedlar's stock in trade. Homemade "torpedoes" were packed in barrels by the farmers or by storekeepers who took them in trade, and shipped to the ports for the sailor market. Many a New England tavern had its cigar barrel and gave away "free" smokes to their patrons. Actually, few beside the sailors would buy them.

Shoestring and stogies

Around the time of the Revolution cigar manufactories took hold in New York City and Philadelphia. At Conestoga, Pennsylvania, which gave its name to the covered wagons or "prairie schooners" which were beginning to open up the West, long slender cigars were made of so-called "shoe-string tobacco." This was the narrow-leaved, coarse variety grown in York and Lancaster counties as well as in the Connecticut Valley. Conestoga cigars or "stogies" came to be the accepted term for cheap cigars (although the Lancaster area was later to grow a type of cigar leaf much superior to "shoe-string"). In New Orleans "Spanish" cigars were being made in 1800 — probably the equivalent of the "clear Havana" cigars now made in Tampa, Trenton and Philadelphia from Cuban leaf. Beginning shortly after the turn of the nineteenth century Cuban cigars were imported through New York and Philadelphia, and in 1810 a Suffield, Connecticut, cigar manufacturer imported a Cuban cigar-roller to teach his skill to American workers. Cigar factories became quite numerous; since all the work was done by hand, a large number of small factories rather than a few large establishments prevailed until machinery was introduced a century later. As the industry took hold, branded goods slowly superseded the former homemade product. The workmanship was not, at first, outstanding: an early New England brown roll carried the brand name of *Paste Segars*, descriptive of the method of fastening the outside wrapper to the filler. The best known brand of this era was *Windsor Particulars*. Long nines were pencil-thin; short sixes not so long; supers were finished off with a twist. Short sixes became a fixture in the taverns, and were the earliest "twofers" (two for a cent). Even at that early date, when tastes for cigars were presumably not too refined, a variant edged into the market at twice the price of twofers. This was known as "half Spanish"; whether it contained 50% Cuban leaf is conjectural, but it did foreshadow today's common cigar, which typically comprises a Connecticut wrapper, an inner wrapping or "binder" of Wisconsin or Pennsylvania or Connecticut leaf, and a filler including some Havana. The practice of using Cuban leaf, whether for wrapper or filler, grew quickly. "Clear Havanas" made of Cuban tobacco only were first manufactured in this country in the 1840s, and retailed at four or five times the price of domestic cigars. In the next decade "half Spanish" became literally true for the industry as a whole: the amount of Cuban leaf imported — mostly through New York City — was about equal to the

California was opened up by clipper ships like the Flying Cloud out of Boston. Early contacts of New England sailors with West Indies and later voyages to California beginning with the gold rush of 1849

amount grown in all of New England.

Two factors contributed to this change in the raw material mix: the growth of cities, industry, and transportation, fostering a more discriminating palate in the average smoker; and the specialization of Connecticut leaf. As cigar production grew and the fuselike qualities of shoestring leaf became more evident, an East Windsor planter experimented with Maryland seed. The smooth, broad leaf this yielded (in 1830) made a more attractive wrapper than the narrow shoestring. Since the visible wrapper is what "sells the cigar," a demand grew up for the new "Connecticut broad leaf," still grown today. Shoestring was quickly abandoned. Some features of the Cuban leaf-cure, which had

furthered Yankee interest in cigars as trade goods. Native Californios smoked cigars almost constantly.

evolved over three hundred years, were also applied to Connecticut tobacco, notably the practice of fermenting the leaf in bulk. The improvement contributed greatly to the rise of the cigar, New England production increasing from 540,000 pounds in 1830 to 9,300,000 pounds in 1859. Other factors played their part — the plentiful supply of hand labor as the tide of European immigrants increased, and the Mexican War of 1846-47, from which soldiers returned with an admiration for cigars. California, annexed in 1848 and teeming with American prospectors the following year, was an eager cigar market; the new arrivals took readily to the old Mexican-Spanish custom practised by the Californios. Yankee clipper ships were quick to take advantage of the lucrative supply trade from Boston and New York around the Horn to San Francisco. Beginning with Israel Putnam's return in 1762, each succeeding contact with the Spanish furthered the concept of the cigar as an aristocratic luxury.

Actually, before 1870 or so, almost any kind of factory tobacco product was more or less an aristocratic luxury. Before the industrial surge of the postbellum years, a good deal of retail exchanging was in kind — cash was not spent even on cheap cigars or plug if homegrown leaf could be had. Every farmhouse had its tobacco patch, big or small according to the size of the family — all of whom chewed or smoked. For this reason statistics on tobacco consumption before 1870, sparse as they are, do not describe the actual extent of chewing and smoking by Americans but only indicate the very slow growth of manufacturing.

There was another good reason why the manufactured article did not catch on quickly — the leaf of which it was made was scarcely different from "long green" fresh from the barn. Virginia turned out dark, strong shipping leaf; New England grew the harsh, narrow-leaved "shoestring"; and the Midwest shipped a leathery Red Burley. There was no blending to speak of, and very little in the way of "value added by manufacture."

A third reason for the failure of consumption to keep pace with population growth was the "mancipation" of women shortly before the War Between the States. (The "emancipation" did not come until the turn of the century.) The ladies of colonial New England were said to "smoke in bed, smoke as they knead their bread, smoke whilst they're cooking."

John Quincy Adams, one of the Boston Adamses and also the sixth President, was a noted connoisseur of Havana cigars, made the brown roll "proper" for

Bostonians. What Adams did for New Englanders, the inveterate cigar-puffer Ulysses S. Grant was later to do for smokers of the United States as a whole.

During the antebellum days, women smoked pipes or chewed just as their menfolk did. Mrs. Andrew Jackson and Mrs. Zachary Taylor smoked pipes while they lived in the White House without being thought bumpkins. But as the nineteenth century passed the halfway point, city manners and the romantic notion of womankind as fragile flowers came in, and women's pipes went out.

Still another factor in the tobacco equation were the immigrants from Europe who swelled the population but did not add greatly to the market for ready-made tobacco. Many, at first, were too poor to buy smokum or quid. Those who passed on through the port cities could obtain or grow "hillside navy" so much better than the manufactured product of Germany or Holland that there was no point in buying factory twist. When the urge to splurge came on, the ordinary man might buy a cigar or two as a special treat. Even so, he was not

likely to derive any special taste thrill; chances were his hard roll of shoestring had to be soaked in rum or wine to make it halfway palatable.

The day of the Spanish cigar

The growth of American demand for cigars can fairly be said to reflect, at least in part, events in Europe. In 1814 British forces engaged the French in Spain, at that time, with Portugal, the only major smoking-ground for the cigar. As a result of this European round-robin on the Iberian pennisula, both French and British revived the simple tobacco cylinder which was the mode first observed by Columbus in 1492. It required no great length of time to demonstrate to the British that Spain controlled all the acceptable cigar leaf. Imported Havanas (or Sevillas), virtually unknown in the tight little isle in 1826, weighed in at a quarter of a million pounds in 1830. In the next few decades

90

the after-dinner cigar established itself in English and French salons, smoking rooms featured every gentleman's club, and smoking cars were introduced on European and British railroads. The influence of this vogue on Americans, just beginning to be citified and, in the narrow sense, "civilized," can hardly be overlooked. For New Englanders, the example of John Quincy Adams symbolized and spearheaded the trend toward cigars. Adams, son of the second President and the sixth President himself, was a prominent connoisseur of imported Havanas, and no family was more prominent or quintessentially New England than the Adamses of Boston. So many Bostonians flourished brown rolls with joyously glowing tips that the city fathers eventually confined them to the "Smoking Circle" on Boston Common. What the younger Adams did for the Yankees, the cigar-puffing General Grant was to do for the nation's smokers generally.

While John Quincy Adams was still in the White House (1825-29), Connecticut seedleaf was known as "American tobacco" and cigars made from it as

"American cigars." Wrappers of a cinnamon red color were preferred, the choicest being a white-specked mahogany leaf known as "cinnamon blotch." Unlike the Spanish cigar, traditionally boxed in cedar, the New England product was packed in chestnut containers. Even at that early date, however, it was clear that the American cigar could not be fully differentiated from the Spanish and still rival the latter's smoking qualities. References are made to the use of Havana leaf as a wrapper or filler and even to the use of grated Spanish bean to finish off a box of New England brown rolls.

Although the cigar is thought of as an appurtenance of the gas-lit decades after the Civil War, it did not spring suddenly to life between the lips of Ulysses S. Grant. Smoking customs rarely do. Like twist, like the later pipe and cigarette, like tobacco itself, the cigar started out as a new-fangled invention, a novelty. It lingered on the fringe of smokers' consciousness for fifty years (1762-1810) and took another fifty years (1810-1860) to develop momentum as an accepted form. For still another fifty

So many Bostonians flourished brown rolls during the years just before the Civil War that the city *fathers set apart a special area for cigar smokers on tree-shaded Boston Common—the Smoking Circle.*

years cigars reigned supreme, reaching their peak in 1907; thereafter they fell off gently to the status of a secondary form.

Yankee heyday

Of these three phases of cigar development, New England dominated the first two. Lest the word "dominate" be misinterpreted, it should be added that Yankee leaf production never ran to really substantial weight compared with the tidewater tonnage. The first phase ending in 1810, marked by the home-rolled torpedo, the town packer and the two-dozen-hogshead shipment to the West Indies, is of historical rather than economic importance. As has been pointed out, the Connecticut Valley crop of 1801—the largest up to that year—amounted *in toto* to a mere score of hogsheads.

The second phase, the Yankee heyday, is of limited interest even to the tobacco historian. New England's leaf output in 1849 totaled about 1,400,000 pounds. This figure is much less impressive than it reads when it is recalled that it was reached more than two centuries earlier by a few

tobacco planters along the James River only fifteen years after they began hacking their clearings out of a virgin wilderness. It was not until the eve of the War Between the States that the Yankee crop achieved the semi-significant level of 10,000,000 pounds a year (a level it rarely exceeded through 1900). But by the time New England had generated real momentum for cigar leaf production and cigar manufacture — 1860 or thereabouts — the brown roll ceased to be Yankee property. In 1860 as much cigar leaf was grown in Pennsylvania and Ohio as in New England, although commercial seed-leaf production did not begin until 1828 and 1838 in the Keystone and Buckeye states respectively. Twenty years later the Ohio cigar leaf crop equaled New England's, and the Pennsylvania crop doubled the Yankee output.

The third phase, or postbellum era, was actually a national phase not only in cigars but in many other lines of consumer products. The regional product and provincial tastes and customs were beginning to yield to nationwide standards; the upheaval of civil war, the inrush of immigrants, the

POPULATION, U. S. (000,000)

POUNDS OF TOBACCO CONSUMED, U. S. (0,000,000)

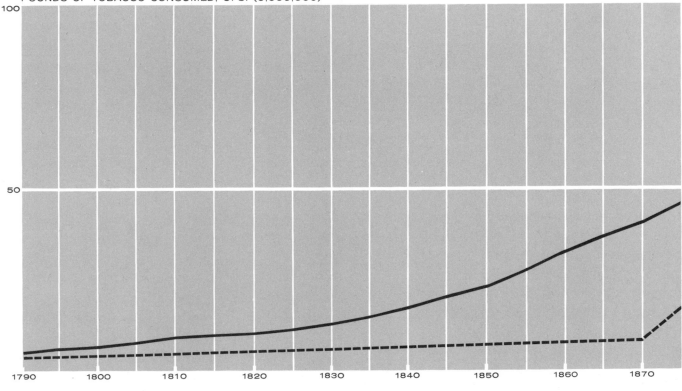

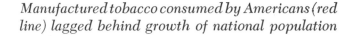

Manufactured tobacco consumed by Americans (red line) lagged behind growth of national population

between 1800 and 1870, when much of it was grown at home and used in home made products. From 1870

92

lure of fresh land and mineral wealth in the West were fusing a nation out of what had been a federation of separate regions.

So despite the limits climate and soil place on the production of leaf tobacco, many states tried their hand—Wisconsin, Illinois, Ohio, Pennsylvania, Indiana, New York and even Florida entered the seed-leaf (cigar) culture, and the growth of chewing and pipe leaf spread to Ohio, Kentucky, Tennessee, Missouri and even as far as the northwest corner of Arkansas bordering on the Indian Territory (now Oklahoma).

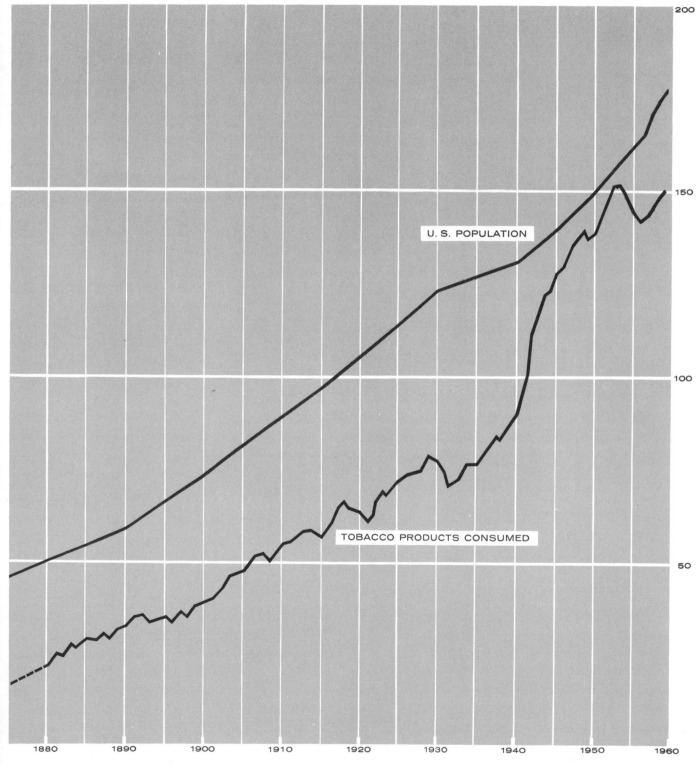

through 1929 consumption roughly followed curve of population increase (black line), fell off the pace during the 1930s and gained faster than the population during World War II and the Korean War.

Seville, world's first great tobacco manufacturing center, made finest cigars. The king of Spain rigidly controlled leaf culture in his colonies, *prohibited export except to Seville. Cigar rollers of that city worked with the best of all tobaccos; "Spanish" became a magic word in the tobacco trade.*

Manufacturing, of course, was not limited as was agriculture. By 1880 there was not a single state or territory, except for Montana and Idaho, which lacked its own cigar factories. Most also boasted plug and pipe tobacco manufacture as well, including even such a sparsely settled place as Arizona.

This explosive spread of manufacturing was a reflection of greatly intensified demand for manufactured items—that is, for better goods. Any old scrap of baccy rolled into a cheroot or crammed into a pipe would no longer do. Discrimination was setting in. The next step, the nationally advertised brand of uniform and dependable quality, was inevitable.

Cigars were to be last among all tobacco products to evolve truly national brands, despite the early appearance of *Windsor Particulars* (before

1820). But cigars were probably the first American tobacco product to generate a clearcut quality distinction, that between domestic and "Spanish" rolls. During the years before the Civil War, pipe tobacco was pipe tobacco and chew was chew. But every cigar smoker knew the difference between a paste segar or stogie and the lordly clear Havana. Moreover, he could taste the difference for himself in spite of the rather loose use of terms like "Spanish" and "Havana" by certain makers of domestic cigars. And the difference was firmly fixed in the minds of the smoking public well before Sumter, a clear indication that by then the brown roll had "arrived."

Thus the rise of the cigar as a national habit came during the first half of the nineteenth century, more or less coinciding with the rise of chew or "fudgeon"

94

as the Yankees called it. Smoking — as distinct from chewing — was therefore never absent from the American scene. The cigar forms the bridge between the calumets and clays of colonial times and the twentieth-century briar pipe and cigarette. Since many brown rolls were homemade, there is no statistical record of the domestic cigar's ascendancy before the War Between the States. But an idea of its rise can be inferred from the figures on cigar imports. These amounted to 4,000,000 or so in 1804, 24,000,000 in 1810; 14,000,000 in 1816 (reflecting the disruption of overseas trade caused by the second War of Independence with Britain, largely a sea war); 24,000,000 in 1830; 74,000,000 in 1840; 124,000,000 in 1850; and 460,000,000 in 1861. Many if not most of these imports were Havanas, a significant fact in an era when hard cash was hard to come by.

However the imports of finished cigars, which may have accounted for as much as a third of factory-rolled consumption in a given antebellum year, do not tell the whole story. Of equal "import" were the purchases of Havana leaf for use in U. S. cigar establishments, a preferred procedure owing to the lower duty on bulk leaf as compared with that on manufactured cigars.

Even the Yankees with their "make do at home" attitude had to admit that Spanish tobacco — i.e., Cuban leaf — was an essential ingredient of good cigars. This marriage between Yankee and Havana leaf was expressed in two ways: first, Havana leaf was used as a filler enclosed by an outer wrapper of smooth New England broadleaf; and second, virtually every New England cigar brand with any pretension of quality carried a Spanish box-mark or "top iron"—*La Gloria de la Habana, El Buen Fuego, La Rosa de Santiago*, and so forth. The use of Spanish verbiage led to some strange brand names, like *La Flor de Chas. F. Kurtz*, made in Millville, New Jersey, and *Velocipede Vuelta Abajo Havanas*,

Beginning around 1800, U.S. demand for Cuban-made cigars — the same as "Spanish" — steadily increased. Shapes or "front-marks" were designated by Spanish words Londres, Regalias, Coronas, etc.

In 1861 cigar imports numbered half a billion. An equivalent weight of Havana leaf was imported by U.S. factories for use in domestic cigars. Guests at fine hotels lit Havanas with gas cigar lighter.

95

Despite obviously American brand name, Velocipede cigar trademark paid label service to the renown of Havana leaf. Everything about the cigar except the brand name, the label seems to say, is Spanish.

Yankee ingenuity outdid itself in this unique box which disguised five-cent cigars as cheese. Brand name was "Cheese It." Head label was inspired by Gilbert and Sullivan operetta, "H.M.S. Pinafore."

made in Detroit. (It should be mentioned that the Havana leaf content of some of these brands, like the actual raw material of Connecticut's wooden nutmegs, was highly questionable.)

Cubans and commons

Over the years it has become fairly well established that Havana leaf is the *sine qua non* of a good cigar, and most of today's big-volume ten-centers include some of it in their fillers. (In 1957 a trade magazine, applauding a reduction of tariff on imported Cuban leaf, declared: "An abundant supply of reasonably priced Havana tobacco is essential for a prosperous American cigar industry.") Nevertheless, a good proportion of nineteenth-century cigars were made without it. At the bottom of the scale was the cheroot, a long and untapered roll of

non-blended tobacco — the kind of simple cylinder made by the Maya or the Tupinambas of Brazil. It was recommended, of course, largely by its cheapness. The stogie was a foot long, tapered to a mouthpiece at one end, made of domestic leaf, and sometimes sweetened with molasses. This last rendered the stogie or toby a two-way item especially useful for travelers; it could be chewed as well as ignited.

What constitutes a "good" common cigar (as distinct from Havanas or "fine" cigars) has changed considerably over the years. The brown rolls smoked by the Carib Indians Columbus saw were, to judge by the early prints, about the size of a policeman's nightstick, twisted rather than rolled. They looked like firebrands and, made of unblended *Nicotiana rustica*, tasted like them too. The cheroot, as rolled in the East Indies, was closer in size and shape to the modern cigar, although still unblended.

Before broadleaf was grown along the Connecticut, the standard cigar had a filler of dark shoestring, no binder, and the cinnamon blotch wrapper speckled in white. Some Philadelphia firms surrounded dark domestic filler with a smooth Havana wrapper and advertised the result as "Spanish." They did not much resemble true Havanas. Fit for a king's taste and fit for a royal purse, real Havanas were accordingly named Regalias, Coronas, Kings, and the like.

After the War Between the States, domestic cigars underwent radical changes. The broadleaf wrapper became a binder. A lighter, more bland wrapper was added — first Sumatra, later Connect-

icut shadegrown. Shoestring was replaced by more savory filler leaf from Pennsylvania or New England. Havana leaf was used in the "bunch" or filler rather than on the outside. The availability of four or more distinctly different types of leaf made blending possible, and the various brands took on distinctive smoking characteristics.

The cigar proper — contrasted with cheroot, toby or black Italian "tobacco stick" — has an outer wrapper, an inner binder, and a filler blended from two or more types of leaf. Since these must be selected and put together by hand, even where the actual rolling is done by machine the cigar is by definition a "custom-made" item. The better grades of domestic cigars include some proportion of

Cigar demand grew spectacularly during last half of the nineteenth century. Average price between 1870 and 1880 was 3c: the "Trade" brand sold at wholesale for 1.2c, retailed at two for a nickel. In 1860, 29c of every tobacco dollar was spent on cigars; in 1870, 45c; in 1880, 54c; in 1900, 60c.

Ritual of curing and processing fine cigar-leaf is a Cuban development. First hung up for a barn cure, tobacco is then piled and ferments in its own heat.

For centuries, bales of Havana cigar leaf traveled by donkey from farm to warehouse to ship. Donkeys are now gone but bark-tied bales remain the same.

Bale cure lasts anywhere from six months to three years. Experts inspect tobacco periodically, often roll and smoke a sample cigar to test baled leaf.

Barrel cure or barbacoa is final cure, lasts six months. While in barrel, tobacco undergoes still more chemical changes, effected by its own heat.

Havana, the term "clear Havana" being reserved for cigars made in the U. S. using Cuban leaf only. At the top of the scale (and bearing the highest import duty) is the Cuban-made *tabaco* rolled in Havana from leaf grown in the renowned Vuelta region.

The Vuelta Abajo

This crook of Cuba west of Havana and nearest the United States — the name Vuelta Abajo means "down turn" — grows a fragrant, rich leaf which neither Connecticut, Pennsylvania, Wisconsin, Sumatra, Jamaica nor Puerto Rico can imitate, although all have tried. In the Vuelta province of Pinar del Rio, brown soil, bright sun and heavy humidity are uniquely suited to cigar leaf. Traditions of cultivation, bred by centuries of Spanish rule, play a ritualistic part. Tobacco seedlings are grown in special beds, transplanted to the fields when they are six inches high. As in the United States, sucker leaves and flower buds are removed as the plant grows, forcing all the strength into the leaves. In two months of continual hoeing, irrigating and fertilizing, the stalks reach man's height; a Cuban *veguero*, like his American Indian counterpart, must be "a father to his tobacco."

The leaves are hung for a barn cure, piled to ferment in their own heat, then sorted into different grades each requiring a different length of curing in bale — anywhere from six months to three years. After this, the leaf gets a barrel cure or *barbacoa*

Customs duty on imported leaf is less than that on finished cigars. Cigars "manufactured in bond" are, in effect, certified by U. S. Customs as all Havana.

Hand-rolling of cigars is still the law in Cuba. Most American factories use machines, which yield a better result in all but the very largest sizes.

lasting about six months. Then, ready for manufacture, the precious brown and tan leaves are packed in exotic bales made of stiff Royal Palm leaves tied with *majagua* bark rope. The basic pattern goes on year after year, changing but little. As demand in the United States shifted from the natural brown or *colorado* wrapper to a light green or *claro*, special methods to increase production of light-colored wrapper leaf were introduced: shade growing under cloth, forced-heat curing.

Until World War II, donkeys carried the palm-leaf bales to merchant ships for export — descendents, possibly, of the same donkeys which carried out Israel Putnam's three loads of Havanas. The best of the Vueltabajo leaf is now manufactured into cigars in the U. S. under bond, the retail package bearing a white U. S. customs stamp to certify that it is all "Spanish." A good part of the rest of Cuba's crop is shipped to U. S. factories for use as filler, or to the clear Havana cigar factories in Tampa, most of which do not manufacture in bond.

The art of cigar manufacture is threefold: blending, rolling and packing. Since the strength of the delivered smoke varies with the diameter of the roll, thick cigars or *perfectos* require a different combination of heavy, medium and light leaves than the long, thin *premiers* or *fancy tales*. The factory foreman who apportions the leaf to the bunchers is the key to blending. Hand-rolling, a virtually lost art in the United States after machine-rolling was perfected in the 1920s, has been perpetuated by law

Precision of manufacture is important, since the dimensions of a cigar influence taste. Different shapes therefore require different leaf blendings.

Traditional pride in craft is carried right down to boxing: cigars are color-sorted before being packaged. Skilled selectors distinguish 70 shades.

in Cuba. Selection of cigars by shade of wrapper is a specialty all in itself; in a well-packed box each individual cigar is almost indistinguishable in hue from the next, although skilled selectors can distinguish 70 shades of tobacco.

This proud, measured progression from one step to the next — working the tobaccos "in their time" — results in an expensive product. In 1956, no more than one out of every fifty cigars bought in the U. S. followed the classic Havana pattern of growth, cure and manufacture. Before the Civil War, the proportion was closer to one in ten. But the field and barn rituals of little Pinar del Rio formed the model for imitation by New England tillers, just as the blend-mastery of the palace-like Havana factories formed the model for the 20,000 cigar establishments scattered through the United States in 1900. It has never been possible to assess the cigar's importance solely in terms of units or poundage of leaf, still less

possible to put a statistical yardstick on the place of the fine, or Havana, cigar. In 1904, leaf used in cigar manufacture represented only 27% by weight of all the tobacco processed in the U. S. Yet 60c of every dollar spent on tobacco products went for cigars (chewing and smoking tobacco accounted for 33c, cigarettes 5c, snuff 2c).

Havana salt and pepper

It is strange that the subtle process of transculturation should so closely interweave people as different as the Yankees and the Cubans. Yet the tobacco culture of New England (and that of Pennsylvania too) came to revolve around the limited amount of Havana leaf that could be added to the fillers of domestic cigars. Normally, the Havana component was not used as "long filler" — that is, as a whole leaf crushed together with the Pennsylvania product inside the binder. Rather, it

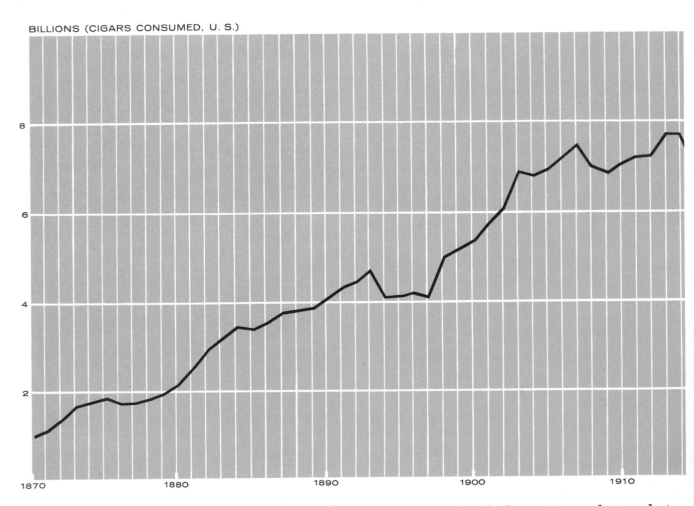

BILLIONS (CIGARS CONSUMED, U. S.)

Cigar consumption came into its own just after the Civil War, accounted for 30% of all tobacco used in manufacturing in 1880. For the next 40 years cigar sales increased with the U. S. population; during that period they accounted for a consistent 25% of leaf used in manufacture. Cigar sales have always

was chopped up and distributed through the filler as H. S. P. (Havana salt and pepper). This permitted a better blending of the inimitable Havana fragrance, and made for more uniformity from one cigar to the next.

At the same time, New England wrapper leaf was grown to be as neutral as possible in taste, so as to allow the Havana-salted filler to dominate. One of the factors that made Sumatra wrapper so desirable to manufacturers toward the end of the nineteenth century was its utter blandness. Connecticut shadegrown was and is bred specifically for this tasteless quality, although it derives from the same seed that produces Havana wrapper, famous for its rich taste and the most expensive tobacco that can be bought in the U. S. (as high as $15 per pound). At that, Connecticut shadegrown is the most valuable domestic leaf; its War II ceiling price was $7.50.

As might be deduced from the mounting cigar imports of 1810-1860, the interweaving of Cuban and U. S. economies was considerable by 1850. In that year Cuban trade with this country exceeded commercial traffic between Cuba and Spain. The long subjugation of Cuban tobacco to the Casa de Contracion de Indias in Seville rankled the Cubans; as early as 1831, fifty cigar makers escaped Spanish domination to set up shop in Key West. They could not take their bottomlands with them, but they could escape with their skills. In 1868, at the start of the Ten Years' War with Spain, another wave of Havana cigar manufacturers fled to Florida. Among them were Vincente Ibor, a Spaniard by birth, and Eduardo Gato; the cities they founded — Tampa and Ibor City — are still major cigar centers. They are also monuments to the easily-forgotten fact that political freedom is inseparable from economic freedom. Like the tidewater planters' resentment

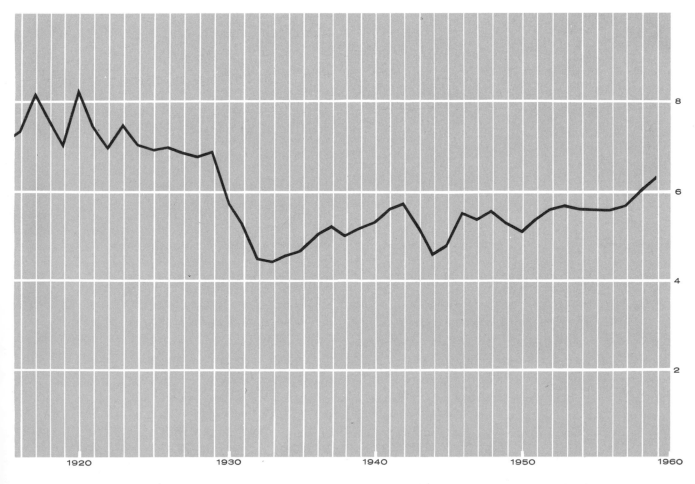

been particularly sensitive to general level of the economy: sharp declines followed the panics of 1893 and 1907, and postwar boom year of 1920 established all-time peak in unit sales. Over the last ten years brown rolls have held steady at around six billion, account for about 10% of leaf used in manufacturing.

Even in the days of the "twofer" (two for a penny) cigars were more or less a luxury smoke. The great weight of tobacco consumption was in quid and pipe form: typical farm woman of 1870s puffed on pipe.

of mother England, the Cubans' resentment of mother Spain eventually burst into a violent war of liberation. One scholar claims that fine tobacco is produced only by free men (unlike sugar, originally distilled from the drudgery of slaves). There is an element of truth in this philosophical position: quality leaf cannot be mass produced, but demands constant pampering. Thus fine tobacco growing is a middle class occupation, more often than not a family tradition, in the U. S. as in Cuba. Sugar, by way of contrast, typically produces a proletariat on the one hand and great wealth on the other.

Politics and panetelas

What was true of the Cuban farmers was also true of the cigar-rollers. They were originally home craftsmen, free and self-employed, who sold their bundles to export dealers; factories with their immense rolling-rooms came later. As the word Havana gained international fame (becoming more widely known than the word Cuba itself), manufacturers aimed for mass production and tried to use slaves and even prisoners in their workrooms. These attempts were not successful; in the end, they had to turn to the free labor market for "cigartists." Filled with pride in themselves and their craft, the cigar-rollers were the free thinkers of nineteenth-century Cuba. Out of their own wages they paid the readers who occupied their minds while their hands were busy shaping cigars in the workrooms. These readers were not hired to divert or to entertain; the books they read aloud were thinkpieces on history, politics, philosophy. This simple institution sharpened the political consciousness of the cigartists, who played a key role in throwing off the Spanish imperialists shortly before the turn of the century.

An exact parallel cannot be drawn between the nineteenth-century Cubans and their Yankee counterparts in the cigar business. New England had achieved politico-economic freedom while the Pearl of the Antilles was still strung on the Spanish necklace. Yet the sequence, though not simultaneous, was the same. On the one hand, civilized men of European stock trying to turn new land and new resources into a new culture; on the other, the dead hand of mercantilism, throttling manufacture and banning free export. Neither Yankee leaf nor Yankee snuff could have become economic mainstays in the sense that Virginia leaf was; yet they bridled under the same repressive measures and generated the same antagonism toward their overseas master.

The tidewater leaf culture of Virginia and Maryland was actually closer to the Cuban sugar complex than to the Cuban tobacco craft. With quality manufacture largely lacking in Europe and England, the Chesapeake colonies strove mainly for quantity. When they produced quality — more or less by accident, in the sandy sweetscented parishes — there was no market incentive to sustain it. So Virginia tobacco, like Cuban sugar, spawned a master-and-slave economy. It was only after the Revolution and the gradual release of manufacturing energy in the U. S. that quality of leaf became a factor. As this happened, the huge plantations

During the 1870s the smoking car became a fixture on the nation's railroads. So widespread was the cigar craze during those years that women took to the brown roll to some extent. This 1877 woodcut in the Illustrated Weekly *was captioned: "A lady on the C.H.&D.R.R. determines to enjoy her rights —she takes her place in a smoking car beside her husband, and joins him in puffing a Havana cigar."*

dissolved and small tobacco patches took their place, with quality by and large replacing quantity as the farmer's incentive. Quality of product was not a workable incentive for a master-and-slave system; instead it gave rise to individualistic enterprise and thereby led to radical improvements in crop and in cure as well as in the arts of manufacture.

From the very first, the limitations of nature prevented any burgeoning of big plantations in New England. The Yankees leafed by their wits, by specializing in what the market wanted and by imitating as closely as possible the peer of tobacco products, the Havana cigar. Only in that way could stony New England keep its precarious toehold in tobacco. Thus the middle-class Yankees shaped

their small but dogged leaf industry around the precious qualities of Havana filler grown by middle-class Cubans.

Cigar smoking showed its steepest rate of climb during and just after the Civil War. Although a number of plausible reasons for this can be cited — lack of access to the Virginia-North Carolina crop for one, the supply of easy money in northern cities for another — this accelerated growth probably reflected nothing more complicated than a growing taste for the product. Chewing tobacco was still on the rise, and by no means in short supply during the war. In fact, the diversion of Burley leaf from the normal New Orleans outlet to New York City made plug manufacture more convenient than ever in the heart of the Northern market.

Mass immigration gave New York City a tremendous reservoir of labor; by 1880, the city had 14,500 cigar workers as against 2,300 in all of the New England states. New York's production was 20% of the national total; New England had 5%, and the original cigar state, Connecticut, was down to 1%.

Northern roll

By the thousands, Americans took to the brown roll. Cigar making had employed 8,000 hands in 1860, as against 19,000 in tobacco manufacture; in 1880 there were 53,000 cigar makers as against 33,000 employed in chewing and smoking factories. It was this final surge that reduced New England to a secondary status in cigar manufacture; there were simply not enough people available to keep up. In 1880, New York City alone had 14,500 people in its cigar factories; in all of New England's 503 establishments the number of workers was only 2,300. New York State made eight times as many cigars as New England's six states; Pennsylvania twice as many. And such states as California, Illinois, and Ohio had as much or more cigar production as the New England states, whose share of the U. S. total fell to a mere 5%.

In all this there was a kind of symbolic division of the tobacco industry. No more than a tenth of the national cigar output was turned out south of the seed-leaf territory of the Northern states. In spite of efforts in the direction of cigar-making,

Richmond manufactured barely ½ of 1% of the national total by 1880. During the war of brother against brother, Grant against Lee, it was the northern cigar on the one side and the flat bright plug on the other. And each side missed the other's specialty, as the soldier-swaps along the front lines proved.

City markets, city makers

Since the largest cities were at once the entrepôts of fashion and the ports of entry for cheap labor, cigar manufacture soon gravitated to New York, Philadelphia and other urban centers. The big cities had both concentrated demand and a concentrated supply of labor; so cigars were rolled on a piecework basis by women in tenements, instead of by farmers' wives in the New England countryside. By 1880 New York City was producing more than a fifth of the nation's 2,500,000,000 output and Connecticut only 1%. Cigar manufacture was dispersed even more by the arrival of additional Cuban firms in Tampa during the 1890s, industrial refugees from the strife-torn Pearl of the

Antilles. Maintaining close ties with sources of Cuban leaf, they spewed millions of Havanas — both clear and not-so-clear—on the American market. Their production, retailing much cheaper than Cuban-made imports size for size, was welcome to the American smoker, but was hardly calculated to spur the demand for Yankee leaf.

Nevertheless, cigars became the gay batons of a civilization on the march toward wealth and comfort. College men discarded their pipes and sported Havanas. In 1876, the nation's centennial year, Currier & Ives ("printmakers to the American people") depicted Uncle Sam not with chew or pipe but puffing on a huge cigar.

This decade of the 70s showed the greatest relative gains for the cigar; in 1870, the brown roll ac-counted for 20% of all tobacco used in manufacture, and in 1880 for 30%. (For the next forty years, cigars were to represent about 25% of all tobacco poundage processed in the U.S., a share which dwindled to 17% in 1930 and 10% in 1955.) The typical cigar of the 70s cost about 3c at retail (vs. today's average of 9c). Aside from price, however, there was very little about the cigar that was typical.

Although it was incubated in antebellum New England, its manufacture spread to virtually every city of any size in the United States. By the end of the nineteenth century the number of chewing and smoking brands were numbered in the thousands, but the number of cigar *manufacturers* was in the thousands. No one tried to publish a complete di-

URKEY.　　GERMANY.　　ENGLAND.　　UNITED STATES.　　FRANCE.　　ITALY.　　SPAIN.

A GRAND CENTENNIAL SMOKE.
History in Vapor.

In 1876 Currier and Ives, most noted chroniclers of American mores, showed Uncle Sam celebrating the centennial year with a huge cigar. Only in England were cigarettes at all popular, as print indicates.

rectory of cigar manufacturers, let alone a listing of cigar brands.

Personal brand names

Aside from the use of Spanish words and phrases to indicate or suggest Havana leaf, there was one tendency in cigar nomenclature that did not appear in other tobacco products. For want of a better description, this might be called the "great man theory" of cigar brand names. Virtually every great statesman found his niche in the cigar lexicon, as is testified by some of the brands surviving today—*Henry Clay, Webster,* and the like. Famous generals and other notables—*Anna Held,* to cite a successful example in the five-cent class—also lent their names, with or without permission. There was, perhaps, a touch of logic to the practise: the cigar was a symbol of personal affluence during the Gilded Age and the Edwardian years. The mighty J. Pierpont Morgan had equally mighty cigars (eight-inch *Kohinoors* at $1.25 apiece) specially rolled for his own use, and the financial barons of the house of Rothschild also had a private shape—*Excepcionales de Rothschilds.* What more logical for a consumer of lesser estate to console himself with one of the many brands allegedly smoked by General Grant, or Senator Clay, or Emperor William, or King Edward? The twin attributes of royalty and Spanishness were combined in a brand name which now leads the ten-cent field—*El Roi-Tan*—although the Roi derived from a man named Roy and the Tan from his partner named Tannenbaum.

Perhaps these personal brand names had their roots in the Spanish culture, where cigar-rolling was a taught skill similar to reading or horsemanship. The ordinary Cuban, the Mexican and the early Californio learned how to fashion his own cigars as a matter of course; the Spanish grandee, like the Morgans of the Gilded Age, had a roller fabricate cigars of distinctive shape for him and for him alone. An echo of this persists in New York City, where a few cigar shops still cater to the

GRANT: NO USE TALKING, THE CAPADURA IS THE BOSS SEGAR.
HAYES: I RECKON, YOUR'E RIGHT, OLD MAN.
BUTLER: YOU BET.

"PUCK"

THE CAPADURA IS NOW, EVER HAS BEEN, AND SHALL CONTINUE TO BE THE BEST FIVE CENT SEGAR IN THE WORLD.

Ill-chosen brand name, Capaduras, was Cuban term for pointed leaves growing from stripped stalks.

A five cent "segar" when Grant and Hayes were in office was the equivalent of today's 15c article.

smoker who likes his Havanas "custom-rolled," perhaps with his own name printed on the cellophane jacket.

This, of course, was the exception rather than the rule during the Brown Decades as now. The trade was personified by the high-hatted, high-spirited cigar drummer, almost as magnificent as the premiums in his sample case and the gilded and embossed decoration of his cigar bands and boxes. Even as he distributed his gaudy gimcracks and lithographed cards, he was uneasily aware that cigarette salesmen were getting their foot in the retailer's door using identical inducements.

The nineteenth-century rise of the cigar, made of Northern leaf, was not slowed by the growth of cigarettes, made of Southern Bright. National advertising was unknown, for there were no national brands. But just the same, cigar manufacturers engaged in "national advertising" of a whispering sort: the cigarette contained opium, was made with tobacco from discarded butts and paper made by

Nellie Bly's 1890 journey around the world, which bore no visible relationship to smoking, was used nevertheless as subject of a cigar advertisement.

Chinese lepers, and so forth. In the long run, this called attention to the competitive product and probably helped rather than hindered its rise.

There was canny economic wisdom in the abruptness with which the New Englanders withdrew from competition in cigar manufacture. They were quite willing to leave the making of cheap cigars — always a low-profit-margin pursuit — to others. This did not mean a retreat from the tobacco trade as such. Rather, the Yankees turned their attention to filling a particular demand created by the growing popularity of cigars. Whatever the filler a given manufacturer uses, he needs an attractive and smooth wrapper leaf to make his cigar sell; and no matter how choice his wrapper,

"Great man theory" of cigar brand names made Clay, Calhoun and Webster logical cigar-box adornments.

Wrapper leaf is carefully hung up in barn for air cure. Despite competition from Cuban and Sumatran wrappers, and despite short summer season, Yankee planters have evolved a highly satisfactory leaf.

he needs a strong, elastic binder leaf to keep the filler from wrinkling or puncturing it. It was to these requirements that the perceptive New Englanders addressed themselves, supplementing the Maryland or Connecticut broadleaf binder with Havana seedleaf and, later, cultivating the delicate and high-priced shadegrown wrapper.

Seed and soil

Without minimizing the part played by Yankee energy and enterprise, the specialized wrapper-and-binder agriculture of the Connecticut Valley is a classic illustration of the part played by geography in tobacco evolution. Although the Valley farms were planted with Virginia seed around 1640, the tobacco they yielded gave rise to home-made cigars. In 1830, the cultivation of Maryland broadleaf along the river produced a successful wrapper for cigars, although the same seed planted in Maryland gave rise to a different leaf useful at first in manufactured tobacco and later as a cigarette ingredient. To put it in reverse, the Connecticut broadleaf was not suitable for non-cigar use; in the same way, the aborigines of Central America who first found and cultivated *Nicotiana tabacum* used it in cigars rather than in pipes, although the pipe was the most widespread form of tobacco consumption throughout pre-Columbian America.

Regional classifications of tobacco are thus not interchangeable. Connecticut turns out cigar leaf whether from Virginia, Maryland or Havana seed. The differentiation can be carried further: the New England types were useful as binder (Connecticut broadleaf, Havana seed) and wrapper (Connecticut

Slatted barn for air cure is used in Burley areas of Kentucky as well as in Connecticut cigar leaf region. In addition to smooth wrapper, neutral in taste, New England grows a strong, elastic binder.

shadegrown), but the Pennsylvania and Ohio crops were used mainly as fillers. (Currently, the development of reconstituted binder sheet is erasing the distinction between filler and binder leaf.) Wisconsin, Florida and Georgia were specifically suited to the growing of binder leaf while the inland valleys of Puerto Rico produced filler leaf. Many of the Ohio filler types were used as short-filler or "grinders" for less expensive cigars. Soil and climate, no less than human enterprise or the lack of it, place definite limitations on the tobacco tradition of a given region.

In general, cigar leaf is air-cured. However, in an effort to starve the leaf into a light, bright color for American smokers, increasing quantities of Cuban-grown wrapper are force-cured with the application of high temperatures. This practise is

somewhat parallel to flue-curing Virginia and Carolina tobacco of smoking and cigarette grades. Sudden application of heat lightens the tobacco, a result first prompted by the market demand for yellow, "colory" plug wrappers. Flue-cured Bright leaf is one of two major classes of tobacco now used in cigarettes; the other class, Burley, grown mainly in Kentucky and Tennessee, is air-cured like cigar leaf. Most air curing is done under shelter, but one type of Virginia chewing leaf, as well as most Turkish tobacco, is sun-cured.

In addition to flue-curing, which applies heat without smoke, and the more natural air-curing, some tobaccos are smoked or fire-cured like smoked ham. Smoked leaf is used in "eatin' tobacco," that is, quid and snuff. (The latter is no longer sniffed but is held in the mouth without chewing.) Fire-cured

Although actual rolling is mechanized, much hand work is needed to make long-filler cigars. Whole leaves—three or four—are twisted together in the "bunch" *or filler. Blending of these according to the shape of the cigar is vital to flavor. Above, imported filler is sorted by type, strength, size.*

leaf is also an export specialty: the historic origin of fire-curing was as a preservative process, and much American leaf grown for export, even well into the twentieth century, was of the smoked variety. Fire-curing played no role in the Connecticut Valley, partly because the valley crop has been a low-volume one which never developed a large exportable surplus, partly because Yankee growers have "babied" their plants in an effort to compete with the costly Cuban leaf.

Despite the excellent burning quality and aroma of Connecticut broadleaf, the influence of fashion reduced the demand for it as a wrapper after 1859, and it did not recover to that year's peak until 1879. The Spanish like their cigar wrappers dark (*colorado or maduro*) and the light-colored Connecticut leaf temporarily lost out to the dark brown variety raised in Pennsylvania. The Miami Valley in Ohio also became a competitive source of cigar leaf, as did Wisconsin. New England acreage seeded to tobacco shrunk by a third, while the Valley planters tried vainly to recapture their market by darkening leaf with licorice. In 1880 fashion swung to the opposite extreme with the importation of Sumatra leaf, light in color (*claro*) and so "light" in

body as to be almost tasteless. (Economics also figured here: a pound of thin Sumatra would wrap many more cigars than a pound of domestic wrapper leaf.) Again the Connecticut growers were caught in the middle, and in spite of high tariffs levied on the Sumatra product, cultivated acreage fell off, although poundage remained at a constant level — around 10,000,000 pounds a year — until 1899. New England ingenuity met this new threat with still another variety — shadegrown wrapper grown from Cuban seed. Filtering the sunlight striking the growing leaf makes it thinner in body and lighter in color.

Connecticut shadegrown stimulated the final spurt in New England tobacco production, from the 10,000,000 pound level of the 90s to nearly 45,000,000 pounds in 1921. Shadegrown, comprising about a fourth of the New England crop, is a highly specialized product, and comes as close as nature will allow to the luxurious wrapper grown in Cuba. Shadegrown is now, however, the most expensive tobacco grown in the United States, and a great amount of hand labor is still characteristic of cigar factories even though most of the actual rolling is mechanized. Thus the cigar, which rode to the height of smoking fashion as a luxury product, has never been dissociated from a luxury price — whether it be rolled from domestic leaf, or made in bond from Cuban leaf, or fashioned in Havana and imported. From 1900 to the present the poundage of tobacco consumed in cigars has varied but little from one year to the next, although America's population has doubled. The peak year for shadegrown, 1921, has not been matched since, for 1921 also marked the ascendancy of another American product as the No. 1 mode of consuming tobaccos — the blended cigarette.

Although the word "cigarette" literally meant a little cigar, the white roll is not a smaller variation of the brown one. While the cigar derives from Cuban leaf types and the Spanish tradition, the cigarette is an outgrowth of southern American leaf and a distinctively American tobacco tradition. This involved first chewing tobacco, then smoking tobacco, and finally the cigarette.

Shadegrown wrapper is New England specialty. It is the most expensive of American tobaccos. Filtered sunlight gives wrapper desirable light color, also yields a milder taste than sun-grown tobacco. Cuba and Puerto Rico also grow wrapper under shade to satisfy American preference for light-hued cigars.

Tobacco, eagerly sought by virtually every Indian tribe, was the white man's passport in opening the Far West. In the Ohio-Mississippi basin a new kind of leaf—Burley—became a major economic mainstay.

ACROSS THE APPALACHIANS

THE westward expansion of the United States is associated, and rightly so, with the dramatic deeds of pioneers like Daniel Boone, death-worshipping gunmen like Wild Bill Hickok and Wyatt Earp, dashing bravos in blue like George A. Custer. Such men "rode point" for the westering; they were the shock troops. But as Captain John Smith and the other skilled soldiers of Jamestown had discovered to their sorrow, shock troops could invade a land but could not really possess it. A territory is held only when economic development is assured to feed the settlers, and only when political structures are set up to safeguard the economic growth.

The real architect of western expansion was Thomas Jefferson. It was he who suggested, in his 1781 "Notes on the state of Virginia" that tobacco would serve as an economic prop to the "western country on the Mississippi." It was he who drafted the Ordinance of 1784, calling for the orderly establishment of provisional territorial governments which would grow into separate states. And it was he, as President, who secured title to the vast valley of the Mississippi by the Louisiana Purchase of 1803 from France.

Land pressure

The need of an agrarian economy for more land had led seven of the thirteen colonies to stake out claims to their west—claims that were denied outright by George III's proclamation of 1763, prohibiting land grants or settlements west of the Appalachians. One victim of this proclamation was the Mississippi Company of Virginia, organized by George Washington and others to develop an outpost at the Ohio-Mississippi junction. Land pressure was particularly strong in Virginia, where tobaccomen realized that the tidewater bottom lands were being worn out by successive years of one-crop cultivation. With the War of Independence over, tobacco began to edge away from the tidewater lands between the fall line and the sea, and into the higher piedmont between the mountains and the fall line. More adventurous planters eyed Natchez, where tobacco had been raised since 1718. In that year John Law's Companie d'Occident brought in 30 settlers to grow tobacco for the French market; two years later Law's overcapitalized venture exploded in the famous "Mississippi Bubble," but the tobacco culture itself was not

uprooted. England acquired the Natchez district after the Seven Years' War, and Spain acquired it during the Revolution. Very much aware of the profit in tobacco traffic, the Spanish government announced its willingness to buy two million pounds a year, to be exported through New Orleans. Since this announcement came just as the War of Independence ended and George III's proclamation went by the boards, quite a few Americans headed for Natchez. Some were experienced Virginia tobacco planters, among them younger sons who could not hope to inherit the family estate.

Even while the Revolution was being fought along the Atlantic coast, pioneer settlers were trickling from the Chesapeake and Carolina colonies into Kentucky and Tennessee. Their routine of settlement was much the same as that followed by the indentured servants of tidewater days, who cleared land on the piedmont "frontier" after working their way out of bond. The big trees were killed (big trees meant rich soil), and a cabin thrown up using pegs if nails were not to be had, as was more often the case than not. Corn and beets were planted before the land was actually cleared, hogs were fattened on wild acorns, and survival thus—it was hoped—insured. The best of the virgin land was saved for tobacco. From a sheltered bed seedlings planted in March were transplanted in May. Harvested, air-cured and bundled, the summer's leaf crop might fill one hogshead—perhaps two. It bought nails and gunpowder, sugar and tea, axes and an occasional "fancy." Shelter and furniture came from the forest trees, food from the land, clothing from animal skins or tended sheep.

The westerner—whether he battled the soil in seventeenth-century western Virginia or nineteenth-century Kentucky—was a different breed than the tidewater planter. The plantation culture of the Chesapeake was a little bit of old England; it enjoyed its lace cuffs, its churchwarden pipes, its books, its Georgian architecture. The western loner was likely to hate England and all it stood for. He had left the built-up East because it offered him no economic opportunity, no real freedom. In Kentucky, the price was right: before 1778, under Virginia statute, anybody could have 400 acres free. (After that year real estate went up—to ten shillings for a hundred acres.) There were no vast tobacco plantations in the Kentucky and Tennessee hills; the pioneers were small farmers by temperament as well as by terrain.

River pressure

So the marginal man of the Atlantic seaboard—the common man of his day—tramped over the Blue Ridge and down, over the Appalachian ridge and onto the wooded Appalachian plateau. This rolling country, stretching from Eastern Ohio through central Kentucky and Tennessee, was a kind of western piedmont. Its soil, rich in limestone and in nitrogen compounds, responded admirably to the hoe. Corn grew tall, tobacco grew strong, and both grew in quantity. Inspection warehouses for tobacco were in operation during the 1780s, but there was no way to export the leaf in volume. Roading hogsheads back over the Appalachians was impossible; floating them down the Mississippi was possible, but not acceptable to the Spaniards who controlled New Orleans. One of the consequences of this frustrating situation was the "Spanish Intrigue" organized by General James Wilkinson, who took an oath of loyalty to Spain and plotted to organize western settlements under Spanish rule. It has never been determined whether Wilkinson's real motive was political or economic. He first broached the Spanish customs barrier in 1787 with a cargo of meat and tobacco, and as the only "American" permitted to use the Mississippi trade route Wilkinson took a magnificent convoy of 25 riverboats to New Orleans the following year. Tobacco was his principal commodity, and on this he made a trading profit, freight, handling fees and inspection fees. The prospect of Spanish colonies on the other side of the Appalachians worried George Washington; and the prospect of U. S. action to prevent it worried Spain, for late in 1788 the Mississippi was opened to trade and American settlers permitted to "export" their tobacco and other produce to New Orleans on payment of duty.

Kentucky 1792, Tennessee 1796

With the historic success of the Chesapeake colonies to inspire them, the Kentucky settlers scattered their seed with a will. In 1790 they shipped 250,000 pounds of leaf to New Orleans and no doubt smuggled in a good deal more. Two years later Kentucky was admitted as a state. The bottom temporarily dropped out of the Mississippi tobacco market about this time as Spain reduced her purchases to virtually nothing—the reasons given were, first, that the royal warehouses in Seville were full and, second, that Kentuckians were "nesting" their hogsheads with trash. The move finished Natchez as a tobacco region, and hit the Kentucky tobaccomen hard. But the pressure for a tobacco outlet nevertheless forced open the mouth of the Mississippi. Spain in 1795 granted Americans the right of duty-free deposit in New Orleans, effective in 1798, and Kentucky boats floated hogsheads by the thousand down river. Tennessee was secured to the U. S. in 1796, when it became a state. With Kentucky it was to become the great transmontane tobacco area, rivaling the Chesapeake states in production.

$11,250,000 bargain

Whatever potency the "Spanish Intrigue" ever had was now dissolved. The Spanish authority at New Orleans withdrew the right of deposit in 1802,

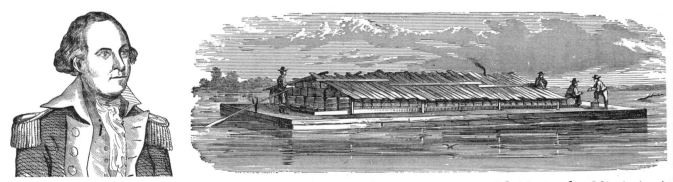

First to pierce New Orleans customs barrier was General James Wilkinson. His "Spanish Intrigue" hastened Kentucky and Tennessee statehood, led to duty-free export of leaf via the Mississippi: early tobacco economy made river shipment vital. Barge trip from St. Louis required four months.

again interrupting the leaf traffic. Meanwhile in Europe the rampaging Napoleon Bonaparte had acquired from Spain the whole Louisiana Territory—an area embracing not only the port of New Orleans but the great plains area west of the Mississippi to the Rocky Mountains. There may have been a connection between the Spanish revocation of free export in October 1802 and the great expedition being mounted in Holland at the same time by Napoleon, aimed at establishing a French colony in the western Mississippi basin. The expedition was icebound in harbor during the winter of 1802-3; meanwhile Jefferson sent James Monroe on his famous $10 million mission to buy the Isle of Orleans. While Monroe sailed for Paris, the groundwork for cession not only of New Orleans but of the great plains as well was being laid by the U.S. minister to France, Robert R. Livingston. Napoleon was becoming discouraged in his scheme for a western empire to match those of Spain and Britain. He failed in his attempt to get Florida from Spain, failed to conquer the West Indian steppingstone of Santo Domingo and faced a war with Great Britain. By the time Monroe reached Paris in April, 1803, all of Louisiana had been offered for sale to Livingston. Before the month was out, Livingston and Monroe had accepted the entire Louisiana package for $11,250,-000. Again the planters of Kentucky and Tennessee stepped up their cultivation; the Mississippi basin had finally been made safe for Americans and tobacco.

Embargo = "O grab me"

The leaf growers of what is now the Burley region (parts of Ohio and Missouri in addition to Kentucky and Tennessee) had Jefferson to thank for the diplomatic coup that assured their economic development. An American merchant marine took shape, and western tobacco began to compete in world markets with that of Virginia, Maryland and North Carolina. But they had also to thank Jefferson for the next serious interruption to their progress—the Embargo of 1807. This was a milestone in international affairs, representing the application of economic sanctions against Britain and France instead of a declaration of war in response to violation of U. S. rights at sea. These violations were crowned by the impressment of American seamen on the high seas by the British Navy, but the blockading

Thomas Jefferson was the architect of expansion to the West. He encouraged westward movement of farms (including tobacco farms), sent Lewis and Clark on mission to explore trade routes, bought Louisiana Territory from France. A tobacco planter himself, he warned against one-crop concentration.

of neutral American ships by each belligerent from the ports of the other was also a severe injury to a fledgling nation. Tobacco and other American staples were seized abroad. After 1807, when the Embargo took effect, they rotted on the wharves of U. S. ports instead. To be effective, the Embargo would have had to continue for several years—that is, until European stocks of cotton and tobacco were exhausted. As it was, the experiment was ended by

Congress after only a year, and the idealistic Jefferson finished his second Presidential term in a storm of bitter abuse. His countrymen jeered that embargo, spelled backwards, read "O grab me."

Americans were not philosophical enough, nor pacifistic enough, to strangle their own export economy in order to chastise the warring empires of Europe. Their reaction, which finally took shape in the War of 1812, was more direct. And among the most prominent advocates of such a reaction were the "War Hawks" of Congress—Clay and Johnson of Kentucky, Grundy of Tennessee, Calhoun of South Carolina. These men were speaking for states committed to the planting of tobacco and cotton, commodities still grown mainly for export, still requiring freedom of the seas. There was poetic justice in the fact that long rifles in the hands of Kentucky and Tennessee militiamen routed the British at New Orleans on January 8, 1815. Although fought two weeks after a peace treaty had been signed at Ghent, the victory of the War Hawks saved the Mississippi valley from invasion. This time not only the Mississippi but the ocean had been made safe for Americans and tobacco.

Era of good feeling

With the departure of the beaten British from New Orleans, the United States was able to settle down to the business of growing for the first time in two generations. The era of turmoil that began with the Seven Years' War of 1756—of which the North American "French and Indian War" was a part—and continued through the Revolution and the War of 1812, was finally over. Boundaries were drawn; land rights and river rights and sea rights affecting the young nation were resolved. This was 'The Era of Good Feeling.' Among other ways, it was reflected in the resumption of steady increase in the tobacco export trade, which had peaked at 100,000,000 pounds just before the Declaration of Independence. This peak was duplicated during Washington's first term as President, but exports fell off by 10% or

Freedom of the high seas for Americans and tobacco was secured by victory over British in War of 1812. Final battle was defeat of British at New Orleans by militiamen from Kentucky and Tennessee who used long backwoods rifles. Peace had already been made, but the Mississippi valley was saved from invasion.

Tobacco manufacturing began with this very simple procedure: pile of cured leaf was roughly sorted, then twisted or spun on a wheel (below) into rope *or roll tobacco like the Spanish colonial product. The resulting "twist," sold by the yard, could be chewed, sliced for pipe, or even powdered to snuff.*

15% in the last ten years of the eighteenth century. During Jefferson's second term (that of the Embargo), the average export poundage dropped below 60,000,000 and between 1811 and 1815 the annual export was less than 40,000,000. The low point, 1814, saw a little over 4,000,000 pounds shipped abroad.

But in 1815, with the seas cleared, leaf exports snapped back to the 90,000,000-pound level as if nothing had happened. Thereafter they increased steadily. By 1830 the pre-Revolutionary peak was being consistently topped. In the next 30 years export poundage doubled.

At the same time the geography of tobacco cultivation was changing. In 1830 the western fields—most of them in Kentucky and Tennessee—turned out a third of the nation's crop, and from 1843 until the War Between the States, about half. Farther west, in the newly-established Republic of Texas, tobacco was raised before 1840 and traded across the Rio Grande for Mexican sugar and coffee. Thomas Jefferson's vision was fulfilled.

More important than the geographical shift, however, was a change in the character of the tobacco industry. Like the United States itself, it was becoming more self-sufficient, making the transition from a supplier of raw material to a manufacturer for home consumption. In 1830 about a fifth of the crop was not shipped abroad but fed into home factories. This proportion grew, and by 1860 about half the leaf grown by Americans was processed and consumed by Americans. Appropriately enough, the new development came about in the place where the tobacco civilization first arose: Virginia. In that state four cities pioneered an industry that was to become the Old Dominion's largest well before the War Between the States. The four cities were Danville, Richmond, Lynchburg and Petersburg; their product, plug tobacco.

Era of good chewing

For the first time, tobacco usage in the United States was not an imitation of some foreign mode, but entirely on its own. The general switch to chew-

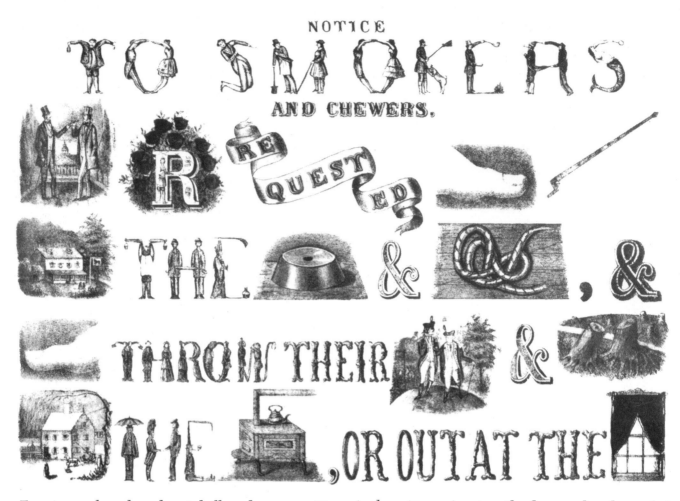

Even in rough-and-ready antebellum days, amenities were important. "Gentlemen are requested to spit in the spittoon & not on the floor, and to throw their butts & stumps in the stove, or out at the window."

ing tobacco was, indeed, a distinctively American departure. After two centuries of aping the pipe-smoking tradition of Europe and, on a higher social level, the Old World's snuff-taking ritual, Americans took the quid in their teeth. There were two explanations. First, the onset of the new habit was partly a matter of psychology: a rejection, final and complete, of Europeans in general and the British in particular, with their inlaid snuff-boxes, formal airs and silk handkerchiefs. It is scarcely an exaggeration to say that snuff was associated with everything Americans detested. The Scotch, who pinched snuff as a means of pinching pennies, manufactured it and used the colonies as a kind of captive market. Led by the prince of state, the Regent, and the prince of foppery, Beau Brummel, fully half of all the hated English took "sneeshin." Snuff went with periwigs and kneebreeches, with the French Bourbons and Marie Antoinette. Later

generations might have described this delicate and dandified sniffing practise as "unAmerican."

As in every change of tobacco fashion, product improvement played a part. Foreign snuff mills of the time used the poorest scrap, stems, sawdust and straw. At the same time plug and twist, fashioned from leaf of light color and pleasant mildness, was displacing homemade tobacco rope. Most Americans could not spell the "retrogression of snuff quality," but they could taste it. It was not the first time, nor would it be the last, that a change in tobacco fashion was based on the development of a better way of bringing out the best in *Nicotiana tabacum.*

Chewing tobacco was also a matter of convenience: Americans were on the move, trundling their wagons to new homesites, building roads and canals, clearing the forests, farming, mining. "Chaw" was the practical thing for the average man, who

118

could not pause in his day's occupation to light up a cumbersome pipe. It was practical for another reason—there was always a spittoon handy, as large as all outdoors. On the eve of Fort Sumter, manufactured tobacco meant chewing tobacco, either plug or twist. Of the 348 tobacco factories listed by the 1860 Census for Virginia and North Carolina, only seven were smoking tobacco producers, and only six of the quid establishments mentioned smoking tobacco as a sideline. And a sideline it was—in most cases the pipe tobacco was a heterogenous mixture of scraps left over from plug production. In the main, if a man wanted to puff a pipe, he could shred his own leaf, or slice up a plug. The universality of chewing is more remarkable in the light of the volume of manufactured tobacco reached by 1860— some 83,000,000 pounds in Virginia and North Carolina alone, or about as much as the nation's total export trade in 1820.

Indian weed

When the tobacco trade moved west after the Revolution, it did not stop at the farthest settlement but went all the way—to the Rockies by land, to California by sea. One reason for its movement beyond the Mississippi and onto the plains (then called "the Great American Desert") was the Indian. To the roving tribes of the buffalo country, as to the more settled hut-builders of the eastern forests, tobacco had always been something special. West of the Mississippi basin there were sedentary, agricultural tribes who cultivated tobacco: along the Missouri River, Mandans and Arikaras; along the upper Rio Grande, the pueblo peoples; along the Snake River of the Northwest, Nez Perces and others. The plains tribes—Sioux, Cheyenne, Comanche, Navajo—were more likely to acquire their tobacco by raid than by trade. Nevertheless, the leaf was prized by all of them. Where the harsh *Nico-*

Era of Good Feeling after War of 1812 saw America on the move, wagoning west, clearing the forests, farming, mining. It was also the era of chewing tobacco, *since few could pause during the day to light up a pipe. Chaw juice was no problem, since every man had a spittoon as large as all outdoors.*

119

Pontiac, who organized many tribes for 1763 revolt against British, was a chief of the Ottawas, one of several tobacco-raising and tobacco-trading nations discovered by Champlain 150 years before. Defeated

Pontiac smoked calumet with English Major Roberts at Fort Erie, was later welcomed to Oswego peace parley with tobacco. From the first, tobacco was a diplomatic offering in dealings with the Indians.

tiana rustica did not grow, even harsher wild tobaccos were smoked, usually blended with mild bark or leaves. Algonquin tribes even had a word for such a mixture—"kinnikinnick," from which a successful Lynchburg tobacco brand took its name.

Like the buffalo and everything else that was valued highly by the Indian, tobacco was a gift of the Great Spirit and, smoked in a straight pipe, a symbol of peace on earth and goodwill toward men. The Indian palate was keener than his agricultural ability, for no sooner had white men begun the cultivation of leaf from Latin American seed than the red man ceased to cultivate *Nicotiana rustica*. This was recorded along the Connecticut River as well as the James and the York. In a sense, therefore, the Indians were the first local "market"

for tobacco. There was never any quibbling about the leaf's acceptability in trading with Indians— only the question of what they could give in return. Thus, in the opening of the West, tobacco was a necessity of travel along with the beads, mirrors and other trading goods used to purchase food and "life insurance."

Tobacco talks

In their sallies across the Appalachians, the empire-building British of colonial times shrewdly spoke to the Indian in his own language, of which tobacco was a part. The Great Lakes tribes, whose regular commerce in tobacco was documented by Champlain and the French explorers who followed him, were "good Iroquois" to the French and, for that very reason, bitterly hostile to the English. These tobacco-trading nations, Ottawas, Hurons, Potawatomies and Chippewas, were organized in 1763 by the great chief Pontiac for a massive revolt against the invading British. Most of the forts in the wild "back country" south of the Great Lakes were seized by the Indians, only Detroit, Niagara and Fort Pitt holding out against the uprising. It required three years to break up the Indian alliance and end "Pontiac's War." Proud in defeat, Pontiac sailed east from Detroit with his fellow-chiefs and stopped at Fort Erie in 1766 to smoke the calumet and parley with the English Major Robert Rogers, commander of the western forts. When Pontiac and his party reached Fort Niàgara on their journey to the peace council at Oswego, New York, the British there welcomed them with tobacco and rum. Tobacco—with or without firewater on the side—became the standard diplomatic gambit for dealing with Indians of almost every tribe as the English soldiery and later American explorers, trappers and fur traders moved relentlessly west.

Lewis and Clark

In the first overland breakthrough to the Pacific, by Meriwether Lewis and William Clark (the former, appropriately enough, having been secretary to a former tobaccoman, President Thomas Jefferson), the trail through Indian country and back was blazed with the aid of tobacco. At every meeting with the native tribes, the young officers presented them with "carrotes" (hands or twists) of tobacco or passed the pipe with them—pausing to do so even on one occasion where a dangerous stretch of white water made them anxious to test their fate. They recorded in their diaries of the two-and-a-half-year trip the attitudes of various tribes toward tobacco. Five months up the Missouri River on the western swing, they described the Arikaras:

> The Nation of the Rickerries is about 600 men able to bear arms a Great perpotion of them have fuseés they appear to be peacefull, their men tall and perpotiend, womin Small and industerous, raise great quantities of Corn Beens Simnins &c. also Tobacco for the men to Smoke they collect all the wood and do the drugery . . .

On their long land-and-water trek from St. Louis up the Missouri, across the Rockies and down the Columbia, Lewis and Clark established "diplomatic relations" with numerous Indian nations, paving the way for later trade and settlement. Gifts of tobacco proved indispensable to win confidence of the red man. So much leaf was given away that the party had no ration of its own during return trip.

This entry would appear to indicate that women cultivated the Arikaras' leaf—either a misconception on the part of the explorers, or an exception to the general rule that braves raised the tobacco.

In August, 1805, the party found itself south of what is now Butte, Montana, and named the Jefferson River "in honor of that illustrious personage Thomas Jefferson (the author of our enterprize)." They worked their way up the Jefferson and ascended the Tobacco Root Range in search of the Snake Indians, with whom they wished to trade for much-needed horses. Just after crossing the continental divide, Lewis and a party got close enough to 60 mounted warriors to communicate peaceful intentions. His account reads:

> bothe parties now advanced and we wer all carresed and besmeared with their grease and paint till I was heartily tired of the national hug. I now had the pipe lit and gave them smoke ; they seated themselves in a circle around us and pulled of their mockersons before they would receive or smoke the pipe. this is a custom among them as I afterwards learned indicative of a sacred obligation of sincerity in their profession of friendship given by the act of receiving and smoking the pipe of a stranger. or which is as much as to say that they wish they may always go bear-

foot if they are not sincere; a pretty heavy penalty if they are to march through the plains of their country.

Two days later he noted in his journal:

> they are excessively fond of the pipe; but have it not much in their power to indulge themselves with even their native tobacco as they do not cultivate it themselves.

The desire for tobacco, coupled for one or another reason with the inability to grow it, was quite evident among the Nez Perces, one of the most advanced Indian tribes. On October 4th Clark remarks

> I displeased an Indian by refuseing him a pice of Tobacco which he tooke the liberty to take out of our Sack.

By Christmas Day of the same year the expedition had reached the mouth of the Columbia and built a stockade, Fort Clatsop. Their holiday began:

> at day light this morning we we awoke by the discharge of the fire arm of all our party & a Selute, Shouts and a Song which the whole party joined in under our windows, after which they retired to their rooms were chearfull all the morning. after brakfast we divided our Tobacco which amounted to 12 carrots one half of which we gave to the men of the party who used tobacco, and to those who doe not use it we make a present of a handkerchief.

The remaining six carrottes not distributed as Christmas presents were husbanded for trading on the trip back. Before leaving the coast, Lewis recorded that the "Clatsops Chinnooks and others inhabiting the coast and country in this neighbourhood, are excessively fond of smoking tobacco." He also found that other English-speaking traders had visited the river mouth to trade; the Indians "give us proofs of their varacity by repeating many words of English, as musquit, powder, shot, nife, file, damned rascal, &c." The visitors were probably British sailors in the Sandwich Island trade, although Lewis suspected that a settlement had been established south along the coast. At any rate the trade goods offered by the whites had consisted of tobacco along with firearms, tinware, beads and sailor's clothing. The Indian commodity was, of course, furs.

The damp winter of the Northwest delayed the departure east until the following March; most members of the party were taken ill. The Indian demand for their dwindling store of tobacco was insistent: one morning three Clatsops turned up and remained all day, the object of their visit being "mearly to smoke the pipe." Rowing their dugouts

William Clark, right, had captained a company of militia, was 34 when he and Lewis left St. Louis to find a Northwest Passage. Clark was an expert riverman, could handle Indians as well as boats. Meriwether Lewis, left, was 30, had been Thomas Jefferson's private secretary, had served under Clark, knew natural science and navigation. He co-commanded the great expedition into the West.

Fur trade keelboat used Missouri route opened by Lewis and Clark expedition of 1805. Tobacco, they found, was an essential trade item. Among several artifacts sent via Missouri boat to their sponsor, President Thomas Jefferson, was a carrotte (twist) of the tobacco cultivated by the Arikaras Indians.

up the Columbia, the whites provisioned themselves along the shore by hunting and trading. The Indians sold them roots, dogs, sturgeon, dried salmon and seal meat, but at high prices: one band refused to accept anything but tobacco in exchange. Consequently,

> we are now obliged to deny the uce of this article (to the men who) suffer much for the want of it. they substitute the bark of the wild crab which they chew ; it is very bitter, and they assure me they find it a good substitute for tobacco. the smokers substitute the inner bark of the red willow and the sacacommis.

This was late in March. By July 8, Clark's group had recrossed the continental divide to find the supplies they had cached the previous August. The "uce" of tobacco no longer had to be denied the men, for tobacco was part of the cache. But at each encounter with Indians—Yanktons, Mandans, and others—protocol required that the pipe be passed, and by September the supply was low again. Near the junction of the Missouri and Big Sioux Rivers (now part of the boundary between Nebraska and South Dakota), Clark and his men came upon a licensed Indian trader plying the river:

> as we were in want of some tobacco I purposed to Mr. Airs to furnish us with 4 carrots for which we would Pay the amount to any Merchant of St. Louis he very readily agreed to furnish us with tobacco and gave to each man as much as it is necessary for them to use between this and St. Louis, an instance of Generossity for which every man of the party appears to acknowledge.

Clark adds, as an afterthought, that Mr. Airs "also insisted on our accepting a barrel of flour."

So far as the tobacco historian is concerned, the journals of Lewis and Clark tell as much about the place of tobacco among white Americans as among red—although in one of the boxes of specimens and artifacts Clark sent to President Thomas Jefferson from Fort Mandan was "a carrote of Ricaras Tobacco" (Arikaras' tobacco). The confidential com-

Indian furs had been object of white traders ever since seventeenth-century tobacco planters sought beaver skins from Virginia red men. "Commerce of the prairies" was a risky business. Tobacco twists were effective trade items, since broadleaf could not be grown on dry plains and Indians generally preferred white man's tobacco to native varieties. Also desirable were blankets, hardware and beads.

mission given by Jefferson was "to explore the Missouri river, & such principal stream of it as . . . may offer the most direct & practicable water communication across this continent, for the purposes of commerce" and specifically to find how the fur trade might best be conducted by Americans. Among their many discoveries, Lewis and Clark found that tobacco was an essential element of that trade.

War and peace

An offering of tobacco as a gift retained a special meaning, because the leaf still held an aroma of sanctity for Indian males. Where the Indians cultivated tobacco, only the males tended the plant and it was the only crop thus dignified. The leaf figured in the life-habits of such non-agricultural tribes as the Comanches, the best horsemen of the plains. When one of their warriors died, a handful of tobacco was buried with him to "quiet the dead." The expression suggests a realization of tobacco's everyday function—to quiet the living. But despite their pride and prowess, the feared Comanches were not above peacefully approaching white wagon trains to beg for tobacco. This practise almost precipitated a war in 1847 when Chief Cinemo of the Cheyenne was shot by a jittery teamster as he advanced asking for tobacco. (Before he died, however, Cinemo counseled peace to his tribesmen.)

The pipe did not always betoken outward peace or inner quiet. Among the plains tribes it often signified an agreement. Before making war, the sacred pipe was sent from village to village; those willing to strengthen the war party would indicate their assent by smoking. And in a somewhat similar way, the long trading-wrangles between white man and red were generally opened and/or concluded with a shared pipe of tobacco.

Leaf passport to Oregon

Long before the Rocky Mountain barrier was breached by land, the mountain trappers were penetrating Oregon from the mouth of the Columbia River. Alexander Ross spent the years between 1810 and 1825 in the Northwest fur trade, and his journal frequently mentions tobacco as an essential tool of that trade. Its principal use was to placate the Indians, smoking being "the introductory step to all important affairs, and no business can be entered upon with these people before the ceremony of smoking is over." Ross describes an attack on a white hunting party "owing to the scarcity of tobacco," and the pleasure expressed by a chief at the return of an old trader friend:

We are rejoiced to see one of our first and best friends come back again to live among us. We were always well treated by our first traders, and got plenty of tobacco to smoke. They never passed our camp without taking our children by the hand and giving us to smoke . .

Ross was careful to use tobacco as his passport. On one trek to the Cascades he found five hundred well-armed Indians, who were observed "to become shy towards us, a very bad sign." At night the crowd was taken into the white party's camp, and

When the ceremony of smoking was over, a few words were addressed to the chiefs expressing the favorable sense we entertained for their character and their deportment during the day. We also bestowed on each a head of tobacco, and to every one of the motly group we gave a single leaf; which took a considerable quantity and some time to distribute. This kind treatment was so different to anything they had met with for years past that all with one voice called out in the Chinook language, "Haugh owe yea ah, Haugh owe yea ah," meaning "our friends, our friends."

Fort Astoria on the Columbia River was the base of operations for fur trader Alexander Ross, builder of the skin commerce with the Indians (1810-1825).

Smoking was "the introductory step in all important affairs, and no business can be entered upon with those people before the smoking ceremony is over."

125

Later Ross describes his answer to one unruly red-man, "a fellow more like a baboon than a man, with a head full of feathers and countenance of brass, having a fine gun in his hand," who called out the one question that was central to the relationship between Indian and Caucasian:

"How long are the whites to pass here, troubling our waters and scaring our fish without paying us! look at all that bales of goods going to our enemies," said he, "and look at our wives and children naked" . . . I turned briskly round, "So long," said I, "as the Indians smoke our tobacco: just so long and no longer will the whites pass here." Then I put a question to him in turn. "Who gave you that fine gun you have?" said I. "The whites," said he, "And who gives you tobacco to smoke?" said I again. "The Whites," he replied. Continuing the subject, "Are you fond of your gun?" said I. "Yes," said he. "And are you fond of your tobacco to smoke?" To this question the reply was "Yes." "Then," said I, "you ought to be fond of the whites, who supply all your wants." "Oh, yes," rejoined he.

As Ross and his trappers made their way toward the Rockies, a little farther east each year, they encountered the Snake nation. "The regularity and order of these people convinced the whites that they were under a very different government to any other they had yet seen in the country." The Snakes were not beggars of tobacco, but preferred their own. Ross thought they were "perhaps the only Indian nation on the continent that manufacture and smoke their own tobacco." By 1820, white man's tobacco had been smoked in most parts of what is now the United States, and Ross' observation may have been substantially correct.

The Snake tobacco plant grows low, is of a brownish colour and thrives in most parts of the country, but is a favourite of sandy or barren soil . . . . it is weaker than our tobacco, but the difference in strength may be owing to the mode of manufacturing it for use. For this purpose their only process is to dig it and then rub it fine with the hands or pound it with stones until it is tolerably fine. In this state it almost resembles green tea. In smoking it leaves a green taste or flavour in the mouth.
Our people however seemed to like it very well . . . yet with all their fondness for the Snake tobacco, I observed that the moment they reached the fort the Snake importation was either bartered away or laid aside; one and all applied to me for good old twist!
The Snakes would often bring it to our people for sale; but generally in small parcels, sometimes

Many tribes of the Great Plains did not cultivate tobacco. Yet they all prized the leaf, using it to signify agreement, to comfort the living and quiet the dead. In 1867 General Hancock, responsible for good order in Kansas and Colorado, was sketched as he "passed the pipe" with Arapahoes. All was well.

126

Westward march of civilization displaced Indians from their lands. In 1870s and 1880s they became government wards, "cheaper to feed than to fight."

Agencies on U.S. reservations handed out regular rations to the subdued tribes. These consisted of tobacco, coffee, flour, sugar and beef on the hoof.

an ounce or two, sometimes a quart, and sometimes as much as a gallon. In their bartering propensities, however, they would often make our friends smile to see them with a beaver skin in one hand and a small bag containing perhaps a pint of the native tobacco in the other: the former they would offer for a paper looking glass worth two pence; while for the latter they would often demand an axe worth four or five shillings!

"Passing the pipe"

In such classic accounts of the early plains traffic as Parkman's 1846 journey on the Oregon Trail, tobacco punctuates almost every camping halt, and "passing the pipe" figures in almost every conversation that follows a meeting with a roaming Indian. For example:

They were the Pawnees whom Kearsley had encountered the day before, and belonged to a large hunting party, known to be ranging the prairie in the vicinity. They strode rapidly by, within a furlong of our tents, not pausing or looking towards us, after the manner of Indians when meditating mischief, or conscious of ill desert. I went out to meet them, and had an amicable conference with the chief, presenting him with half a pound of tobacco, at which unmerited bounty he expressed much gratification. These fellows, or some of their companions, had committed a dastardly outrage [murder] upon an emigrant party in advance of us . . .

And again:

On the prairie the custom of smoking with friends is seldom omitted, whether among Indians or whites. The pipe, therefore, was taken from the wall, and its red bowl crammed with the tobacco and *shongsasha* [red willow bark] mixed in suitable proportions. Then it passed round the circle, each man inhaling a few whiffs . . .

When Parkman and his party arrived at Fort Laramie, then a trading post of the American Fur Company, he relates that the Indians of the vicinity pushed into their quarters and sat silently in a semi-circle. "The pipe was now to be lighted and passed from one to another; and this was the only entertainment that at present they expected from us." The use of a pipe by Indians and whites does not imply that smoking tobacco was carried. Pressed plug was easier to carry and keep and almost as convenient when the smoking-time came, since the red willow bark was usually sliced on a flat board and the tobacco at the same time.

There was nothing about this haphazard Indian trading to push up the price of tobacco, or to move it across the plains in any volume. But when fifty thousand men trekked west during the Colorado Gold Rush of 1859 ("Pike's Peak or Bust"), tobacco, coffee and sugar were sold for their weight in gold dust.

Tobacco continued to play a part on the great plains even after the free trade with roaming Indians had given way to a death hunt by the U. S. Cavalry. When the surviving tribes were rounded up and herded onto reservations, tobacco became an instrument of government policy, aptly expressed in the phrase "cheaper to feed than to fight." Its value as a pacifier was reflected by its inclusion in the government ration distributed by Indian agents; tobacco was one of the five staples regularly issued, the others being coffee, flour, sugar and beef on the hoof.

Seegaritos and Santa Fe

Unnoticed and largely unchronicled in the penetration from the Appalachians to the Rockies was the much older penetration of white settlement from the South, up to the headwaters of the Rio Grande. Smoking was not brought to the Santa Fe area by the Spanish whites; the ancient peoples of

The old city of Santa Fe, reached during the 1820s by American wagon traders, had a tobacco tradition of its own. Early settlers, defying the rigid laws of Spain, rolled cigars from homegrown leaf. Pueblo people of ancient times used pipes and cigarettes, permitted only proven male hunters to smoke pipes.

Around 1820 American traders "discovered" Santa Fe, were surprised to find señoras and señoritas using "seegaritos, to which all females of the Capital, regardless of age or condition in society, are subject."

the pueblos had long before smoked red willow bark and coarse *Nicotiana rustica* in clay pipes, the custom being permitted only to men who had shown their prowess as hunters. But among the precious stores dragged up the hundreds of miles of hot desert from Mexico during the seventeenth and eighteenth centuries was tobacco: it was against the law for any province of Spain to manufacture cigars with homegrown leaf. Nevertheless, the rigid law of Spain was not enforceable in so remote an outpost as old Santa Fe. A Spanish Padre, reporting on the ways of the settlers around 1650, wrote:

> They are content if they have a good crop of tobacco to smoke, caring for no more riches, apparently under a vow of poverty, which is saying much for men who in their thirst for gold would enter hell itself to get it.

During the 1820s, when American wagoners broke open the Santa Fe trail, they described the señoras and señoritas with their black lace, lavender face powder, and "fearsome vice of employing the *seegarito* to which all females of the Capital, regardless of age or condition in society, are subject." The Americans' response to cigarette smoking did not indicate anti-tobacco sentiments, for almost every trader and trapper carried tobacco in his sack of "possibles" strapped to his horse. And American trade goods exchanged in Santa Fe often included

wagonloads of tobacco—contraband under Spanish rule. More likely, the frontiersman—like the midwestern farmer of 1900—could not understand why anyone would take to cigarette smoking when quid and pipe were to be had.

General Stephen Kearny, who used Santa Fe as a staging area for his 1846 expedition to California, also observed that all the local women smoked "seegaritos," and that at night the fandangos were danced through clouds of cigarette smoke. Many of these cigarettes were wrapped, not in scarce paper, but like those of the Aztecs, in cornhusks. At the public dances, cigarettes were lighted from flints; in the Governor's palace, the women ate from silver and held their cigarettes in pincers of gold.

On July 4, 1876 Santa Fe, now part of the Territory of New Mexico, U. S. A., celebrated the hundredth anniversary of independence with a grand parade. One of the most popular floats carried workers from the cigar factory, who rolled cigars as they rolled and presented them to the crowd. In addition to commemorating freedom from Britain, the town was also marking a freedom long denied under Spain—freedom to "roll their own."

California

When Americans began arriving in California early in the nineteenth century they found, as Sir

Early "Californios" from Mexico brought Spanish preference with them, considered cigar-making a necessary skill. Although state could not grow fine tobacco, it was for a time a big center of cigar and cigarette manufacture.

Francis Drake had found in 1578, that the tobacco tradition had preceded them. In the later instance, however, it was civilized Mexican settlers rather than savage Indians who were consuming the leaf. Vallejo of Sonoma, commander of Mexican troops in Northern California in 1839, was trained in tanning, brickmaking, shoemaking and cigarmaking. American arrivals a few years afterward found an unnamed monk in Monterey printing religious tracts on cigar wrappers. And in 1847, a year before

When this sketch of San Francisco was made on the spot in 1848, the town was booming and Americans were pouring in, some seeking gold, others seeking to live off those who found it. Among the thirty or forty professional men who set up in business were three doctors of medicine, one cigar-roller.

130

California was annexed, the mushrooming city of San Francisco contained only three doctors but at least one cigar maker.

As might be expected, the Mexican-Spanish tradition governed California manufacture, even while the Forty-Niners introduced the Eastern mode of consumption. Its cigar establishments grew quickly as Americans poured in; by 1880 it was fourth in value of cigars produced, after New York, Pennsylvania and Ohio. With this background, and in view of California's importance as a growing market, San Francisco soon boasted a sizable cigarette output as well. Until World War II and its squeeze on overland freight transport, the city was a manufacturing center for one of the top three companies. Attempts were made, in view of the long leaf haul from the East, to grow tobacco in the Golden State shortly after the Civil War. But in 1880 the poundage was negligible—scarcely more than a thousandth of the national crop, and well under that of stony little Vermont. Except for modest production in Missouri and Wisconsin, tobacco cultivation did not cross the Mississippi. Irrigation, so successful in converting sandy barrens into luxuriant fruit groves, does not suffice for tobacco. Subtropical in origin, tobacco needs natural rainfall and humid summers to attain richness of flavor. So the story of Americans and their tobacco was to unfold in terms of the arch-rivalry between the Ohio Valley and the Virginia-Carolina piedmont.

Plug spark

Although Virginia accounted for half the nation's non-cigar tobacco manufactures during most of the antebellum years, there was plenty of market to go around. The newer Western cities followed the lead of Virginia and the second largest producer, New York. Chewing factories went up in Louisville, Clarksville, Tenn., and St. Louis. A pioneer plug-maker of the last-named town, the Foulks factory, took on a son-in-law named John Liggett and later evolved into Liggett & Myers.

Just as leaf-growing west of the Appalachians was an offshoot of the tidewater colonies and eventually overtook their production, so the western states first imitated and later (after the War Between the States) outstripped the Virginia District in plugmaking. The reason for this success lay in the nature of Burley leaf itself. Unlike the Eastern plant, Burley has little or no content of sugar. As plugmaking grew more elaborate, flavoring was added to the cured leaf—licorice, rum, sugar, honey, or some other sweetener. The low-sugared Burley leaf could absorb a considerable amount of this

Highly-absorbent western Burley was used in plug by some eastern manufacturers even before the War Between the States. Lucky Strike plug was made in Richmond during late 1850s, was a Burley product. Brand name reflects Gold Rush excitement, as does the scenic label for Pike's Peak chewing tobacco.

131

Licorice was first used in Virginia as a preservative, came to be appreciated as a sweetener. But Bright leaf, with natural sugar content, could absorb only a little.

"casing," and thus Burley permitted many more variations of flavor than Virginia tobacco, which has an ample sugar component to start with. It required time and seasoning—as it does for most tobacco products—for Burley plug to acquire its reputation, and meanwhile the power of the name "Virginia" was a strong sales influence. The lack of repute was so much of a handicap for western manufacturers that some used the names of Virginia and North Carolina towns as box stamps, or even appropriated the names of well-known eastern brands.

Nevertheless, special merit in a particular form of tobacco does not remain unknown very long. One of the first to capitalize on the particular virtues of Burley plug was an alert young manufacturer in, of all places, Richmond, Virginia. In 1850 Dr. R. A. Patterson dropped his medical satchel to learn the tobacco business in his uncle's factory. Six years later he and a fellow-employee struck out on their own with conspicuous success, using the brand name *Lucky Strike* to describe their principal product, a Burley plug. Like *Pike's Peak*, a chew made by Winfree and Loyd of Lynchburg, the name capitalized on the gold fever that was sweeping the East.

Bluegrass boom

The upswing of planting and manufacture in the Middle West was scarcely disturbed by the four years of civil war. The closing of the Mississippi, which had dealt the Kentucky pioneers a severe blow fifty years earlier, merely shifted the export route of Burley tobacco—from the New Orleans river trip to a New York train shipment via the new Louisville and Nashville line. Although Tennessee threw in its lot with the Confederacy, Kentucky sided with the north, and thus the Ohio River valley was a protected area in the Union's Zone of the Interior. Kentucky superseded Virginia as the top tobacco state during the war, although this would probably have happened sooner or later in any event. Between 1860 and 1870, the burley crop in the Bluegrass State held its volume of more than 100,000,000 pounds. The Virginia-North Carolina total dropped from 156,000,0000 to 48,000,000 pounds. Ten years later the so-called "western crop" of Kentucky, Tennessee, Ohio and Missouri was nearly 250,000,000 pounds, up about 25% from the prewar figure, while the Virginia-Maryland-North Carolina total was 133,000,000, about 25% less than before the war.

White Burley

Of greater significance than the rise in Burley quantity was a sudden improvement in quality that began in 1864 along the fortunately-protected Ohio valley. This was the accidental cultivation of so-called White Burley in Ohio, presumably the result of a botanical mutation. "White" in this usage was a synonym for "Bright"—a word that could hardly find willing acceptance along the Ohio! Within fifteen years the lighter leaf (which was not white but soft brown) had completely replaced the dark, gummy Red Burley formerly grown. The startling change, plus the shift of wartime leaf traffic toward the east, made Cincinnati a thriving market town. Averaging receipts of about 6,000 hogsheads a year through 1860, the Queen City received 50,000 hogshead in each of the last two war years, a figure that went to 100,000 by the winter selling season of 1880-81. Louisville, eighty miles farther west, handled 63,000 hogsheads in 1864 but averaged no more than that number through 1881. "Cincinnati," wrote the United States censustaker of 1880, "is foremost in the distribution of this new and popular product, and in this trade knows no competitor except Louisville."

Battle of the sweet tooth

The "new and popular" Burley, having bested the Atlantic states in crop volume, was now challenging the older eastern centers in plug manufac-

ture, still the big item of the tobacco business with 60% of the total processed poundage. By 1880, the Middle West had gotten within striking distance of the Bright states, with 26,400,000 pounds of plug against 45,800,000 pounds for Virginia-North Carolina. (The New York area produced virtually all the rest, 16,400,000 pounds.) Taking full advantage of the porous, absorbent quality of the new strain of White Burley, the midwesterners pressed the "battle of the sweet tooth." Plug made in St. Louis and Louisville was 25% licorice and sugar by weight. The Bright leaf of the east could not absorb these quantities; the "flat plug" of North Carolina averaged only 4% of sweetening, some die-hard manufacturers holding the line with an absolutely unsweetened product.

The Bright "purists" denied to themselves the possibility of such mouth-watering copy as the following, carried in an 1885 advertisement to the trade by Harry Weissinger, a Louisville plugman:

PRUNE NUGGET
is made of the highest grade of White Burley *Leaf* and *Fruit*. The fruit, by a process known only to

Absorbent qualities of Burley tobacco, which has little natural sugar, led to wholesale flavoring of chewing tobacco. Mass output of sweet Burley plug resulted. Heart of each plug tobacco factory was its "kitchen," where top-secret flavoring was mixed. Only trusted employees were allowed inside.

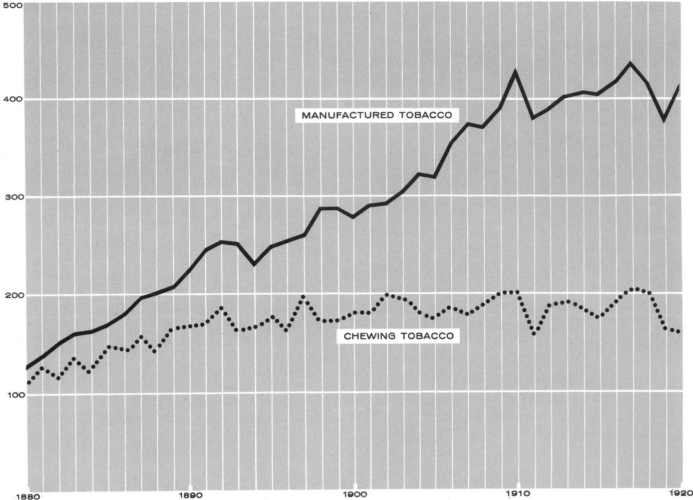

MILLIONS OF POUNDS (MANUFACTURED TOBACCO CONSUMED, U. S.)

MANUFACTURED TOBACCO

CHEWING TOBACCO

Consumption of manufactured tobacco — chewing, smoking tobacco and scrap—tripled between 1880 and 1910 (solid line). However, the peak use of chew (dotted line) was reached in 1897, which was also the climactic year of the "plug war" in the West. Market for chew remained static for twenty years.

us, becomes a component part of the manufactured article, and thus a delicately delicious flavor is imparted never heretofore obtained outside of a *French Confection*.

Tobacco is of itself a positive quantity and a pronounced flavor, and hence the difficulty of imparting a taste to it which is more delicate in its character than the tobacco itself. This from the very obvious reason that sufficient quantities of that which was more delicate could not be used to overcome that which was more strong. Hence manufacturers, in order to flavor tobacco, have had to use that which was more potent than the tobacco itself, and consequently the "drug store" taste and smell which pervades all flavored navy tobacco.

To impart a delicate flavor to tobacco and yet not destroy the identity of the tobacco itself has been the dream of our manufacturing life. That we have been awakened to a realization of this

dream in the production of *"Prune Nugget"* no one who chews the tobacco will doubt.

In the chew of *"Prune Nugget"* the acme of our hopes has been realized; we have taken an advance step in the manufacturing art, and have left all competition behind.

This great success is not without cost, and the process is expensive; hence *"Prune Nugget"* can not be sold at a low price. It runs 9 to the pound and is packed in twelve-pound boxes. The lumps are of a novel and attractive shape. We have fixed the price at sixty-two cents per pound, which is as low as the quality will admit.

The battle of the sweet tooth was thus a war of words as well as flavorings. But not all the words were as sugary as Weissinger's. Early in the game Bright manufacturers had labeled Burley plug as "navy goods," a term of opprobrium, since the Navy was alleged to buy cheap, common tobacco for its ration. One Virginia manufacturer went so far as

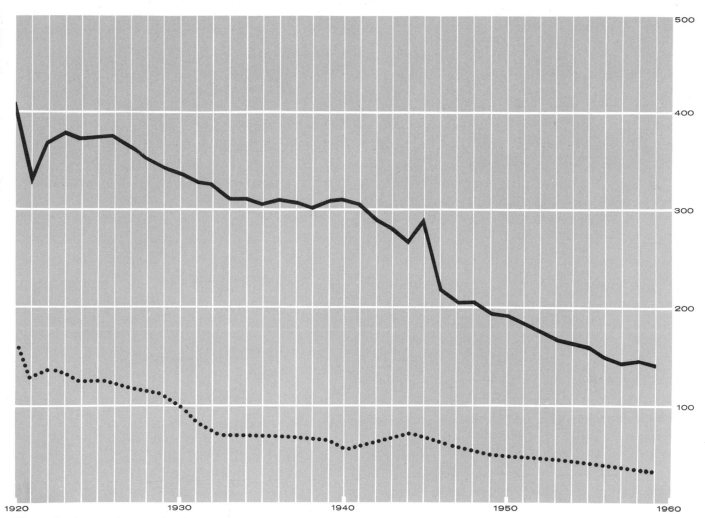

Growth of manufactured tobacco from 1900 through World War I was sustained by increase in smoking tobacco consumption. After the Armistice chewing *and pipe-smoking fell off sharply, then declined steadily except for emergency revivals during the depression of 30s and cigarette shortage of 1945.*

to label his brand *Anti-Navy*. But on this point the South was by no means solid. Richmond, still the largest plug town, averaged a sugar-and-licorice content of 17%, indicating that a goodly number of manufacturers had followed the lead of R. A. Patterson and gone over to a Burley filler. Great pains were taken in that city to burn the slats and staves of tobacco hogsheads bearing evidence of midwestern origin.

Despite the best, if belated, efforts of the Richmonders, the West came into the manufacturing business just as it had come into farming—with a rush. Huge factories went up in Louisville and St. Louis. There was no tradition of gentle handcraft in sleepy country establishments to overcome, no fussing over golden wrappers. Missouri produced about one-third as much manufactured tobacco as Virginia in 1880, Kentucky about a fifth. Ten years

later the "show me" state was even with Virginia in pounds produced, even though the Old Dominion had stepped up its total by 25%. (Ohio just about matched the smaller Kentucky output of plug and smoking, but was turning out cheap cigars in the hundreds of millions and in 1880 ranked third in brown-rolling behind New York and Pennsylvania.)

By 1890 the Midwest had a corner on manufactured tobacco, with St. Louis and Louisville placing one-two. Even before that year, however, the old rivalry of East vs. Midwest, Bright vs. Burley, flat plug vs. navy, was superseded by fierce competition within each class of product. Around 1875, manufacturers of plug began to concentrate on differentiating their brands from those of the competition. This brand identification was achieved in two ways: first, by the art of flavoring—exact formulas, almost impossible to duplicate and guarded like

Flat plug (left) usually referred to a product of Bright tobacco or one with a Bright leaf wrapper. Burley chewing tobacco of same shape was called "navy." *Burley twist (right), popularly known as* "pigtail," *evolved from the old Spanish tobacco rope, was first woven or spun, then compressed.*

crown jewels, made the taste of each product more or less distinctive; second, by brand name packaging. In the plug field this took the form of tin tags — usually an inch or less in width — having two sharp prongs that bent into the plug and proclaimed its trademark and/or origin in bright yellow, red, blue and green enamel. Before the genius of the Machine Age evolved tagging devices, small boys were hired to affix the tin tags.

It is interesting and probably significant that the tin tag, an important merchandising advance, was originated not in the West but by the Lorillard company of New York and Jersey City, about 1870. Appropriately enough, the first Lorillard plug to wear the novel disc was a brand named *Tin Tag* (see page 193). The company attempted to patent the device for its exclusive use but the courts ruled that tin tags were not patentable and in short order tags were used by plugmakers generally.

Tin tags

The gaudy identification of tobacco goods was not in itself new: fifty years before, rival cigar brands had begun to sport fancy names and embossed, gilt bands and boxes of a regal splendor no tin tag could match. But the tin tag served a purpose beyond mere identification; as plug volume worked upward toward its 1897 peak of 200,000,000 pounds (which it was to approximate for the better part of 20 years), the manufacturers offered premiums for the tin labels. Resembling coins in size and sometimes in shape, the tin tags were the equivalent of currency. Not only prizes but cash could be had; in 1902, one manufacturer spent $1,567,000 in redeeming plug tags, no small sum in the day of

the pre-inflated dollar. Some tags were worth as much as half a cent apiece in trade-in value, although one-eighth of a cent was closer to the average.

Fighting brands

In the flush of the rush to "big business," the entire plug industry dedicated itself to volume, letting the profit margins fall where they may. Each ambitious manufacturer turned loose at least one "fighting brand," sold to the trade for as low as 13c or 14c per pound (of which 6c represented federal tax). At the height of the plug war, in 1897, it was scarcely possible to make the product, even in volume, for less than 21c per pound including tax. During 1896, 1897 and 1898 more than a fifth of the nation's plug was sold at a loss! The sole mission of the fighting brands was to cut into the other fellow's volume, and they were aptly branded: *Battle Ax*, the most famous, made by Louisville's National Tobacco Works; *Scalping Knife*, made by Liggett and Myers in St. Louis; *Crossbow*, made by the Drummond Company in the same city; *Quality and Quantity*, made by Sorg in Middletown, Ohio.

These fighting brands were not, at first, popular favorites or profit-makers. Nor, in spite of their economy appeal and subsequent volume, did they become so. After the plug war, an attempt was made to restore *Battle Ax* to the 40c per pound needed to show a profit, but in three short years ending in 1900 its volume dropped from 29,000,000 to 12,000,000 pounds. The big brands of the day were *Star*, put out by Liggett, and *Newsboy*, turned out by the National Tobacco Works. Another brand, Brown's *Standard Navy*, was famous for exceptional keeping qualities and gained success on a smaller scale.

Verbal warfare

The brand names used for plug ranged, in retrospect, from the whimsical to the incredible. The National Works had a *Lic Quid* and a *Monkey Wrench Plug.* Myers of Richmond offered *Little Swan Rough and Ready* and *Darling Fanny Pan Cake,* either name enough to curdle the lustiest masculine appetite. For every action there was an equal and opposite reaction. When Pfingst, Doerhoefer & Company of Louisville registered *Piper Heidsieck,* the "gentleman's quid," it was only a matter of time before a rival—in this case McNamara, Sealts & Mullen of Covington, Kentucky—registered *Champagne* and *Mumm's Extra Dry.* Chewers whose salivary conditioning resembled that of Pavlov's dogs were not intended to take the latter brand name literally.

As late as 1885 trade marks could not be registered in the patent office unless they were used in commerce with foreign nations or with the Indian tribes. Redress could be had at common law, but this was no great deterrent to imitation. There were at least nine manufacturers with a *Legal Tender* plug, three with *Honey Suckle,* six with *Strawberry,* four with *Pine Apple,* eleven with *Honey Dew* (and one slyly branded *Mountain Dew).* There was, inevitably, a plug tobacco named *Durham* in an effort to borrow some of the sales appeal built up by Durham smoking tobacco. This *Durham* plug was made in Richmond.

In imitation or outright theft of names there was a kind of piratical logic; there was none in some of the plug designations used even by the largest companies. Thousands of pounds of palatable tobacco were sold under such names as *Hard Pan, Plank Road, Grit, Old Slug, Jaw Bone, Old Brick, Alligator, Ring Coil Hot Cake, Leatherwood, Sailor Knot, Ironsides, Sam Jones' Vest Chew, Red Hot,* and *Marline Spike.* Lacking even this grisly imaginative character was a brand put out by Wilson & McCallay of Middletown called *That.* So desperate for a name was Thomas C. Williams of Richmond that he titled one of his plugs *Little Worth.* A small plugger of Chillicothe, Missouri, bucked the trend by calling his brand *No Tag.*

Weird nomenclature was by no means confined to the cheapest form of tobacco. Fine-cut chewing mixtures, a comparatively expensive specialty, bore names as repulsive as *Mule Ear, Lime Kiln Club* and *Susin's Excelsior Tarred Chewing.* Nor was humor of a sort lacking: one fine-cut brand name was *Its Naughty, But Oh How Nice.*

Chews to choose

The term "chewing tobacco" covered several kinds of product. "Flat plug" meant compressed rectangular cakes of Bright tobacco, sweetened lightly or not at all. "Navy" also referred to flat, rectangular cakes but was reserved for Burley leaf, highly flavored. "Twist" accounted for about one-twentieth of plug volume and was a tobacco rope braided by hand like the ancient West Indian roll and then compressed. "Fine-cut chewing" resem-

Tin tags served two purposes: pronged into plug, they constituted a trademark identification and *some assurance of consistent quality; they were also premium tokens redeemable for prizes, cash.*

Like the Virginia tobacco towns, Louisville was a natural leaf market and manufacturing center owing to its river location, near the confluence of Ohio and Mississippi. During and after the War of 1861, Louisville handled some 60,000 hogsheads per year and was rivaled as leaf market only by Cincinnati.

bled long cut smoking tobacco in that it comprised shredded stripped leaf (not sliced plug) and was not compressed; it was made specifically for masticating, however, using dark Green River leaf in addition to Burley. Fine-cut was just as expensive as long-cut pipe tobacco (about 1900 smoking and chewing tobaccos alike averaged about 35c per pound to the trade, with granulated Bright priced 5c or so higher). The volume of fine-cut chewing generally ran close to that of twist.

Navy was not usually wholesaled in bite-size squares but in rectangles averaging a pound in weight and three inches by sixteen in size. These were indented for the retailer's convenience into five or six "cuts" which sold ordinarily for a dime per cut. Some brands were "two-spaced" or "two-faced"—divided on one side into five cuts, on the other into six. Armed with his fearsome plug chop-

per—one widely used slicer was designed to resemble a battle axe to promote the brand of that name —the retailer had his option as to how big a cut to sell for a dime.

Naval victory

During the 80s and 90s the small quidmaker faded from the scene, as large volume with microscopic unit profits became the order of the day. As the century drew to a close there were only ten sizable plug manufacturers: Liggett & Myers, Drummond, and Butler in St. Louis; Finzer and the National Tobacco Works in Louisville; Sorg in Middletown; Scotten in Detroit; Lorillard in Jersey City; and in Winston, so-called "Storm Center of the Plug Industry," Reynolds and Hanes. These ten companies alone did 60% of the nation's plug manufacture. The giants among them were Liggett

War closed the Mississippi but hogsheads went to New York by rail. Small plugmakers vanished; in 1890s ten companies made 60% of all U.S. plug.

& Myers and National Tobacco Works, each with a cool one-seventh of total production. This listing alone tells the story of the battle of the sweet tooth: it was a "naval" victory for the Midwest, whose seven leading pluggeries accounted for 52% of national poundage.

There were fine old firms of some consequence outside the big ten: Brown in St. Louis, Mayo, Patterson, J. Wright in Richmond; S. W. Venable in Petersburg, and others. But their annual output ran to one, two or three million pounds each. They did not rank with the 26,000,000 or 27,000,000 pounds turned out by Liggett and National, or the 10,000,000 figure approached by Drummond, Butler, Lorillard and Sorg.

Actually, the victory of the West was not so overwhelming as the plug situation alone would indicate. During the last quarter of the nineteenth

LOUISVILLE, KY.
SCENES IN THE TOBACCO MARKET.

ONE of the leading branches of trade in Louisville is that of leaf tobacco. In this commodity, Louisville ranks as the first inland market in the world.

The Kentucky crop for 1872 amounted to over 100,000 hogsheads.

The leaf is prepared for shipment by the planter, who packs it into hogsheads containing from 800 to 2,000 pounds, the average being about 1,200 pounds. When these arrive at the warehouses, and before they are offered for sale, the tobacco is stripped—that is, the hogshead is reopened and the entire contents are exposed. It is then inspected, by being broken in three or more places, fair samples are taken out, and by these the various lots are sold, each hogshead upon its own merits, to the highest bidder—the warehousemen being responsible to the buyers that the tobacco purchased shall be in all cases equal in quality to the sample. A sample is then delivered to the buyer. The tobacco is again placed in the hogshead, well coopered, and made ready for shipment to any part of the United States or the world.

Very little do the lovers of the "weed" in our Northern cities know of the many ins and outs, ups and downs, the leaf of tobacco takes before it reaches them in the shape of a fine "Havana" or "plug."

One of our sketches presents an interior view of the Louisville tobacco warehouse. Purchasers are seen at the "breaks," or auction, buying; also, the planters are looking after their interests. Near by are the negro hands, packing and coopering hogsheads for shipment.

The second engraving is a picture of the colored hands loading the drays, while others are waiting for freight. One notorious character, "Old Uncle George," is whipping a juvenile negro for some rascality. The youngster does not seem to consider the operation any **too** pleasant.

Plug tobacco was made in rectangular slabs about an inch thick, three by sixteen inches or so, and a pound in weight, scored for cutting into small chews. Star brand typified "Missouri manufactured."

century, while the West concentrated almost wholly on quid, North Carolina and Virginia were riding upward on a new, fast-selling product—bagged smoking tobacco for pipes. This product was soon to replace plug as the common man's 'baccy, and ultimately to spawn an even greater growth item, the cigarette.

Thus, even within the manufactured tobacco field, Virginia and North Carolina were able to maintain their position and weather the assault of sweet Burley plug. In 1890 the two Atlantic states accounted for 33% of the nation's smoking and chewing output. During the 90s the western plug factories dented this to 28%, but by 1904 the Virginia-North Carolina volume was back to its customary third, where it remained until World War I. After that conflict, the 33% increased to 40%, although total manufactured tobacco production had begun a

National market was "tied" together in railroad-building rush of 1862-1883. Work train of Union Pacific inched across the plains of Nebraska and Wyoming guarded by soldier and Indian scouts, was called "Hell on Wheels." National brands, uniform quality developed concurrently with railroad net.

sharp decline that continues to the present day.

Not that the mighty plug towns of the Mississippi did not make an effort in the field of smokings. Almost every sizable plug plant added pipe mixtures to its line. But the leaf requirements, the flavoring touch, the cutting, the packaging were all different from those of chew processing. Missouri never exceeded a 7,000,000-pound annual output of pipe tobaccos; Kentucky—meaning Louisville—achieved twice as much volume as Missouri by

1906, but even this was less than 10% of the national total, and no threat to the Virginia-North Carolina poundage (40,000,000 pounds in 1904, 55,000,000 in 1909, 68,000,000 in 1914).

National ties

The frenzied pursuit of volume by the midwestern plugmakers, and the more profitable growth of smoking tobaccos centered in the East, marked the emergence of tobacco as a national industry.

While cigar brands were still regional favorites rather than national brands (to a considerable extent, they are still); and while cigarettes were incubating as an exotic novelty in the big cities; bags of smokum and boxes of plug were achieving national distribution and national reputation. This changeover from local factories spewing forth thousands of brands to the nationally advertised, widely known trademarked product was not peculiar to the tobacco business. The factor which brought it

Mississippi packet, operating on schedule under a responsible pilot, replaced the brawling boatmen on whom leaf transport once depended. But rise of *railroads meant that water routes no longer fixed the location of tobacco markets or factory towns. New Orleans, for one, saw tobacco output dwindle.*

about had nothing to do with the tobacco evolution: railroad-building.

The breakdown of sectionalism and the uniting of the country with steel ribbons was attempted as early as 1855, with Stephen A. Douglas, the great debater and political opponent of Lincoln, devoting his forensic talent in Congress to the matter of a transcontinental railroad. Legislation was not passed until 1862. For seven years afterward the track gangs sweated; Chinese by the thousands carved the Central Pacific right of way out of the Sierra Nevadas and spurted eastward across the Nevada-Utah desert.

Meanwhile, rolling westward from Council Bluffs, the "Hell on Wheels" work train under military escort fought monotony, supply shortages and rampaging Indians across the Nebraska and Wyoming plains. Parallel and connecting lines came thick and fast after the Central Pacific and Union Pacific met in 1869 at Ogden, Utah; by 1883 there were four transcontinental railroads. The old reliance on canals and rivers was ended; railroads made the U. S. a single whole, not only by making all corners of the nation accessible to settlers but by providing rapid and regular communications and deliveries to virtually the whole population. National brands, in tobacco and

in other consumer goods, could not be launched until the steel ways were laid down to receive them.

The quitting of the quid

But the very process by which the big plug sellers were made available to every American made most Americans less interested in "eatin' tobacco." Radiating outward from the city factories, the railroads carried such intangibles as good manners, good dress, and cosmopolitan taste along with the stacked commodities in their rattling freight cars. The imaginary line with townfolk on one side and half-wild pioneers or prospectors or rivermen on the other disappeared. Pride in isolation and self-sufficiency, symbolized by the ruminant clenching of teeth on wad, remained only among the old-timers—and they were losing their teeth. The tendrils of the city, with its refined tastes and broad outlook, reached out to all but the most remote hillfolk.

In part, chewing tobacco—whether on Margarita Island or on the scattered homesteads of nineteenth-century U. S.—was a function of space and solitude. Space, because of chaw's juice-generating character; solitude, because chomping was a substitute for chatter. In varying degrees the cigarette, the pipe and even the cigar were less offensive to non-smokers (although the last-named form sometimes resembled chewing tobacco in the mouths of particular consumers). They were, certainly, more conducive to conversation. If the philosopher Hobbes was correct in describing life in the natural state as "solitary, nasty, brutish and short," then the passing of chew signaled the arrival of civilization. In other words, the ascendancy of chawin' terbacker could not be assigned solely to the physical circumstances of the chewer; plenty of it was molared in crowded cities. Chew was supreme when the city was dominated by the frontier and when Americans gloried in being common men, in the ancient Latin sense of the *vulgus*. Toward the end of the nineteenth century, as the industrial revolution set in and the city came to dominate U.S. culture, Americans no longer played the prideful bumpkin but acted like urbane men of affairs. The quitting of the quid meant simply that men were no longer proud of their resemblance to animals.

If life on the land became an extension of city existence, so did life on the water. The rivermen on whom the movement of leaf tobacco once depended—and who sometimes stole as much as they delivered—were supplanted by the Mississippi steamboat pilot. He was no thief, nor was he "half horse-half alligator," but the responsible operator of a city-sponsored transportation factory. It was altogether proper that Mark Twain, who learned life on the Mississippi as a river pilot, was not a cussin', spittin' savage but a cerebrator careful in his choice of words and careful in his choice of pipe tobacco and cigar. As a thoughtful man, it was inevitable that he should consider giving up smoking; and as a connoisseur of life, it was natural that he should do so not once and for all but "hundreds of times."

For the tobacco historian, the significant thing about Mark Twain was that he—perhaps the most

Best known of Mississippi pilots was writer Mark Twain, perceptive chronicler of American life in the nineteenth-century Midwest and the author of "Huckleberry Finn." *Twain was a devoted pipe and cigar smoker, said he could give up smoking with ease and had in fact done so "hundreds of times."*

cosmopolitan citizen of the postbellum West—was a smoker and not a chewer, a thinker and not a "natcheral man." The pendulum of tobacco fashion was swinging back to the East.

Plug war aftermath

The abrupt tax increase of June 1898, from 6c to 12c per pound, followed a year of tremendous volume in plug sales. Much of the volume of 1897 may have been artifically inspired by the "bargains" offered in the course of price competition. No doubt many customers found it more convenient to buy a pound of plug for 25c and slice it into their pipes than to pay 65c for a pound of plug-cut or granulated mixture. Whatever the reason, chewing tobacco in 1897 accounted for exactly half of all leaf used in manufacturing—an amount equal to the weight of smoking, snuff, cigars and cigarettes combined. That this was attributable more to price than preference was shown in the first year of the higher tax: plug consumption dropped by 10%. Although the 12c tax was halved early in 1902, chewing tobacco never significantly exceeded its 1897 peak in later years. In terms of per capita consumption or percentage of leaf used in manufacture, quid rode steadily downward after 1897.

The great plug years of 1890-1910 were to represent the high-water mark of tobacco manufacturing west of the Appalachians. During these years Missouri, Kentucky and Ohio kept 60% or more of the plug market. Toward the end of that period only one eastern plug town—Winston—held an important concentration of volume. In 1906 the Reynolds Company and its subsidiaries turned out well over 20,000,000 pounds of flat Bright chew—about a seventh of the nation's plug total—and boosted their share to a fourth by 1912. But because of the close relationship between smoking tobacco

Midwest plug factories were oriented toward mass production. Louisville's National Tobacco Works, above, was one of the largest and accounted for a seventh of U.S. output. Plugs weighing one pound, measuring 3 x 16 inches, were sliced by retailer into five or six "cuts" each selling for a dime.

and cigarette blends, Louisville, St. Louis and the other midwestern states never seriously challenged the East in white-roll output. Today 80% of cigarette volume originates in Richmond, Durham, Winston, Reidsville and Greensboro. Only Louisville remains as a midwestern making center with substantial volume, accounting for nearly a fifth of cigarette production.

The exuberant growth of Burley and the thickly-sweetened navy plug processed from it had been more or less natural phenomena. When Virginia soil was worked-out and weak, the virgin acres of Kentucky, Tennessee and Ohio luxuriated in sheer productivity. When the burned-out manufacturers of Richmond were groping to revive the past in the bitter smoke of Reconstruction, the lusty plugmen of Louisville and St. Louis, unharmed by war, were reveling in a frenzy of mass production. In their processing as in their planting, the westerner quid-men were oriented toward quantity.

Possibly for that very reason their sway was brief. The new era, the era of national brands, the era of new developments and higher living standards for all, was not to rest on volume alone. Competition in quality, as distinguished from crude price combat, was to play a part; invention—agricultural and mechanical—was to play a part; alertness to the subtle ground swell of changing consumer preference was to play a part. Actually, Kentucky and Tennessee and Missouri and Ohio had learned their leaf cultivation from the experienced East. They had also learned prizing and preserving and flavoring from the handcraftsmen of antebellum Virginia.

While they were occupied in applying these lessons with characteristic western vim, the older tobacco centers were acquiring new knowledge and new techniques faster than the transmontane tobacco-men could absorb them.

Quantity was the word among Burley planters just as it was among plugmakers. This warehouse, built in Owensboro, Kentucky in 1890, was among world's largest wood frame structures of its type. Wooden superstructure has been removed; same foundation now supports two-story cigar manufacturing plant.

145

Flue-curing of Virginia and North Carolina leaf, developed just before the War Between the States, gave the tobacco industry a new impetus. Southern tobacco was swapped for Northern coffee. Soldiers of both armies, mustered out in 1865, stimulated a national demand for the sweeter Bright tobacco.

BLUE, GRAY AND BRIGHT

THE difference between a colony and a self-sufficient nation shows vividly in the story of tobacco. For the better part of two centuries, Virginians and their neighbors to the north and south had been, in effect, field hands to His Majesty. The dark "shipping leaf" they sent abroad improved but little during the export years — it only increased in quantity as the tobacco fields climbed beyond the tidewater and over the fall line. As chance would have it, part of the tidewater soil produced a naturally Bright leaf — the sweetscented. But as a slavish supplier of raw stuff, Virginia had no opportunity to develop its potentiality, to experiment, to specialize.

Early in the nineteenth century, the second War of Independence was followed by a transformation of the tobacco trade and other economic pursuits. For this, the term "Industrial Revolution" has been coined, but it is perhaps just as accurate to describe it as a spiritual revolution. The widespread rejection of pipe and snuff-box in favor of chewing was a surface manifestation of the new spirit. But the essence of the change lay deeper. In a mere generation or two, without losing their export trade, the liberated Americans developed a wholly original mode of manufacture (plug) and at the same time perfected a new, superior kind of leaf tobacco (Bright) which in turn completely changed the world's tobacco tastes. All this occurred in the threescore and ten years following the War of 1812. And it was accomplished by people whose fathers and grandfathers and great-grandfathers had worked the very same soil year after year after year without let, plunging deeper into debt as they repeated the seasonal round.

The Tobacco Sack

These people were the Virginians and North Carolinians living in what was called the "Virginia District" or the "Tobacco Sack" — the central belt of piedmont Virginia with a tier of half a dozen North Carolina counties forming the sack's flat bottom and the Fredericksburg-Madison line constituting the narrow neck. They began making "homespun" twist for chewing in much the same way as the New England farmers evolved the homemade cigar. Tobacco growers did not find it difficult to form dry leaf into a coarse, sometimes

146

sweetened twist for their own use. Storekeepers who took tobacco in payment for trade goods processed it for sale at a profit without much trouble. As the population increased and the demand for worked tobacco grew, the rush to manufacture was on. Leaf dealers naturally turned to fabrication; a negro slave set up a small shop and bought his freedom with the profits; even gentlemen of the cloth entered the trade.

Twist to lump

During the eighteenth century, a wheel was used to fashion tobacco leaves into a rope or twist, sometimes yards long. After a little aging, the twist could be sliced into shavings for a pipe, ground up for snuff, or chopped into bite-size chunks for chewing.

The first step in this procedure was to strip the entire midrib or stem from each leaf, and for this reason the factories of Virginia were often called "stemmeries." The wheel was abandoned, and the delicate strip tobacco was fashioned into a twist by hand labor. The twist then went into a press for a few days, and was "prized" or compressed as tightly as wooden or iron screws would permit. The

purpose of "prizing" — which was very similar to hogshead prizing on the plantation by lever or screw—was to distribute the moisture evenly throughout the final product. As pressuring devices were refined, the basic twist gave way to a lump, still shaped by hand and then compressed mechanically into a cake or plug.

As chewing became a national pastime, the demands of the market added infinite variations to the simple choice between twist and flat plug. Some liked their "chaw" natural, others wanted it sweetened. The number of possible sweetening recipes was infinite, and each manufacturer took infinite pains to keep his formula secret. The most important "casing" or flavoring ingredient was licorice, which was in use around 1830 by some of the 119 factories in the Virginia District. ("Cavendish" entered the tobacco lexicon as the term for licorice-cured leaf, from the name of a Norfolk exporter who used it as a preservative.) But rum, sugar, tonka beans, cinnamon, nutmeg and a host of other spices and condiments were measured into the dipping vats as the number of chewers, brands and factories increased.

Principle of plugmaking derived from the prizing or compressing apparatus used to pack hogsheads on the farms. Purpose of pressurizing chew was the even distribution of moisture through finished product to prevent spoilage in warm weather. Moisture control is still key to quality tobacco making.

As is still the case in tobacco making, the most important single factor in quality control was regulation of moisture. Dried-out tobacco is brittle and harsh; overly moist tobacco is subject to mould and decay. Many a box of plug and twist manufactured during the damp Virginia winter held enough moisture — impossible to detect in cold weather—to spoil in the warmth of summer. Some selling agents refused to buy "first quarter plug" or "winter work" and it was frequently proposed that the plug factories should shut down from December through March in order to preserve the good repute of Virginia tobacco.

This was not done to any great extent, for the simple reason that the concept of brand names and its corollary, uniformity of product, had not yet taken hold. Here and there a manufacturer's name or that of a particular town stood for outstanding quality, but the bulk of factory output was unbranded, anonymous merchandise and the brands that did exist were small and local. Most tobacco was grown for export; in the early years of the nineteenth century rotten and waterlogged tobacco that could not pass inspection for export was plowed into domestic manufacture. If a consignee complained that last winter's production had turned mouldy, the obvious recourse was to change the consignee, or the brand name, or both. This

approach to the market was inherent in an industry comprised of many small businesses; it still characterizes the fringe of the cigar industry. Where the advertising investment is negligible, as in the one-man shop or family enterprise, it is simpler to change trademarks than to maintain set standards of leaf quality or precision of manufacture. Conversely, where a well-advertised trademark has won a sizable portion of the market, ordinary prudence and self-defense dictate a special effort to preserve consistent quality.

Gray land for Bright

The connoisseur of "eatin' tobacco" soon came to demand that his quid be not only delectable to the tongue but also pleasing to the eye. Manufacturers began to search out hogsheads of smooth, light-colored leaf for use as wrappers; the more golden the leaf, the more it brought on the leaf markets. This was the circumstance that led to the development of true Bright leaf, rendered lemon yellow by a combination of sandy soil and forced curing of the fresh tobacco in barns heated by flues. Oddly enough, the clamor for bright-wrapped Southern chaw arose at about the same time dark-wrapped cigars in the Spanish mode were finding favor in the North. While Virginia manufacturers were steeping plug filler in licorice as a sweetening,

Yankee leaf growers were using it to darken their broadleaf!

There had always been a demand, more or less sporadic, for "colory" tobacco, that is, a light, mild leaf of a yellow or golden hue and sweet aroma. Edward Digges satisfied it as early as 1650 from his gray land on the York, and some of the other tidewater planters, similarly favored, commanded premium prices for sweetscented leaf in colonial times. The belt of sandy soil extending through the center of Virginia came late to cultivation, as it was part of the less accessible piedmont.

For two centuries the European market showed no great interest in Bright tobacco, for the very reason that it commanded premium prices. In France, for instance, the Farmers-General maximized the profit from its tobacco monopoly by feeding strong scrap to its captive market. Most smokers, Frenchmen included, would rather smoke shag than nothing. Napoleon's campaigns through Europe, however, brought considerable numbers of

French soldiers into contact with Russian ("Turkish") tobacco, and generated a demand for milder, more aromatic leaf.

As this overseas demand for colory leaf strengthened following the War of 1812, the naturally light color of Maryland leaf attracted attention. As a result, Maryland tobacco in general brought a higher-than-average price right through to the Civil War, and "Maryland" became a term used abroad to describe light-colored leaf. Around 1825 the best "Maryland" was grown in the vicinity of Zanesville, Ohio. Some years later a sandy stretch along the Kentucky shore of the Ohio River, called Yellowbanks, turned out colory tobacco sweet enough for the English buyers.

Revived interest in yellow leaf provided extra incentive for the movement of tobacco out of the tidewater and up onto the piedmont. The tobacco wharves of the Chesapeake were no longer the exclusive support of merchant fleets, for in 1803 cotton passed tobacco as the nation's leading export.

Manufacture of chewing tobacco developed in four Virginia towns—Danville, Lynchburg, Petersburg, and Richmond. Choice lemon yellow leaf was sought for wrappers, which enhanced the sales appeal of "Virgin" chew. Search for colory led to flue-cure of Bright leaf and rebirth of Virginia-Carolina.

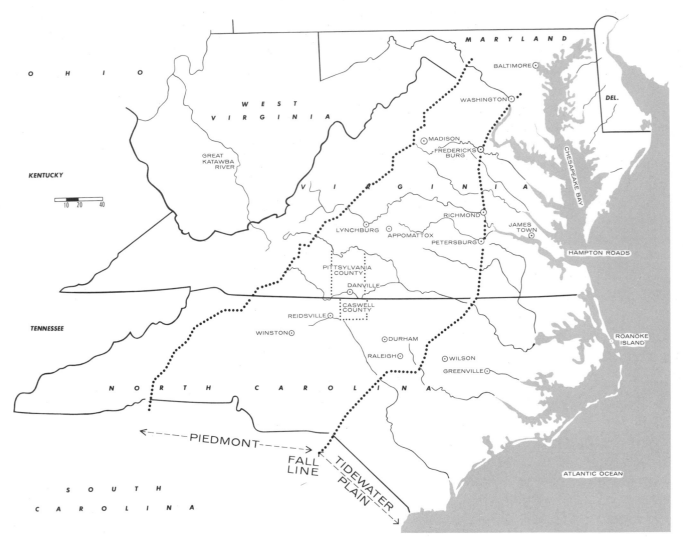

"Tobacco Sack" comprised central belt of Virginia and north-central belt of North Carolina, bounded on east by the fall line and on west by the Blue Ridge (dotted lines). Antebellum Virginia tobacco towns were all on rivers; postbellum centers of North Carolina—Durham and Winston—were not.

This was the combination of circumstances that shaped the Tobacco Sack in central Virginia.

But it was the poor, sandy soil of North Carolina—known during the tidewater's golden years as "the land of tar, pitch and pork"—that contributed Bright leaf. Lightness and mildness in tobacco is achieved, literally, by starving the leaf as it grows; and the siliceous ridges of the Carolina piedmont, too thin for almost any other crop, were exactly suited to this purpose. The choice qualities of tobacco grown on these ridges was to transform the "Rip Van Winkle State" into a world center of tobaccomaking. This, however, was not to transpire until after the War Between the States. During the years when Virginia manufacturers were spreading the use of Virginia leaf in plug form,

North Carolina was being deserted, many of its exhausted farmers leaving its exhausted soil to join the trek to the West.

Slade's cure

In 1839 an eighteen-year-old Negro on the Slade Farm in Caswell County, just south of Danville, Virginia, was curing leaf in a barn heated by wood fires. When the fires were almost burned out, he fed them with charcoal ordinarily reserved for the blacksmithing forge, since the woodpile was soaked by rain. Under the renewed blast of heat supplied by the charcoal, Stephen's leaf "kep' on yallowin and kep' on yallowin' and kep' on yallowin'." It also sold for forty cents a pound, as against the average ten cents. Such curings, achieved not entirely by accident, had cropped up on the Tobacco Sack markets before. As early as 1823 in Louisa County, Virginia, one planter was heating his barn from an outside firebox which delivered heat inside via a stone-lined tunnel. In 1832 Dr. Davis G. Tuck of Halifax County (also Virginia) patented a curing method which used a stove in a tight barn. Charles E. Gage, director of the first comprehensive compilation of tobacco statistics for the U. S. Department of Agriculture and an authority on the history of tobacco cultivation, has noted that Tuck's schedule of daily temperatures, as published in an 1832 booklet, closely approximates modern practise. So the Slade cure, though accidental in itself, was the continuation of a long effort rather than a sudden change of direction.

The essential feature of the cure was not necessarily charcoal but a thorough drying out of the leaves ("sapping") before the final intense heat was applied. This was accomplished, as yellow leaf production evolved, in two ways: (1) using ventilated barns, permitting the escape of moisture driven out of the leaves by the first gradual application of heat; (2) using flues to introduce heat without smoke.

Danville's day

Although this method — "flue-curing" — was not standardized until after the Civil War, the farmers in the Tobacco Sack region turned out fair amounts of colory leaf during the 1850s. James Thomas, Jr.,

MAKING THE VIRGINIA TWIST.

Twisted tobacco rope gave way to lumps, also made by hand. "Lumpers" of Danville became famous for their accuracy, shaped lumps without using scales.

Richmond's leading manufacturer, set up a second factory in Danville so that he could get first crack at such fine gold leaf as was brought to that market. (Caswell County, just south of Danville and Pittsylvania County, formed the first incubator for the new, true Bright leaf.) If Jamestown was the

General View from across the Dan.

Early manufactured tobacco center was Danville. The town was close to sandy piedmont farms which yielded naturally bright leaf even before advent

of flue-curing. Small manufacturers moved to the place in order to get first crack at the limited supply of light-colored wrapper leaf grown nearby.

151

THE SALE.

A small town in the Blue Ridge foothills, Lynchburg became a tobacco center of first rank after 1840, when it was linked by the James River Canal to Richmond. Buyers were summoned by trumpet to the leaf markets or "breaks," so called because the first item of business was breaking open hogsheads to get samples on which purchasers based bids.

cradle of America's leaf export tradition, Danville was the cradle of leaf marketing and manufacturing. Pittsylvania County was, in number of factories, the nation's tobacco capitol early in the nineteenth century (although Richmond was probably the leader in weight of output from the first). The reason for Danville's prominence was nearby White Oak Mountain, which guarded a pocket of land especially suitable for growing Bright leaf. As the planters moved inland across the fall line, the Danville region was one of the first piedmont places to support tobacco culture. This in turn led the small manufacturers of the day to set up their factories in town or in Pittsylvania County, where they could be within shouting distance of the choicest

wrappers for their plug products. And this, of course, made Danville a capital leaf market, hundreds of farm wagons trundling in long lines across the covered wooden bridge over the Dan River during the season.

Richmond's reign

As the century wore on, tobacco manufacturing mushroomed. Factories in Virginia and North Carolina multiplied from 119 in 1840 to 348 in 1860. In the latter year tobacco products made in the United States weighed more than 100,000,000 pounds (about one sixth of the total being exported). Almost all of it was plug or twist, shipped in 125-pound wooden boxes with the maker's name and city stamped on the bare wood. The manufacturing capital soon came to be Richmond, which had all the requisites—leaf markets, transportation, and banks. It also had shrewd businessmen like James Thomas, Jr., the "uncle" who taught young Dr. R. A. Patterson the tobacco trade. Patterson's daring use of Kentucky Burley in Richmond-made plug was about the only trick his Uncle Jim missed. Thomas was among the first to recognize the importance of "bright yellow lumps." He was among the first to ship quality chewing tobacco (i.e., mould-proof quid) to California during the Gold Rush years, thereby achieving a virtual stranglehold on that state's business.

On hearing about the firing at Fort Sumter, Thomas shipped all the tobacco he could lay his hands on to his agents abroad and at the same time laid in as large a leaf inventory as his facilities could hold. In the years of blockade and shortage that followed he profited handsomely enough to equip a battery of Confederate artillery at his own expense, and became an unofficial financial adviser to Jefferson Davis' government.

Another well-known Richmonder, Robert A. Mayo, supplied the navy with plug under the logical brand name—much-imitated later on—of *Navy Tobacco.* Because of his contractual relationship with the Federal Government, the local Whig newspaper objected to his candidacy for public office in 1850. The reply of the Democratic newspaper is a classic of tobacco lore: "Mr. Mayo simply sells his tobacco to the United States Government and gives a *quid pro quo.*"

Lone Jack of Lynchburg

Lynchburg, where James Thomas, Jr., started his career as a leaf buyer, was comparable to Richmond and Danville in antebellum importance and was known as "The Tobacco City." In addition to its forty plug and twist factories—almost as many

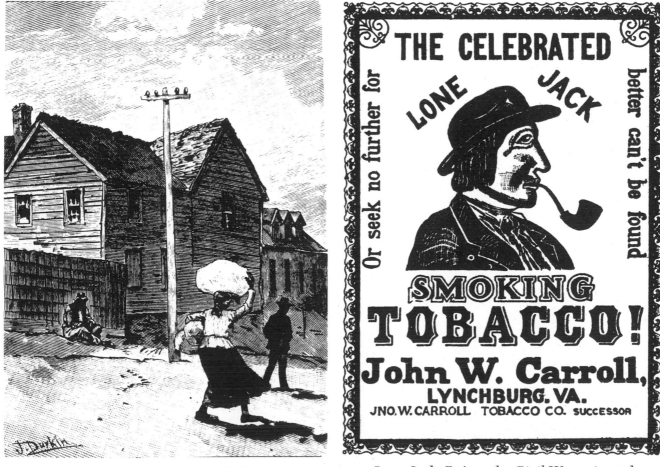

Lynchburg turned out the only antebellum smoking tobaccos of any consequence. One was Killickinick and the other, made in the modest building above, was Lone Jack. Before the Civil War, pipe tobacco was a byproduct of chew; outside Lynchburg there were few firms devoted purely to smoking mixtures.

as in Richmond—Lynchburg witnessed the remarkable growth of Maurice Moore as a manufacturer, starting from scratch. Moore concentrated on what was then a specialty — granulated tobacco for pipe smoking — and captured half of the market in that category by the outbreak of War Between the States, his big brand being *Killickinick.* Another colorful Lynchburg figure was John W. Carroll, supposed to have staked his all on a lone jack in a card game and to have repaid the kindly fates by naming his principal tobacco brand *Lone Jack.* Others advanced a simpler explanation, Jack Carroll having wandered into Lynchburg alone and fundless, prospering as a lone Jack.

The New York factor(s)

But if Richmond, Danville, Petersburg and Lynchburg had leaf, New York (which got in on everything) had money and salesmen. Owing to its vast labor pool, the Big City was already taking the play away from New England in cigar manufacturing. It also developed a concentration of plug factories second only to Virginia's. More important, New York was the financial center for all industry and the marketing center for many—including tobacco products. Most of the Virginia output went on consignment to New York factors, who in turn sold it to wholesale jobbers throughout the nation. To the antebellum Virginia manufacturer, the concept of salesmanship was quite remote; he expected his quality product to "sell itself," as, indeed, tobacco always had. Consequently his selling was confined to occasional horse-and-wagon trips to nearby towns; many southern retail houses actually got Virginia plug from New York distributors! This consignment system played a part—by no means a minor one—in turning the Era of Good Feeling into the Era of Civil War. The difficulty with the system was mainly the long credit—up to twelve months—extended by the factor (present-day practice is, on the average, thirty days with a discount for payment in ten). This long recovery time often forced manufacturers to turn over their factors' acceptances to Richmond banks, at a discount, for needed cash. During the panic of 1857, New York factors failed to meet their acceptances and the burden of meeting or guaranteeing them fell on the southern manufacturers. Seven out of eight in Richmond were reported to have suspended operations in 1857 as a direct result of the defaults of their Northern agents. A convention of Virginia and North Carolina tobacco processers resolved to "require" their agents to limit credit henceforth to four months. But the differences between South and North were too great to be solved by resolutions.

Split leaf land

It was significant that the Confederate States of America chose as its capitol Montgomery, Alabama. Economic determinists would call the struggle between North and South a cotton war, not a tobacco one. Despite the difficulties of long-range marketing on consignment—reminiscent, to a degree, of the ill feeling between the tidewater planters and their London agents—the custodians of the pivotal tobacco-making industry saw no solution in war. Nevertheless, it was time to choose up sides, and the tobacco states split: Maryland, Kentucky and Missouri to the Stars and Stripes, Virginia,

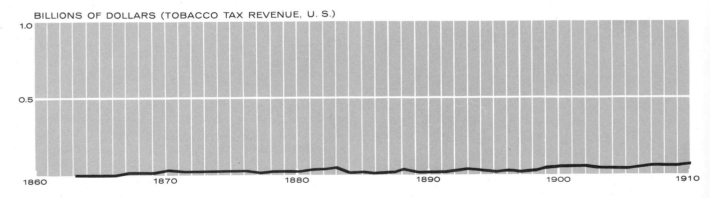

BILLIONS OF DOLLARS (TOBACCO TAX REVENUE, U. S.)

Although manufactured snuff was taxed as early as 1794, the first non-sumptuary tobacco excise was levied by the U.S. Government in 1862 in order to raise funds for military operations. The earliest rates were 5c per pound on manufactured tobacco—now 10c—and 40c per thousand cigarettes—now four

North Carolina and Tennessee to the Stars and Bars.

Exports dropped, but not enough to jeopardize the European market. Kentucky, finding the New Orleans gateway closed again after fifty years of Mississippi riverboating, sent its hogsheads to the New York docks by rail. Louisville and Cincinnati became the big tobacco markets, and Kentucky the No. 1 source of leaf.

Taxes for the troops

The War Between the States may not have been a tobacco war, but it developed something which has influenced tobacco and its market ever since: the U. S. excise tax. Enacted on July 1, 1862, it was originally intended to raise funds for the government's military operations.

The tobacco tax was official recognition of the fact that manufactured tobacco had "arrived." Alexander Hamilton's investigation of 1794 had generated only a "luxury tax" on snuff: common tobacco was untouched. The ostensible reason was a reluctance to place a burden "upon the poor, upon sailors, day-laborers, and other people of these classes." At the same time it was true that snuff could not be ground conveniently at home but had to be manufactured, while quid and pipe tobacco was homegrown leaf more often than otherwise. So the decision to tax snuff was at least partly based on the practical consideration of enforceability.

Similarly, when Union Army support was needed, the very existence of factories invited a manufactures tax. A leaf tax was first proposed, but "the machinery for collecting a tax of the grower would be too extended to be practicable." Policing factory output, on the other hand, was easy. So "manufactured tobacco"—the term for smoking and chewing—paid 5 cents a pound to the U. S. Treasury during the war, an amount raised to 35 and 40 cents as the war ended and lowered to 16 cents fifteen years later. The wartime levy was eight-tenths of a cent on a penny cheroot and four cents on a nickel cigar (then a high-priced item), but these were reduced in 1867 to half a cent per cigar regardless of value. Cigarette taxes were 40 cents per thousand at first, went to $2.00 per thousand in

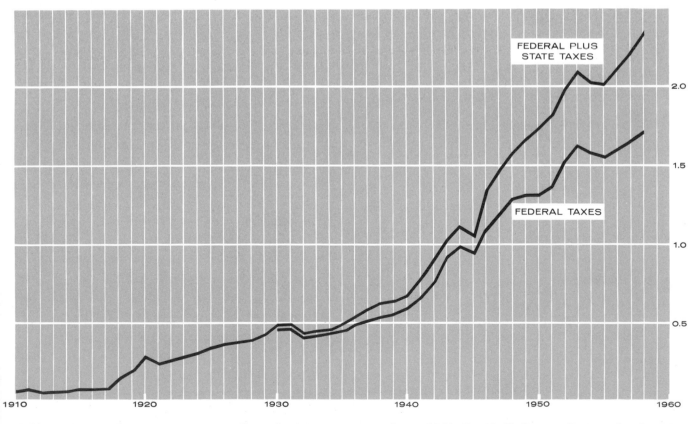

dollars. Before the income tax was levied in 1913, tobacco taxes were the chief source of government revenue; they accounted for 31% of total receipts as early as 1880. In 1958 the total of Federal and state taxes on tobacco products was more than 40% of their value at retail—over two billion dollars.

The Confederate States discouraged tobacco growing very early in the war. Food and most manufactured articles were in short supply from the first. So were transportation facilities. Troop movements on *the James River Canal virtually halted the traffic in tobacco. This alone was a severe blow, for in a normal year between a fifth and a fourth of the eastern crop floated into Richmond via the canal.*

1865, $5.00 in 1867, and $1.75 in 1875. (The 1960 rates are 10 cents a pound for smoking and chewing; one cent for a ten-cent cigar, two cents for a "fine cigar" retailing at 20 cents or more; and $4.00 per thousand on cigarettes, or eight cents per pack of twenty.)

By 1880, when tobacco taxes were more or less stabilized, smoking and chewing accounted for 50% of collections, cigars and cheroots for 40%, and cigarettes for less than 2%. At that time tobacco revenue to the U. S. amounted to $38.9 million, or some 31% of total tax receipts. It can be said that manufactured tobacco "took over" in the early 1880s, for in 1883 Congress put strict limits on the traffic in home-cured leaf. Farmers could sell no more than 100 pounds of their own growing directly to consumers in a year. Also, a tax was not required of a farmer or lumberman "who furnishes rations of tobacco to his laborers, not to exceed 100

pounds during each tax year, provided he is not engaged in the business of a merchant, selling to others beside his own laborers." Such a regulation would scarcely have been passed had not home consumption dwindled to practically nothing.

Although the excises on the several forms of tobacco were varied from time to time, total tax receipts from tobacco manufactures rose steadily—from $1.3 million in the first full year, fiscal 1864, to $58.1 million in 1910, $462 million in 1930, $705 million in 1940, and more than $2 billion in 1957. Before income taxes were constitutionalized, tobacco was the chief support of the federal government, accounting for more than a fifth of total U. S. revenue in the years leading up to World War I.

In 1930 another kind of army—the army of the unemployed — posed financial problems which led individual states to add their own excises to the federal tax. In the next 25 years forty two states imposed tobacco taxes (Virginia, North Carolina and Maryland being conspicuous exceptions), the aggregate receipts reaching close to half a billion dollars a year. In 1958 Maryland levied a tax.

In recent years cigars and manufactured tobacco have turned in less than 4% of all federal tobacco collections; their current taxes are about the same as the first levies enacted in 1862. Cigarettes account for more than 95% of federal tobacco revenue, about $1.7 billion, the present federal tax of eight cents per pack being ten times the original levy.

Shrunken tobacco sack

The Confederate Government decided early in the war to discourage tobacco growing. Leaf production in the Old Dominion, 123,000,000 pounds in 1860, dropped so sharply that by 1870, after five years of reconstruction, it was only up to

37,000,000. Blockaded by sea, the South needed food even more than foreign exchange. Furthermore, its chief tobacco regions were border states, directly under the Union guns. Richmond plants and warehouses became hospitals—one became the famous or infamous Libby Prison. Towns which did not figure directly in the fighting, like Danville and Lynchburg, suffered from dislocation of people and transportation facilities.

Although the tobacco trade had come a long way since the days of Rolfe, Bacon and Culpeper, it was still dependent in large measure on water transport. Roads were rudimentary, and railroads limited. The era of the Virginia Tobacco Sack—1800 to 1860 —coincided with the age of canal-building, and the James River canal was a vital link between the piedmont farms and the markets at Richmond, located just at the Fall Line. This waterway, begun in Richmond in 1795, was gradually extended west-

In Richmond itself, the largest and best buildings were tobacco plants and warehouses. Many of these were converted into hospitals or to other wartime use. One brick tobacco plant, occupied at the war's outbreak by Libby and Sons, ship chandlers, was to be known and hated by thousands as Libby Prison.

157

ward, reaching Lynchburg by 1840. Since it conveyed up to 20,000,000 pounds of leaf each year to Richmond, between a fifth and a fourth of the eastern crop, the James canal contributed much to the opening of the piedmont for planting and to the growth of Richmond into the top tobacco town. In 1835 it was renamed the James River and Kanawha Canal, the new title implying an intention to extend navigation to the Ohio via West Virginia's Kanawha River. This could have brought the Kentucky crop within the Richmond-Lynchburg manufacturing orbit, but despite the ambitious name the James canal never got farther west than the Blue Ridge Mountains.

The canal's importance within Virginia was amply demonstrated by the requirements of war. Troop movements to the Richmond bastion virtually ended hogshead traffic and this, together with the conversion of Richmond's warehouses into hospitals, dumps and prisons, directly affected Virginia tobacco manufacture. Production began to shift southward to the small, out-of-the-way towns in the leaf areas of North Carolina.

It is clear that tobacco manufacturing in the four big river towns of Virginia was seriously crippled, where it was not paralyzed, for the duration. It is not so clear exactly what happened in the rural leaf areas, but there is no doubt that quite a few planters were left with considerable tobacco on their hands at the outbreak of war. There was no ready market in which to sell it, and in fact not much could be purchased with the currency the tobacco might bring. Aparently what took place was a farmers' holdback of tobacco similar to the farmers' holdback of milk and eggs in Britain during the blitz years of the 1940s. Manufacturing tech-

The burning of Richmond a week before Appomattox was accidental. Confederate troops intended only to burn valuable leaf tobacco before withdraw- *ing from the city, but the fires got out of control. This Currier and Ives lithograph of the holocaust somehow fails to convey any real sense of tragedy.*

nique was not at that time a mystery outside the city factories, and doubtless many farmers were able to make acceptable flat plug at home from the bright yellow leaf they had started to grow and cure.

One result of this was a "temporary" wartime shift of production from the established centers to out-of-the-way country towns, particularly in the Old Belt of North Carolina. Like many such measures, they ended up by being anything but temporary.

Aside from the farmers who took temporarily to manufacturing, there were those who seized on the wartime shortage as an opportunity to set up a rural business, perhaps raising the leaf themselves.

Gray rations for Blue

It was possible to commandeer a factory and divert freight cars, but it was not possible to destroy the taste for tobacco. Realizing this, farmers in the beleaguered Southern states continued to plant and cure tobacco against the recommendation of the Confederate Congress. As in earlier centuries, sheafs of tobacco served as currency, being used by country folk to purchase what supplies were to be found in the retail stores. Morale among the troops made tobacco essential, and the Confederate States recognized this in 1864, when it authorized a tobacco ration to enlisted men. This was an act more symbolic than substantial, for the army ration by all accounts was of miserable quality. But Gray troops, deploying and fighting through the Bright tobacco country, were often well supplied with good tobacco by those who grew it, and a considerable "export" trade in tobacco sprang up through the front lines. Coffee was the usual "import" from Blue troops anxious for the scarce Southern leaf.

The new science of photography provided realistic evidence of what had happened. There was hardly a downtown building that escaped total ruin. These structures had constituted the capitol of tobacco manufacture. To the left of the charred lamppost at right a sign remnant reads "---ctured ---acco."

159

After Appomattox, General William T. Sherman with 50,000 Union troops entered Raleigh, halted there to negotiate surrender of Gray army near Durham.

While General Joseph E. Johnston parleyed, 30,000 of his men had nowhere to go but Durham's Station. There they met and mingled with Sherman's soldiers.

Some manufacturers were still operating in beleaguered Richmond. As in all wars the demand for tobacco was strong, and a few tobaccomen were fortunate enough to possess inventories within the city. In spite of the astronomical price of leaf tobacco, it may have been possible to turn a profit from manufacturing even without a large inventory cushion.

Before Richmond was reborn, it had to die. On the night of Sunday, April 2, 1865, the end came for the proud center of tobacco manufacture. In a sense the final holocaust which cremated the city was a suicide; Confederate troops put the torch to the city's downtown tobacco warehouses to deny valuable leaf stores to Grant's advancing Army of the Potomac. Out of control, the blaze raged for days. It was still burning on April 9, when the surrounded Robert E. Lee sent his flag of truce to Ulysses S. Grant at Appomattox.

Surrender to Carolina Bright

The soldier demand for tobacco, a notable fact of military life in every war, combined with the southward shift of manufacturing to produce another surrender — a surrender by both Blue and Gray to the new Bright leaf grown, granulated and bagged in North Carolina. Lee surrendered the Army of Virginia to Grant on April 12 at Appomattox, but he did not take it upon himself to negotiate for Confederate troops elsewhere. General Joseph E. Johnston and his army of 30,000—a force larger than Lee's — were taking a position a few miles northwest of Durham's Station, North Carolina, while General William T. Sherman had come up through South Carolina with 50,000 Union troops and entered Raleigh. It was not until April 26 that a military surrender was concluded in North Carolina. Meanwhile 80,000 men had nothing to do but forage, an activity in which both Blue and Gray were well practised. Durham's Station lay squarely between the two armies who mingled freely in a mutual effort to dissipate boredom and find what creature comforts they could. The tobacco factory of J. R. Green could hardly be missed, being only a hundred yards from the railroad depot. Green made his product of the new Bright tobacco (Durham's Station was only 40 miles from the Slade farm where the famous accidental cure was effected). Unlike the average manufacturer Green

"Sherman's bummers" had foraged their way through Georgia and South Carolina (above). Johnston's men were also used to living off the land. When these armies milled through Durham, they "sampled" the tobacco in J. R. Green's factory near the rail depot. Weeks later, mustered out, they were writing back for more Durham smokum. So a national demand arose for granulated Bright, called Bull Durham.

did not press his leaf into twist or plug but shredded it, believing that a trend toward smoking and away from chewing was in the making. As luck would have it, Green's factory was chock full of his *Best Flavored Spanish Smoking Tobacco,* and the entire stock, with or without his consent, was consumed by soldiers of both sides. The result was that Green's little factory experienced the most amazing "run" in the history of tobacco manufacturing. In a few weeks letters came into Durham's Station from mustered-out soldiers throughout the nation, all desirous of getting more of the *Best Flavored Spanish.* In order to protect himself against the numerous *Durham Tobaccos* and *Best Flavored Spanishes* which immediately appeared, Green adopted a picture of a Durham bull as his trademark. The official name of the product was *Genuine Durham Smoking Tobacco,* but it has always been known as *Bull Durham.* For the next

fifty years it was the world's best-known tobacco brand; Green and his partner W. T. Blackwell were smart enough to nourish the wide demand with advertising, not only on billboards and posters, but also via newspapers, comic books, and with the inevitable premium clocks. Green's advertising campaign was almost as significant for the industry's future as the overnight renown *Bull Durham* brought to Bright leaf; the emergence of a national and international brand (it was truthfully advertised as "The Standard of the World") marked an abrupt departure from the hundreds of brands that preceded it, all depending mainly on local renown and word-of-mouth recommendation for sales growth.

Bull run

A great many competitors — some of them Virginians — rode the broad back of the spirited

Bull. There were *Old Bull, Black Bull, Jersey Bull, Bull's Head, Brindle, Bison, Bully, Buffalo, Wild Buffalo* and *Buffalo Bill; Durham Gold Leaf, Magic Durham, Rosebud Durham, Pride of Durham, Billy Boy Durham, Ram Durham, Nickel-Plated Durham,* and *Ten Cent Durham.* Some rival brands combined the idea of the Bull with his Spanish predecessor, as *El Burro, Eureka Spanish Flavored Durham,* and *Los Toros Tobaco de Fumar.* Perhaps the most far-fetched variant was *Sitting Bull Durham.* But the Genuine Bull reigned supreme, and by 1884 the four-story white stone *Bull Durham* factory alongside the Durham railroad tracks was the world's largest tobacco plant.

Carolina renaissance

In the Bright Belt of which Durham's Station immediately became the manufacturing center, the big plantation pattern of the tidewater culture was not repeated. There were several reasons. First, and probably most important, slave labor was no longer to be had. Second, not all the soil is the gray type suited to Bright leaf: a given field might produce the finest lemon tobacco, and the next one full-bodied "greasy green" tobacco fit only for scrap chewing. Third, the new method of flue-curing and the handling of the delicate leaves after the cure required constant, careful attention; raising the better grades began to require intensive effort (and still does). Yet, small farms or no—the average size was not much over 100 acres—the cumulative result of the Bright surge was, as the Census of 1880 put it, "one of the most remarkable transitions in the annals of agriculture." The town of Winston, in the ten years ended 1880, added a leaf market and fourteen plug factories and grew from 443 to 2,854 inhabitants: most important of these was to be the R. J. Reynolds plant, started up in 1875 by the former tobacco pedlar of that name. Reidsville, which did not exist in 1870, had a population of 1,316 in 1880 who ran nine plug and two smoking-tobacco factories. Durham's Station, a whistle-stop of 256 souls in 1870, grew to 2,041 by 1880 and 5,500 by 1885; its growth in factories—from one to a dozen—occurred earliest, between 1865 and 1872. The manufacturing transition in North Carolina was quite as remarkable as that of its agriculture. By 1880, the Virginia manufacturing industry had recovered from hostilities, show-

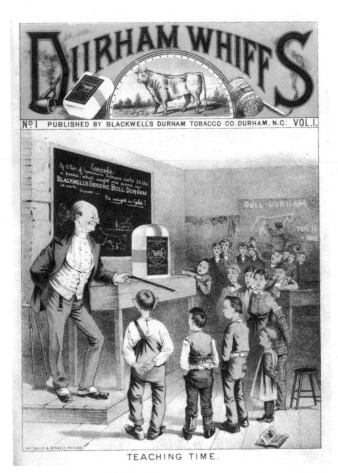

TEACHING TIME.

The rage for Bull Durham was unprecedented. Also unprecedented was the national advertising placed by the Bull's makers to maintain national demand. Promotion included newspaper ads, premiums, billboards and even comic books like the above. Also pictured (top right) but hardly big enough to be visible was a package of Golden Belt Cigarettes.

ing an increase of 8% in value of product over 1860. In the same span, the increase for North Carolina was 100%.

Duke of Durham

Among the small farmers who participated in the explosion of Bright was a mustered-out widower of 45 named Washington Duke. Returning in 1865, he found his 300-acre farm near Durham's Station fairly well foraged. However, before being conscripted in 1863, he had become convinced that Bright leaf had a bright future, and had stockpiled as much of it as he could. Some of the tobacco remained; with his children he flailed it in a small cabin, packed it into bags, and made a mule-and-wagon selling trip toward Raleigh. For a while

Duke was a planter-manufacturer on his farm, and in 1874 Duke and Sons moved their factory into Durham near the railroad. This simple adjustment, logical as it now sounds, was not at all typical of Southern tobacco-making up to that time. Most country manufacturers regarded their plants as sheltered extensions of the farms and expected them to flourish wherever they grew. It was this rural impracticality that left many to wither and die as costs and competition rose and the margin for error grew smaller. To their *Duke of Durham* granulated tobacco the Dukes added, in 1881, *Duke of Durham* cigarettes. The growth of their business was steady but not spectacular until 1883, when they leased and improved a cigarette machine devised by James Bonsack of Virginia. This was the last link in the chain of developments which was to make possible the American blended cigarette (though that product was still thirty years off): flue-cured Bright tobacco; Burley leaf of cigarette grades; and precision machinery.

Chaw to smokum

Although the Blackwell *Bull Durham* company responded to Duke's challenge by putting out a line of cigarettes, the big growth item of the day was smoking tobacco. Prior to the war, smoking tobacco had consisted simply of scraps left over from plugmaking, plus leaf that would not chew too well. A plug establishment was a different proposition altogether from a smoking product plant, and its smoking tobacco by-product not at all comparable to the sacked Bright leaf that was sweeping the nation — *Bull Durham* and its stampede of imitators.

The transition from chew to smoking tobacco

The 1839 flue-cure for Bright leaf was adopted by many Old Belt farmers before the war. Washington Duke had stockpiled Bright before he was drafted, found some left on his 1865 return. In this little cabin he flailed and bagged the leaf, a beginning typical of many a country tobacco business. A few years later Duke made the uncommon transition to a factory proprietor in the bustling town of Durham.

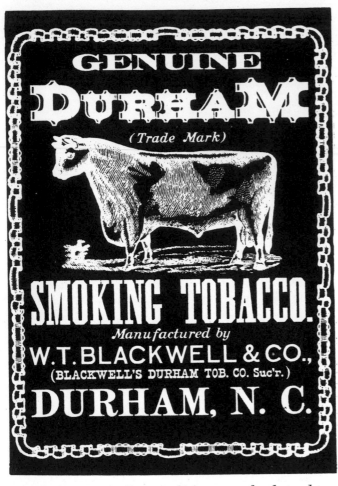

Smoking tobacco lent itself more easily than chew to mechanized production and packaging, thus held out a higher hope of big volume and high profits. Bull Durham with its head start led all the rest.

was, in simple terms, a mass refinement of tobacco taste. Chewing leaf was, and is, a dark, coarse, product that required virile taste buds. Originally, licorice water was added to transoceanic leaf cargoes as a freshener or preservative; early in the nineteenth century licorice and other sweeteners were added to improve the taste of quid. As the midwestern plug factories capitalized on the absorbency of Burley leaf, loading it with sugars and spices, the "improvement" came to be almost self-defeating. In warm atmospheres, the heavily confectioned navy product would not keep; in colder climes, the sugary surfeit may have contributed to the popularity of cigars and pipe mixtures offering a more honest tobacco flavor.

From the manufacturing viewpoint, the change from chew to tumblings was not entirely a radical one. Prior to the Civil War, pipe tobacco was simply shaved plug; many smoking tobaccos are still literally labeled "cut plug." The art of blending originated, in a sense, with plug and was elaborated in the more easily mixed smoking tobaccos; dark Burley filler held in a Bright wrapper leaf was probably the first non-cigar "blend." The sweetening or casing, if not overdone, was found to add to the pleasure of tobacco long before the age of Burley chew. Cuban cigarettes were wrapped in cinnamon-flavored paper or cased with molasses before the white roll was accepted on the mainland; cheap cigars used rum, wine or molasses more or less as a camouflage.

There were four basic types of smoking tobacco. Plug cut was the original "sideline" form, more or less accidental in its beginnings. Sliced from a compressed, flavored cake of tobacco—usually, in later years, the porous Burley—it lent itself to a wide range of textures: cube cut, curve cut, straight cut, wavy cut, Cavendish cut, granulated plug cut.

Granulated or "flake cut" was worked through toothed cutters and sieved for uniform fineness; almost always this was straight, naturally sweet Bright leaf, cased lightly or not at all.

Long cut, or ribbon cut, was shredded strip leaf. More often than not it was dipped Burley or a Burley blend, and could be made in a variety of strand widths. Cigarette tobacco is a variety of long cut.

The last and least category, scrap, was a byproduct of cigar manufacture; these cigar cuttings (leaf ends) and clippings (cigar ends) were both chewed and smoked.

There were numerous advantages to the smoking tobacco business. It lent itself more easily to machinery, and thereby held out a higher promise of big volume to the successful entrepreneur. Credit for the first mechanization of tobacco production is given to the Richmond makers, who began "thrashing" leaf almost immediately after Appomattox (a method now used by some cigarette manufacturers in lieu of hand or machine stemming). The thrasher took the place of hand-flailing with a sassafras stick. Packaging, too, was mechanized in a way impossible with plug or twist; various packing presses and bag fillers were used in Richmond and Durham with greater or less success until the "bag jack" was invented by Rufus Patterson in 1895. This contrivance weighed the tobacco into its muslin sack, applied the label, and stamped it so efficiently that some 1900 models are still running (more accurately, shuddering) today.

All this gave the smoking tobacco maker a wider profit margin than the plug maker: specialized hand-work like that done by the famous "lumpers" of Danville—who could gauge the weight of a plug lump as accurately as a scale — was not needed. Also, the winter season did not carry the same risks of spoilage in making pipe mixtures as it did in the pressurizing of plug. For these reasons there was an early tendency for smoking factories to be urban, few and big, as against the tendency of the early country pluggeries of Virginia to be many and, relatively, small.

Richmond revival

While it required a hardy palate to chaw raw leaf, pipe tobacco can yield a good smoke with little flavoring or none at all. This recommended it to the hard-pressed Richmond trade during the War Between the States when sugar was in short supply. The idea of converting from chew to smokum was half-realized years before in the recapture of damaged or half-rotted plug; as a sideline, many factories took to flaking the bruised quid and selling it as pipe mix. These practical considerations were not lost on the resourceful tobaccomen of 1865, anxious to rise like Phoenixes out of the rubble of Richmond. By 1880 the city was turning out nearly a million pounds of smoking tobacco a year — far less than the four million pound rate of Durham and Baltimore, but at least comparable to the million-plus of New York and Jersey City.

Interest in the exciting new item was particularly strong because the plug trade, antebellum mainstay of the Bright region, was being invaded by the Burley "pigtailers." Virginians were prone to blame the damn Yankees for not being able to appreciate fine (i.e., Bright) tobacco and thereby falling prey to the highly sweetened Midwestern twist. Nor were they as quick as manufacturers of New York, Kentucky or North Carolina to hitch their production wagon to the rising stars of salesmanship and national promotion.

In retrospect, it appears that Richmond's tradition of successful manufacturing prevented or delayed its adoption of new, vigorous selling methods. The following letter, written in 1886 by one of that town's "fine old name" firms, suggests an inability

Typical smoking tobacco was granulated to "pour" freely, sold in drawstringed sack for easy pipe loading. Plug cuts like Woodcock were also bagged.

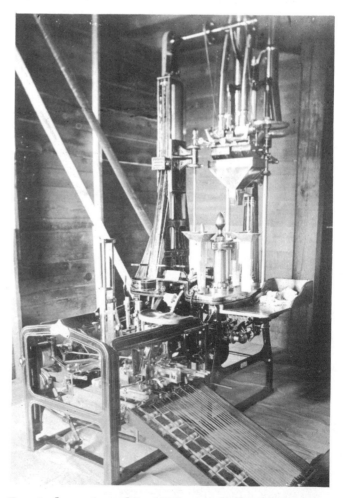

Bag jack, perfected in 1895, weighed tobacco into muslin sack, applied and stamped the label; 1900 bag jacks are still operating efficiently today.

Reopening of James River Canal to freight traffic after Appomattox was hailed as a great event. But resumption of leaf tobacco supply was not enough to insure revival of Richmond as top tobacco town. Mass production of navy plug was threat from West, vogue for Carolina smokum a threat from the South.

to cope with the tidal wave of premiums on which cigars, cigarettes, smoking tobacco and plug were riding upwards:

> Dear Sir
>   Your attention is called to certain imitations of _____ _____ tobacco which are being pushed by travelling salesmen under the stimulus of a large gift offered them by the manufacturer. Will you allow goods to be forced upon you by these salesmen whose only object is to secure the costly presents offered them as a reward for imposing upon you? Bear in mind that these expensive premiums have to be paid for out of the pockets of the retailer and consumer, by having their full value taken out of the quality of the tobacco. Any article that will not sell upon its own *honest merits* should be entirely avoided for they are only deceptions. If your wholesale dealer will not furnish you with the genuine _____ _____ tobacco, order direct from us.

Between the lines of this letter one can sense a nostalgia for the days when reputation meant everything, combined with a certain bewilderment about salesmen's inducements in a free-for-all market.

In many respects, the Richmond men erred in staging a revival rather than a revolution. They aimed for a return to the *status quo ante bellum*, selling on consignment to factors; the North Carolinians sent their own men to canvas not only the wholesale trade but the retail. At first, it appeared that Richmond was taking its old place as kingpin of the eastern region; four years after Appomattox, it turned out more than half of Virginia-North Carolina tobacco products, a sixth of the national manufactured tobacco total. In ten years more the sixth had been whittled to 10% while North Carolina had come up from 2% to more than 7%. Before the Revolutionary War, tobacco prominence meant planting; before the Civil War, planting and processing; after the Civil War, a third element was required: salesmanship. It was by selling, inspired by the accidental sampling at Durham's Station, that North Carolina was to take the play away from proud Richmond. At the same time the smoking tobacco "Bull fight," focused in little Durham, made the Old North State not only the manufacturing center but the center of Bright leaf growing as well.

Cotton to cutters

Although tobacco was always a staple in Maryland and Virginia, the art of leaf cultivation was

Makeshift tobacco exchange was set up in Richmond, the former market building having been destroyed in the 1865 fire. Hands of tobacco from hogsheads in the warehouse nearby (below) were taken to the exchange by leaf dealers. While buyers sniffed and felt samples the auctioneer (seated, right above) conducted the bidding. Dispatch which accompanied sketch above reported that "the growth and sale of this staple in Virginia is just now but a mockery of what it was at the outbreak of the war," though "still of sufficient importance to be one of the leading items in the commerce of the State, if not its most important one." The observation proved a prophetic one. Although Virginia tobacco planting and manufacturing regained an important place, the center of Bright leaf cultivation shifted to North Carolina. Eventually, the Old North State became a leading manufacturer of tobacco products as well.

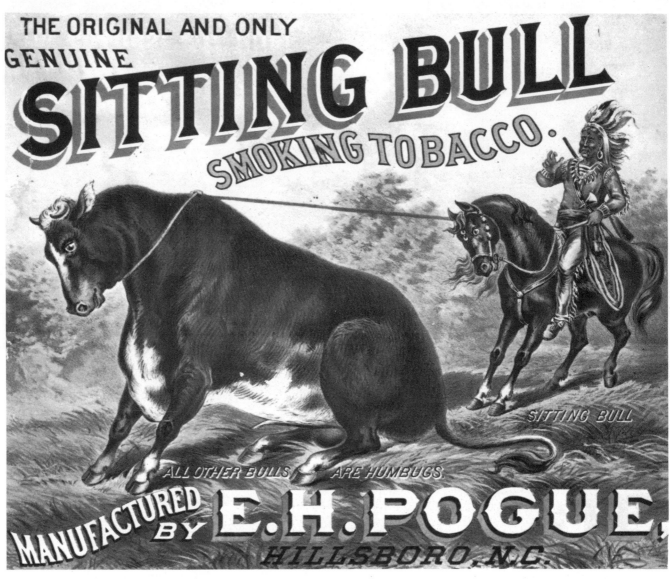

THE ORIGINAL AND ONLY
GENUINE
SITTING BULL
SMOKING TOBACCO.

SITTING BULL

ALL OTHER BULLS ARE HUMBUGS.

MANUFACTURED BY E.H. POGUE,
HILLSBORO, N.C.

Success of Bull Durham led to a stampede of bull imitations. The "original and only" Sitting Bull *tobacco was one of the most far-fetched of these, airily disparaged all other bulls as "humbugs."*

largely confined to the James, York, Rappahannock and Roanoke (Dan) valleys. Diversified crops became the watchword following the Revolution, and after cotton became king in 1803, tobacco planting moved upriver, found its niche in the "Tobacco Sack" area and stayed there. Granulated tobacco in Durham and gritty adherence to Bright flat plug in Winston changed this completely. It took some doing: in 1885, for instance, the citizens of Winston organized their own company to complete a rail line connecting with the Roanoke and Southern. North Carolina became a rich agricultural state; roads and railroads laced the once-deserted piedmont, and fingered their way into South Carolina and Georgia as well.

The excitement of the 1880s in the North Carolina piedmont could hardly go unnoticed in the coastal plain. Cotton was still king below the fall line, but his subjects were restive as prices dropped to eight cents a pound. Bright tobacco *averaged* over thirteen cents a pound during four crop years in the 80s, and in the other years did not dip much below ten cents. The farmers of eastern North Carolina, however, were not thinking in terms of averages. During the heyday of the Virginia plug-makers, wide publicity attended the sale of fancy yellow wrappers for 40c, 50c and even more. The smoking tobacco trade generated a demand for yellow cutters—so-called because the leaf was thin enough to be shredded — and it was found that cutters good enough to bring 25c a pound could be grown almost within sight of the Atlantic Ocean. Tobacco, which a hundred years before had climbed laboriously up and over the fall line, now spread downward to the North Carolina "tidewater." The whole story can be told in two jingles, both circulated during the 90s:

> Fi-cent cotton and ten-cent meat —
> How in the world can a po' man eat?

And, from the poetic pen of a promotion-minded warehouseman of the new Eastern Belt:

> Cotton was once king
> And produced Carolina's cracker;
> But now we have a better thing —
> The glorious Bright Tobacco.

It would be inaccurate to describe the spread of Bright tobacco culture as an overnight revolution. Human perception, in agriculture or manufacture or even consumption, is not that quick. During the entire thirty-five years from Appomattox to the turn of the century North Carolina Bright averaged about 10c per pound on the leaf markets; during the same period the old-fashioned dark, fire-cured Virginia — smoked like that state's renowned ham — never reached the 10c level, averaging somewhere near 6c. The handwriting was on the wall a long time before it was read by the farmers en masse, for the main sweep of tobacco into the coastal plain did not take place until the 1890s.

Once started, it overreached itself, as most mass social and economic movements seem to do. In an attempt to build up in western Carolina lucrative warehouse businesses such as those in Durham and Winston, entrepreneurs of the 60s and 70s distributed a pamphlet of instruction and panegyric to farmers in the Blue Ridge counties. With the unerring instinct of promoters, they secured the

Market growth of granulated flue-cured Bright led cotton farmers of coastal North Carolina to raise tobacco. Large warehouses like this at Greenville in the Carolina "tidewater" owed their existence partly to Bull Durham, partly to five-cent cotton. Common tobacco averaged over ten cents during 80s.

authorship (or signature,) of a former member of the state legislature. "Conjecture is lost," wrote one Asheville prophet, "in the contemplation of what the tobacco industry will do for this county in a few years, at the present rate of increase." But the tobacco produced in Buncombe county proved strong and rank, and after a few wild years the tobacco fever passed, leaving only bitter memories and bald hillsides.

Social register of tobacco

The positions occupied by plug, cigarette and smoking tobacco during the postwar revival of the Bright region are best suggested by their brand names. The placename "Durham," with or without a variant of "bull," dominated the pipe brands and told its own story; it was not necessary to consult the census of 1880 to realize that Durham led all the rest in smoking tobacco (although Maryland, which originated many of the rival "bully" brands, was second). In the wide-open smoking sweepstakes, consciousness of brand name — inspired, no doubt, by the commercial magic of the word "Durham" — became quite as painful as it was in plug competition. All the obvious names were used and blithely re-used: in 1886 the *Bulls* were too numerous to count; there were thirteen *Spanish Mixed* made in as many different plants between Detroit and Durham; and there were at least ten *Old Kentucky* mixtures and sixteen variations on the old Indian word kinnikinnick, somehow transmogrified into *Killickinick* (*B. & O. Killickinick, Tip Top Killickinick, Capital Killickinick, Virginia Killickinick, St. Jacob's Killickinick*, and so on). Daniel Scotten of Detroit, one of the few big plugmakers to achieve big volume in smokings as well, boasted an especially piquant array of labels, designed to play on every chord to which the fickle customer might respond. One brand was named *What are Ye Givin' Us*, another *Who Says We Haven't Got It Now*, and a third, simply, *We Got*. There was *Get There Eli* and *Eli Got There After a While; Dats de Stuff, Live and Let Live, I've Caught You*. In a self-deprecatory spirit Scotten marketed *Same Old Thing, Old Hat, Good Common Smoking, Glass Blowers' Choice, Cheap John, Buncombe, Stunner, Buzz Saw, Gold Brick* and *Barbed Wire*. In prouder vein he offered *Just a Little the Best, Its a Daisy, I Cry For It, Give Us Some More, Kerect,*

" **I DID NOT** "

J. H. CLYPFIN, JAYE ST. PHIL.

Tobacco manufacturing started up in almost every large city after the Civil War. Brand names were

and *Beats the Dickens*. In cryptic mood were *Mother-in-Law, Shoo Fly, Come and Fan Me, Put It There* and *Ish Dot So*.

Scotten was not unique in this verbal competition. Gail & Ax of Baltimore offered *Toodles;* Kimball of Rochester, *Rock Bottom;* Catlin of St. Louis, *Solid Shot;* Schwartz of Louisville, *Paralyzer;* Durvel of Cincinnati, *Little Bone;* Tolman of Chicago, *Eye Opener;* Beck of Chicago, *To Please The Boys;* and Allen, also of the stockyard city, *Dinah's Big Quarters*.

In their infatuation with the power of words, manufacturers of the 80s labeled their factories as well as their products. The Daniel Scotten factory in Detroit was the "Hiawatha Tobacco Works"; August Beck & Co. of Chicago named their four-story plant on Dearborn Street "Eureka Tobacco Works"; and the huge gabled establishment of

I Smoke "GOLD FLAKE" Cigarettes
and Chew "GLOBE" Fine Cut.

J. H. CAMP PHIL'A

no more whimsical than advertising, as the above display on behalf of Globe of Detroit indicates.

William S. Kimball in Rochester was "Peerless Tobacco Works." It was not pure coincidence that the three firms made, respectively, *Hiawatha* plug and fine-cut, *Eureka* fine cut, and *Peerless* chewing and smoking tobacco. Daniel Scotten was not one to let his rivals steal a march in the name game, however, and his Hiawatha Works produced a *Eureka* fine cut and a *Peerless* chewing tobacco. Not that this gave him a decisive advantage: there were thirteen plugs and smokums traveling under the *Eureka* trademark, nine *Peerless* brands beside the two made at the Peerless Tobacco Works, and some *Hiawathas* which did not originate in Detroit.

Fancy versus folksy

Cigarettes had fancy names, being intended for fancy city folk: *Union Club, Opera Puffs, Vanity Fair, Entre Nous, Town Talk, Cameo.* The majestic

sophistication of these names suggests the narrowness of the cigarette market. In 1880, Richmond and Baltimore were the only cigarette-making cities of any consequence outside New York State. Each accounted for about a tenth of the nation's output. Cigarette-making was a newfangled novelty outside New York; fewer than 500 persons were employed in the Virginia cigarette establishments, compared with 14,000 hands in the chewing and smoking factories. The restraining factor was not any reluctance on the part of Richmond businessmen to enter the new market, but rather the difficulty of training and keeping handrollers. A year later, one Durham manufacturer had to import 125 experienced rollers from New York — most of them Polish and Russian immigrants—in order to achieve a beginning in cigarette production.

As befitted common cud, most chewing tobaccos carried folksy appellations: *Old Country Twist, Honest Ben, Big Chunk, Black Bass, Mountain Dew, Dixie Queen, Poor Man's Comfort.* The average plugmaker offered anywhere from 40 to 140 brands, and in the search for new names was easily carried away with himself, as with *Otto of Roses, Ring Coil Hot Cake,* and the like.

The mad proliferation of names was to continue beyond 1900, but a narrowing influence was already at work. Unlike the early plugmakers who depended on consignees and commission merchants to do their selling — often to their sorrow — the postbellum tobacco men, more and more, sold their own. As time went on this tended to cut down on the number of pipe brands offered.

This brand paring was no reflection of complacency: on the contrary, the exuberant competition that inflamed North Carolina was unlike anything the South had ever known. It was as if the ruthless spirit of Yankee enterprise had been wafted south of the Mason-Dixon line by the clouds of war. The word of the day, as proclaimed by the proprietors of *Bull Durham*, was "Let buffalo gore buffalo, and the pasture go to the strongest!" Enthusiasm for Bright tobacco was boundless. In its flush the Durham manufacturers subsidized a company for the production of tobacco ointments, a three-century flashback to the prescriptive pretensions of Jean Nicot. A great horn, tuned to resemble the bellowing of a supernatural bull, was mounted atop the Bull Durham factory and cried a deep-throated

THE WONDERFUL EFFECTS OF JACKSON'S BEST

MANUFACTURED BY C.A. JACKSON & CO.

MY WORTHY FRIEND, IF EVER YOU
SHOULD WANT A REALLY FIRST CLASS CHEW,
USE JACKSON'S BEST, OR YOU WILL BE
AN ASS, LIKE I WAS FORMERLY.

I WAS A MOST CONSUMMATE ASS,
FOR NOTHING HUMAN COULD I PASS,
I GOT A CHEW OF "JACKSON'S BEST,"
INVERT THIS CARD AND KNOW THE REST.

Virginia fought hard to keep her chewing tobacco volume against the Burley onslaught. Depending on the point of view, this trade card for Jackson's Best chew is describable as ingenious or asinine.

challenge to the countryside at intervals during the day.

Storm center of plug

The excitement infused new life into the old flat plug business, especially in the town of Winston at the western edge of the original Bright Belt (now called the Old Belt). Undaunted by the challenge of Burley, the Reynoldses and the Browns and the Haneses stuck strictly to Bright leaf. While Danville and Lynchburg wasted away for lack of enterprise, the Winston companies sent indefatigable salesmen through the back country where proud Richmond plugmakers disdained to tread. In 1880, ten years after Winston became a tobacco

town, it ranked eleventh in plug production and eighteenth in leaf converted to manufacture. Seventeen years later, the "Storm Centre of the Plug Industry," as Winston proudly described itself, was the third ranking city in manufactured tobacco (the "navy towns" of St. Louis and Louisville were first and second).

Yet the success that came to Winston had its offsets elsewhere in the Bright tobacco region. The onslaught of Burley and the decline of Richmond, Petersburg, Lynchburg and Danville as chewing tobacco centers of the first rank led to this classic lament, published in a Richmond trade paper of 1898:

> Fifteen and twenty years ago every factory in Virginia and North Carolina, every one in Richmond, worked bright filler brands twist and plug, cable coil and lady finger, and other styles. The South was not the only great field of sale, but the demand came from California and Canada, from Maine to Texas. But smoking twist gave way to fine cut and plug-cut and fancy cuts, and soon business was cut to pieces as literally as the tobacco was. The burley juggernaut journeyed hither and crushed the life out of our fine fillers. We capitulated with little effort at defense, burley captured crew and craft, and went on crashing and cruising until it owned the country, and with this the transfer and transformation of business on tobacco has moved West until it centered there. . . . That it might have been held by strategy and effort is proven by the progress of Winston, N. C., manufacturing, which in face of the fact of lost prestige in older larger markets, that market has created and held business, bucking against burley on all sides, and Winston wins the day that way; and is a winner still, holding her ground not only but gaining . . .

The "strategy" Winston used to buck Burley was the use of a little saccharin to sweeten its flat plug. In this way the absorptive advantage of Burley leaf was completely overcome, saccharin being several hundred times as sweet as sugar. This innovation, begun in 1895, enabled Winston to increase its flat goods business in a period when eastern plug sales generally were falling off and the national use of quid leveling out.

Stage set for the cigarette

Actually, the desolate outlook portrayed by the Richmond trade journal did not turn out to be valid for the Bright region as a whole. In 1880, Virginia and North Carolina made a third of the nation's chewing and smoking tobacco; during the not-so-gay 1890s — a decade of depression — this share dropped to 28%. But early in the twentieth century the Bright country regained its third of manufactured tobacco output and held it consistently through the first World War. True, the region's share of chewing tobacco alone declined from 43% in 1880 to 25% in 1899 (it recovered and maintained a 30% level until the first World War, after which plug-taking fell off abruptly). But the swelling sales of pipe tobacco easily compensated for the loss of plug business, even before growing cigarette volume was taken into account.

In the minds of the Southern plugmakers, though, this was beside the point. Along with the tobacco-man's cherished traditions goes a kind of stubborn pride. This pride manifested itself in many ways; the names *Stonewall* and *Stonewall Jackson*, for example, became quite popular for Southern quid during the time of the Burley challenge. Brands

Winston, North Carolina, was "storm center of the plug industry," stubbornly stuck to flat plug made of Bright leaf in the face of spectacular increase in Burley plug sales. Winston became third-ranking city in manufactured tobacco output, rejected old consignment system to develop its own sales force.

Southern pride in flat Bright plug, heightened by war and the threat of Western Burley, manifested itself in Stonewall label. Montreal imitator, above, used Stonewall brand name to get Southern "flavor."

with this name were made during the 80s and 90s in North Carolina, in Tennessee and in Virginia — but not in Kentucky or Maryland. (One Montreal manufacturer tried to give his brand a bit of Southern flavor by using the *Stonewall* name and a handsome label of the dashing general on a black charger.)

The same streak of pride, sometimes described as "cussedness," typified many of the small manufacturers. One such was William Taylor, raised during the war years in the Richmond area. After a

teen-age start as a horse and mule trader, Taylor went to work for Cameron, then the largest Richmond tobacco firm. By 1879 he had eleven years of factory experience to his credit and was plant manager. After a journey to Australia, where he set up a tobacco factory in Sidney, Taylor set up in business with a partner in Bedford. Three years later he moved again, this time to Lynchburg. As senior partner of Taylor and Gish, Taylor made $22,000 his first year, invested all of it in leaf tobacco, and lost all of it when his factory burned. In 1883, at 32, Bill Taylor followed the drift to North Carolina, choosing Winston for a fresh start. At that time there were more than thirty tobacco firms in the town; but helped by his brother Jack, who came down from Richmond to join him, Bill Taylor hung on. Despite recurring offers to merge with larger firms, he kept Taylor Brothers Tobacco Company independent and remained "boss in my own little puddle."

Bill Taylor expanded his plant, acquired brand names like *Ripe Peaches, Red Coon* and *Foot Prints.* Like most of the independents, he was represented in the great "bull fight," with an entry named *Bull of the Woods.* Although Taylor was a seasoned hand at plugmaking, his biggest asset in the fight for survival was promotional ability. In a time of plug price wars, he went after the goodwill of jobbers and retailers. In 1907, when Confederate veterans passed through Durham on the way to a reunion in Richmond, Taylor was on the spot to hand out samples of his *Stars and Bars* tobacco. He even "sold" his own employees, by cutting the workday from twelve hours to ten and then to eight: this enraged not only his competitors but also the newly organized unions who were trying to cut the workday from ten hours down to nine.

In his social life as well, Taylor became known for his "cussedness." When the local preacher sermonized that "Money is the root of all evil," Bill rose in his pew to shout "I challenge that, sir! *Love* of money is the root of all evil, Doctor." Such interruptions of Sunday harmony were more the rule than the exception; at one time the entire Taylor clan was dropped from the congregation.

However detrimental to his religious standing, Taylor's stubborn streak lent strength to his little company. Taylor Brothers continued as an inde-

Richmond, still striving to regain its former top position in tobacco, followed New York into hand-rolling of cigarettes. Production was primitively *slow, for the best cigarette girls rolled only 4-5 per minute. To start cigarette production one Durham firm brought foreign rollers from New York.*

pendent plug firm until 1952. In that year, nineteen years after Bill's death, his son Arch came to the end of the family line. With Arch's only son a missionary in Japan and with no other Taylor man to take over, the "last of the independents" sold out to one of the large snuff corporations.

Although Taylor and others like him were bold enough to move into new locations, they were not bold enough to move very far from the traditional

Bright chew which was the pride of the Southeast. The future would belong to men willing to venture into new markets — first, smokings and later, cigarettes — in a wholehearted way. In the big cities capital was drawn to the mass-produced items (it took as much labor to make $1,000 worth of plug as it did to make $20,000 worth of cigarettes). In Durham, in Winston, in Baltimore, in New York and even in proud Richmond there were tobacco-

"QUITTING TIME"

Main difficulty was in training and keeping girls skilled in cigarette rolling. Virginia population in 1880 included 14,000 workers in smoking tobacco *and chew, 500 workers in cigarette factories. But "Virginia cigarettes" made exclusively from Bright tobacco enjoyed growing demand in U.S. and abroad.*

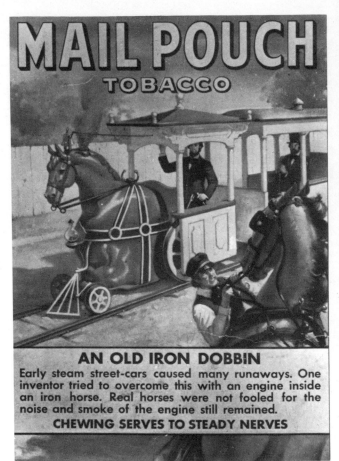

For Richmond, chewing tobacco was still the chief product. Trade cards tried ingenious sales appeals: Jackson's Best was advertised as "Bright navy"—a

contradiction in terms. Mail Pouch chew mixed the history of the trolley car with a slogan sounding rather modern: "Chewing serves to steady nerves."

men who were not too proud to drop quid for smokings.

Smokum to cigarette

In point of taste and in point of manufacture, the cigarette developed not from the cigar but from smoking tobacco. Cigarette grades of leaf, though lighter, are intrinsically akin to the pipe grades. The cigarette blend evolved directly from blended smoking tobaccos — and, by and large, in the same factories. *Prince Albert* pipe tobacco was the antecedent of *Camel; Lucky Strike* sliced plug was the advertised forerunner of *Lucky Strike* cigarettes. The factory-blended cigarette may well have been inspired by the common practise of using blended pipe tobaccos in roll-your-own handmades. Even the mighty *Bull Durham,* always a straight granulated Bright, had to take cognizance of this preference; by 1917 it was to be advertised not as "the makin's" but as an ingredient of the

do-it-yourself blend — "like sugar in your coffee." Cigarette recipes are direct derivatives of flavoring formulas used for pipe tobaccos.

Where the plug and the plug cut were laminated "cakes" in their finished form, the cigarette mixture consisted of single-thickness shreds. This difference posed the biggest problem in making a blended cigarette, for shredded Burley quickly loses its flavor. Separate dipping and overnight bulking of the Burley component — a cumbersome and expensive interruption of the production stream — solved this.

Oddly, the cigarette making machine was "perfected" for commercial purposes ten years before the bag jack for smoking sacks. But the cigarette machine was born 30 years too soon — in 1883, while the first big-volume national cigarette, the blended cigarette, did not debut until 1913. It too can be considered an offshoot of the smoking tobacco business, a precocious by-product of the long and intensive search that finally led to the bag jack.

Although this search was focused in Richmond, it went on in other places which would now be called "cities" rather than "towns" — Detroit, Chicago, Jersey City, St. Louis, Cincinnati, Milwaukee, Rochester. All had one or more avid enterprisers who were trying to attain big volume in tumblings by intensively applying the new formula for big business — mechanization, direct selling, advertising — along with many different formulas for pipe blends and casings.

Baltimore transition

Although the surge of smoking tobacco was a free-for-all, only one tobacco town kept pace with Durham's pipe poundage in the fifteen years following J. R. Green's soldier-sampling of granulated Bright. This was Baltimore. The robust rise of its smokum business had nothing to do with the geography of yellow leaf, as was the case with Durham. It was, rather, a reflection of enterprising spirit. Baltimore society would never so describe it, but the place was changing from a southern town into a northern city.

Several aspects of Baltimore's tobacco tradition set it apart from that of Virginia-North Carolina. Maryland leaf had always differed from the Virginia; in Europe, it had the reputation of Bright leaf before true Bright leaf was flue-cured in quantity. The term "Maryland" had long symbolized better-than-average leaf, and this was no hindrance

Richmond made valiant efforts to gain a foothold in newer tobacco products, and with some success. In 1886 the Kinney Company of New York built this *sizable Richmond factory to make smoking tobacco and cigarettes. Renovated in 1930, same building now stems leaf for an adjoining cigarette plant.*

Every large city had tobacco factories soon after Civil War. August Beck of Chicago specialized in Eureka fine cut chewing, made in four-story plant.

the U. S. crop in 1830, 11% in 1840, 9% in 1850, and 5% in 1880. In fifty years the second-largest tobacco state became the sixth; Maryland leaf in 1880 was not a major crop but a specialty, outranked in poundage by Pennsylvania cigar filler. Maryland tobacco, as such, was no more suited to pipe mixtures than any other. It had a good rate of burn, was attractive to the eye and could absorb flavoring sauces, but it was rather neutral in flavor. Thus no "Maryland cigarette" or "Maryland mixture" ever gained great fame; instead the leaf was commonly used as a leavening ingredient in smoking mixtures (and later in cigarette blends).

To a greater extent than Richmond, Baltimore adapted to the hectic postbellum years. The city on the Chesapeake was matching Richmond's cigarette output in 1880; it was the nation's sixth largest cigar-making center, while Richmond could not get a foothold in the lucrative brown roll business. Baltimore firms, in fact, were among the "northern factors" selling Richmond plug and twist even before the War Between the States. It was a Baltimore man, George Watts, who risked $14,000 for a 20% interest in the Duke firm of Durham in 1878, while that company was struggling in the shadow of Blackwell's mighty Bull. So it is not surprising that Baltimore should have captured

in Baltimore's entry into pipe tobacco making. There was also an independence of action in Baltimore's past that dated back to the palatinate days; while Virginia leaf was restricted to London sale, Maryland for a time shipped direct to Holland, France, and Sweden.

As the massive Burley trade grew up beyond the Alleghenies, Maryland's status as a leaf producer was drastically changed. The state raised 30% of

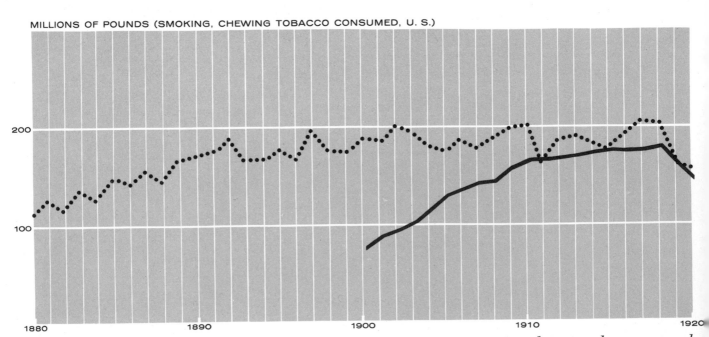

MILLIONS OF POUNDS (SMOKING, CHEWING TOBACCO CONSUMED, U. S.)

Despite all the promotion given smoking tobacco (red line), it did not match chew (black line) in poundage until 1911 and did not exceed chew until the 1920s. In terms of product poundage consumed, smokings did not achieve the 1897 plug peak until 1940, although it reached its peak of consumption

about 15% of the new smokum market — almost identical with Durham's share — while Richmond, rich in plug, turned out less than 3% of the country's smoking mixture. During most of the 1890s Maryland was the leading state in smoking tobacco output, with Baltimore's Gail & Ax, Marburg and Felgner companies as the bellwether producers.

Baltimore's smoking output ran the gamut from plug cuts to long cuts to granulateds and "German smoking," a coarse, heavy product. It included a goodly number of "high-grade" blends, a term which generally meant finer leaf grades, often including such expensive ingredients as the smoke-cured Latakia from the Middle East and the strong-sweet Louisiana Perique, cured black by stewing in its own juice under pressure. As a natural tobacco market, the port of Baltimore received leaf from every part of the country and offered a complete selection of smokum, from *Red Indian* and *Miners Extra Long Cut* to *Fashion Plug, Old English Curve Cut, Continental Cubes* and the inappropriately-named *Seal of North Carolina.*

Between 1895 and 1910 Maryland-mixed smokings went from 9,000,000 to 20,000,000 pounds. Even so, the state yielded first place to North Carolina, whose output went from 6,000,000 pounds to 43,000,000 pounds in the same fifteen years. (Ac-

Kimball factory in Rochester, N. Y., the "Peerless Works," made smokings and plug. During 1880s this was also one of the top five U. S. cigarette plants.

tually, Maryland dropped to third place in the latter year, Ohio ranking second by virtue of its yearly spew of 30,000,000 pounds of scrap, then classified as smoking tobacco.)

The auctions

It took the better part of a century — the nineteenth — for the tobacco trade to work up to such versatile blending and manufacturing centers as

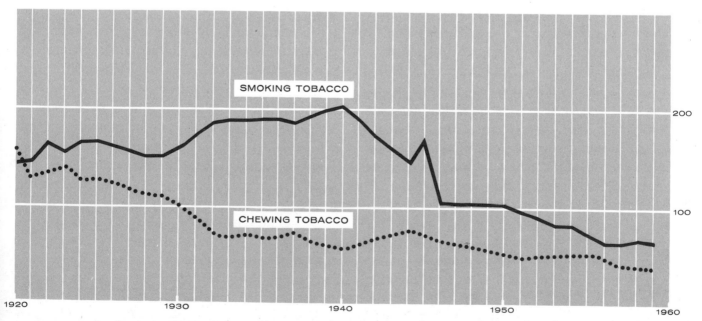

on a per capita basis in 1918. Depression years of the 30s gave pipes and roll-your-own cigarettes a last push. The trend of the market to tailor-made

cigarettes during and immediately after World War II is reflected in the disappearance of half the demand for smoking tobacco between 1940 and 1946.

Baltimore and New York. Differentiation of product, not only into cigar, smoking, chew and cigarette but also into the many types within each category, required precise differentiation between many grades of leaf. Thus, very soon after the War Between the States, "Baltimore agents" and "New York agents" were on duty more or less continuously in Danville, in Lynchburg and in Richmond watching for specific types of tobacco.

During the export centuries, one hogshead was pretty much like another. "Ducked" (waterlogged) tobacco was burned or thrown out; a rough distinction was made between Oronoko and sweet-scented, between Virginia and Maryland, but that was all. Leaf was leaf, and all the "tobacco note" represented was a specified weight of it. By the very nature of the system, picking and choosing grades was the exception rather than the rule.

As small factories began to sprout in the "Tobacco Sack" after the War of 1812, this system no longer sufficed. Individual manufacturers began to buy not just hogsheads but particular hogsheads. Hence the picturesque trumpeter of Lynchburg, announcing that the hogsheads had been broken open for inspection. The official inspector gradually became the auctioneer—in many cases he was one and the same gentleman. Sometimes he was also a leaf merchant. But like the stock exchange broker who is not supposed to mix his customer's interests with buying and selling on his own account, the last function seemed unethical in an objective arbiter of sales, and after a while the role of auctioneer was separated from that of commission dealer.

The original purpose of prizing leaf into tight hogsheads on the farm was for protection in shipping tobacco over long distances (a mile over a "rolling road" was, to all intents, a long ride) and to economize on shipping space. Markets like Richmond, on the edge of the piedmont growing area, continued to do business on a hogshead basis. Markets like Danville and Lynchburg, smack dab in the middle of the tobacco fields, experimented with a loose-leaf type of selling. This was a convenience to the plugmaker who wanted to dress up his quid in choice light wrapper leaf; and it was bread and butter to the planter, who might realize four times as much money for colory tobacco undamaged by prizing and suitable for wrapper as he could from common tobacco bought for filler. The particular

In the Bright leaf country, warehousemen tried to increase their share of the "wagon trade" by paid advertising (above), prizes and barn signs (right).

town where small manufacturer and Bright leaf planter could meet face to face to deal in tobacco was Danville, the only important loose-leaf market before the Civil War.

In Richmond, where manufacturing requirements and leaf sales both mounted into big-volume totals, the custom of "breaks" became cumbersome: it took too long to break open each and every hogshead in its turn. So in that city an Exchange took the place of the auction warehouse. Leaf samples instead of whole hogsheads were inspected to save time and space. This method of selling was an expedient practised mainly in Richmond and New Orleans. The reason for auction sales as against state inspection to a single standard was to permit each manufacturer to do his own inspecting, and the exchange system did not serve this purpose too well.

Today's curing barn resembles the type used since Civil War emergence of flue-cured Bright tobacco. Basic requirements include a supply of fuel, flues to conduct heat without smoke from an outside fire into the barn, vents to let out moisture before it can condense on the hotted-up tobacco and stain it.

In the country towns space was not so much of a problem, and huge sales sheds (which retained the export name of "warehouse") could be erected in central locations. Time was saved by the development of fast-talking auctioneers on the one hand and quick, keen-eyed buyers—"men who know tobacco best"—on the other. The latter were, at first, the small manufacturers themselves who frequented the warehouses throughout most of the year. Their ranks were swelled in the heavy season by speculators skillful enough to turn a slim but fast profit by gauging the ebb and flow of supply and demand. Aware of the dislike of manufacturers for mixed lots, these small dealers could make money by buying up such lots and reclassifying them for more lucrative sale—all done in a few minutes on the warehouse floor. Some of them, called "pinhookers," bought leaf in the street from impatient growers and resold it in the warehouses. These pinhookers were not above scouting the leaf country and frightening farmers into distress selling with rumors of overproduction, disappearance of important buyers from local leaf centers, and the like. The amount of this "barn door buying" was not very great, however. For most farmers it was a matter of pride (plus the fun of a trip to town) to take their chances on the auction floor.

Warehousing in volume was not an unprofitable occupation, since fees were fixed by the hundredweight. Accordingly each proprietor did his best to attract as much of the "wagon trade" as possible to his own establishment. There were three major inducements: a short distance for the farmer to travel; a quick cash payoff; and promotion of the auction house via poster, painted barn messages, and even paid advertisements in periodicals. Of

181

Turn-of-the-century auction was messy by current standards. Tobacco was piled on floor, picked up dirt. Today, the white-haired gentleman squatting on the tobacco would be requested to sit elsewhere.

these the first turned out to be the most important, especially after the hogshead yielded to the carefully-arranged basket of loose leaves. Mahomet went to the mountain, and leaf markets gravitated to small or medium-sized towns in the tobacco country (where they still remain). The big city leaf markets — Richmond, Petersburg, Louisville and Cincinnati—lost their big volume.

After the turn of the century, refinements were added. Loose-leaf sales made literally "on the floor" proved somewhat messy in the day of the horse; baskets were introduced, and these not only got the piles up off the floor but could be quickly whisked out of the way as they were sold, making room for fresh ones wheeled out for sale. The traditional tin bugle gave place to a bell. Sales which were originally spaced somewhat unevenly throughout the twelve months were compressed into a few weeks, buyers making the "circuit" from one market to another and procuring the variegated assortment of types and grades needed in

modern blending and manufacture. This greatly increased the speed of transactions; from a pile-a-minute pace in 1870 the chant of the tobacco auctioneer accelerated to a dizzy rate of a pile every six or ten seconds.

More specialized than the auctioneer himself was the highly trained buyer of "cutters" for use in smoking mixtures and, later, cigarette blends. In a few seconds, with a glance and perhaps a quick brush of his hand, he had to make an estimate of leaf qualities described as "body," "flavor," "finish," "strength," "slickness," "burn," and "aroma," relate these to the needs of his own company, and translate the two into a bid. Instilling the necessary skill and judgment into a leaf-buyer now requires in the neighborhood of five years. Nor is the language of leaf an esoteric mumbo-jumbo without precise meaning: as chemical analysis of tobacco prior to market openings became general, the laboratories confirmed in scientific terms what the buyers had known for decades.

Beginning in 1929 the Department of Agriculture was to recognize up to 60 or more grades in each of seven cigarette leaf types: Burley, Maryland, Georgia Belt, South Carolina Belt, and the Eastern, Middle and Old Belts of North Carolina. Even this wide range of distinctions, though useful in fixing support prices, did not embrace all the shades of difference used by company leaf men.

Mores of tobacco

The complex routine of the auction sale, now an established institution of big business, was built up year by year as part of the everyday "cake of custom." The tidewater leaf inspector, weeding out rotten leaves, became a state official. The state official became an auctioneer as the manufacturer did his own "weeding." The hogshead, built to compress the leaf for stowage and to protect it in transit, gave way to the basket where the manufacturer and planter were not separated by distance, as in antebellum Danville.

Manufacturing itself grew out of day-to-day mores. The twisting of leaf into rope for convenient carrying by Indian, Spanish slave or plains traveler led into the pressed pigtail. Licorice as a preservative evolved into the art of flavoring. Hogshead prizing was duplicated in miniature by the screw press used in plugmaking. Both warehouse and factory are end-results of accumulated experience —in the sociological sense, traditions. The slow

Baskets were introduced to keep the leaf in clean, neat piles. Leaf is now wheeled quickly up to the selling rows, whisked out of the way to speed the auctions. Pace has increased from a pile-a-minute in 1870 to a pile every six to ten seconds today. Judging leaf quality in that time takes training.

Transition from the age of chew to the present tobacco industry was led by three manufacturers. J. R. Green's granulated smoking tobacco spread the fame of Bright leaf; J. B. Duke mechanized cigarette production and organized his company along "big business" lines; R. J. Reynolds made and marketed the first of the "American blends." Their state, North Carolina, became industry hub.

process that made them what they are was a universal one, repeated in many tobacco regions.

Interwoven with this slow growth of tobacco custom was an occasional "invention," accelerating the onward crawl of the leaf industry with a sudden leap. Such inventions seem to have occurred only where there was a great need for them coupled with a conscious awareness of that need. Perhaps Rolfe's experiment with Trinidad or Orinoko seed was the first important one, shifting the tobacco balance from the Antilles to the Atlantic coast. Another came out of the dogged ingenuity of New Englanders forcing their valley land to yield a cigar leaf roughly competitive with that of the favored tropics. But the most impressive series of innovations, the sequence which turned tobacco into big business, took place in the most barren area of all— the Old Bright Belt of Virginia and North Carolina.

In colonial days, this sandy ridge of stunted pine scrub was scornfully dubbed "the land of tar, pitch and pork" by clergymen who preferred their pay in leaf tobacco grown in more fertile parishes. It was nearly abandoned by weary farmers during the westering years; stripped of its thin manpower during the Civil War; disrupted afterward by the emancipation of slave labor and the consequent migration to cities. Still, it was this unpromising pocket among the foothills that led the nation out

of the age of rubbery cud and into the appreciation of light smoking and cigarette grades.

The Old Belt inventions filled three basic needs, the want of which reduced Richmond to second rank in tobacco: better leaf, mechanized production, and efficient distribution.

In a narrow sense, the famous "yaller cure" on the Slade farm in 1839 might be regarded as a mere accident that happened to a dozing slave. Yet the result would have passed unnoticed (as it had during tidewater times) if Caswell and Pittsylvania counties had not been straining hard to produce Bright leaf in every rustic way they knew. Flue-cured Bright was the first American leaf that could be smoked directly — that is, in pipe or cigarette form — by the majority of Americans. Before the spread of flue-curing there was straight chaw for the cast-iron jaw, with syruped quid for queasier palates; and there was harsh northeastern cigar leaf, doused in molasses or rum even for teamsters' tastes but ameliorated with, or replaced by, imported Havana for city connoisseurs.

The cigarette machine was developed in the stress of dog-eat-dog or rather, bull-gore-bull, competition in tiny Durham—not, as might have been expected, in cosmopolitan New York or in proud Richmond. In its train came the mechanical packers, stampers, sealers and baggers which made possible mass consumption of tobacco products and, in broader perspective, led all industry into the age of automation.

And it was the half-deserted land of tar, pitch and pork that seized the golden opportunity to capitalize on golden leaf and new contrivances by creating the image of the national brand. Even the knowledgeable cigar and cigarette firms of New York City, with their alluring premiums and flamboyant drummers, did not achieve this until *Bull Durham* set the example. The tactics and execution of national selling and distribution were perfected, to be sure, in New York; but the strategy was first conceived in Durham. The results tell their own story. The three largest tobacco makers (Reynolds, American and Liggett) make the bulk of their product in Durham, Reidsville and Winston-Salem, and in 1956 another of the large companies (Lorillard) concentrated almost all its manufacturing in nearby Greensboro.

While the quid-conscious Richmond ruminator of 1898 was bewailing the loss of plug prowess in his city, the cigarette business had begun to gather momentum. This momentum had just been checked rather severely by a tripling of the Federal excise from 1c per pack of 20 before August of 1897 to 3c after June of 1898. Half of cigarette production originated in North Carolina and Virginia, a proportion that was to rise to 80% by 1930 and remain at that level through 1960.

Although cigarette making had increased sixfold in sixteen years of machine production, he could not have foreseen that the little white roll would increase a hundredfold in the fifty years to follow. The impetus of that growth had already been generated right under his nose, in the Bright tobacco country. But the cigarette surge was to require, in addition to flue-cured leaf and White Burley from the Ohio Valley, a generous flavoring of New York City enterprise.

Center of bright leaf revolution after the Civil War was Blackwell Bull Durham plant (four-story portion of building above). Granulated straight

Bright tobacco in a sack, Bull Durham was first truly national tobacco brand. The building now is Durham headquarters for American Tobacco Co.

New York has been a prime consumer of tobacco ever since the pipe-smoking Dutch defied a no-smoking edict by Governor Willem Kieft. Alert to foreign fashions, the city rivaled Philadelphia during the snuff and cigar periods and led Americans into the age of the cigarette. It was the nation's selling center and, for a time, top tobacco manufacturer.

THE FLAVOR OF OLD NEW YORK

NEW AMSTERDAM was settled in 1625 by a company of Netherlanders looking for new business. And ever since then, its citizens have continued to look for new consumption goods, both for their own sake and for their business potential. After three centuries, New York is still a giant marketplace whose biggest customer is itself: it is the nation's industrial connoisseur.

It was fitting, therefore, that the first New Yorkers should have been smoking tobacco on their arrival; they did not have to take instruction about it from the Indians, like the settlers who came to the Connecticut Valley a dozen years later. The bustling, business-like Hollanders of the sixteenth and seventeenth centuries who were to give Manhattan its "personality" were quite as enthusiastic as the Spaniards about tobacco, and just as quick to make it a national custom. In 1590, just as the Soverane Herb was penetrating England, Holland was not only puffing the clay pipe but was growing the plant on a large scale. And Dutch merchantmen were crossing the Atlantic to load cargoes of *tabak* for sale in Europe well before the end of the sixteenth century.

Dutch uncles vs. Indians

Like the English under James I, the settlers of New Amsterdam had to contend with a ruler who thought tobacco a waste of time. He was Willem Kieft, director-general of New Amsterdam between 1637 and 1647. Kieft, a soldier of fortune on the order of Captain John Smith, felt belligerancy was the best policy in dealing with the native Indians and earned the sobriquet of William the Testy. In 1639 he issued an arbitrary ban on smoking, whereupon the city's smokers — virtually the entire male population — camped outside Willem's official doorway and produced a massive smoke screen by way of silent protest.

As might be expected, pipe smoking was conspicuous all during the New Amsterdam phase. "The women . . . entertain each other with a pipe and a brazier; young and old, they all smoke." The Dutch lived almost wholly on trade, in which tobacco played its part. Leaf stores came from Connecticut, Massachusetts, Long Island and, of course, Virginia.

Kieft's successor, Peter Stuyvesant, also treated the Indians like a Dutch uncle and, partly because

of the trouble this caused, was forced to yield the city to the English in 1664. Under its new name of New York the city added snuff-taking to its original custom of pipe-smoking. For the next hundred years or so, New York rivaled Philadelphia in such tobacco manufacture as there was. This was a business of little consequence compared with the mammoth exports of the tidewater planters. From the first, however, hogsheads of tobacco were coastered along the seaboard from the Chesapeake estuary and the Carolina inlets. Most of it was reshipped, but enough was put ashore at Philadelphia, New York and Boston — legally and otherwise — to supply the small shops and snuff-mills of those port cities.

Minimized manufacture

The Crown's imperial policy did not favor colonial manufacturing activity, however, and most of the snuff inhaled by its American subjects in New York and elsewhere was made in Scotland.

In 1760, about the time Gilbert Stuart's Rhode Island snuff mill was forced to shut down, Pierre Lorillard, a French Huguenot emigre, established a tobacco business in New York City on the high road to Boston at Chatham Street, near Tryon Row, and the present P. Lorillard Company traces to this beginning. At that time New York's small tobacco shops were not entirely dependent on their own manufactures, since they were retail houses primarily. Possibly for this reason, this type of business was still thriving after the Revolution, and some added substantial factories to their retail establishments. During the early 1800s their principal manufactured product became chewing tobacco. Later emphasis was shifted to cigars, to pipe tobacco, and, after 1880, to cigarettes.

As in Virginia and New England, the rise of manufacturing establishments in New York and Philadelphia began with the departure of the King's men. Ten years after the Treaty of Paris, when Congress was weighing the question of excise taxes on tobacco, one Samuel Russel of New York City submitted this information on behalf of the city's manufacturers:

The price of tobacco by the hogshead, in New

York, is four-pence one farthing per pound. . . . This is cash; no credit ever being given on leaf-tobacco, in any part of America. The expence of work is two-pence three farthings per pound, on what is called spun or plug tobacco; only two-thirds of the leaf, on an average, can be made into this kind of tobacco. The loss in stems and dirt will amount to one penny per pound. Every pound of good plug tobacco, therefore, costs the manufacturer eight-pence per pound; and the general selling price is nine-pence. . . . This leaves a profit to the manufacturer of twelve and an half per cent out of which he must pay shop-rent and be supported. The remaining one third is made into the coarser kinds. . . . The profits on this part, are not far from thirteen per cent.

It is significant that Russel, while speaking for both snuff and tobacco manufacturers, emphasizes the "spun or plug tobacco," which was the all-purpose ropelike twist made on a tobacco wheel. Snuff

was obviously ground from the scrap residue, including the stem, and the tenor of Russel's report indicates that it was declining in importance as early as 1794.

These were the years of great rivalry between New York and Philadelphia, in tobacco-making and in almost every other form of enterprise. Throughout the entire colonial period, New York had run a distinct second to the City of Brotherly Love. Now, however, New York was overtaking its rival as America's No. 1 commercial city. A visiting French politician named Charles Maurice de Talleyrand-Perigord, who was to achieve considerable fame as Napoleon's foreign minister, cast his objective eye on the reasons: "Its good and convenient harbor, which is never closed by ice, its central position to which large rivers bring the products of the whole country, appear to me to be decisive advantages. Philadelphia is too buried in the land

Philadelphia preceded New York City as political, cultural, commercial capital of America. In "Old London Coffee House," men like Benjamin Franklin and Thomas Jefferson discussed state policy. Later the place housed one of the numerous tobacco firms which made Philadelphia the leading tobacco center.

Erie Canal, brainchild of Governor DeWitt Clinton, spurred development of New York as leading commercial city. Opened in 1826, "Clinton's Ditch" linked New York with Buffalo and the rich Great Lakes area. Fifty years afterward, picture of Clinton appeared on the federal cigarette excise tax stamp.

and especially too inaccessible to wood of all sorts. Boston is too much at the extremity of the country, does not have enough flour, and has not a large enough outlet for the commodities of the West Indies, except molasses."

Clinton's Ditch

The one factor — if one can be isolated — which insured New York's rise to pre-eminence was the Erie Canal, opened in 1826. At once, the city on the Hudson became the natural outlet for the produce of upper New York State and all the states bordering on the Great Lakes. It was to the Canal that New York owed its victory over Philadelphia; and it was to the indefatigable DeWitt Clinton that the Canal owed its existence. The national Congress was indifferent to the waterway, which became a state project. Clinton never emerged as a national political figure, having left the U. S. Senate to become Mayor of New York City and then Governor of New York State. He was an avid follower of Jefferson and Jackson, although he died in 1828 before he could share in the fruits of Old Hickory's victory. More important, he had a vigorous faith in America's future, rejoiced in the passing of the powdered hair and cocked hat, and devoted his personal funds to the drive for a canal, 363 miles long, from Buffalo to Albany. Like his fellow Americans of that rude but patriotic period, he was full of enthusiasm, encouraged Robert Fulton and his steamboat, John Jacob Astor and his fur trade, was active in founding the College of Physicians and Surgeons. He took the inevitable jeers about "Clinton's Ditch" while the canal was under construction and died, $6,000 in debt, only two years after the "wedding of the waters" of Atlantic and Lake Erie. His great project benefited not only the tobacco trade but commercial traffic of all kinds; and his

Tobacco & Snuff of the beſt quality & flavor,
At the Manufactory, No.4, Chatham ſtreet, near the Gaol
By Peter and George Lorillard,
Where may be had as follows :

Cut tobacco,	Prig or carrot do.
Common kitefoot do.	Maccuba ſnuff,
Common ſmoaking do.	Rappee do.
Segars do.	Straſburgh do.
Ladies twiſt do.	Common rappee do.
Pigtail do. in ſmall rolls,	Scented rappee do. of dif-
Plug do.	ferent kinds,
Hogtail do.	Scotch do.

The above Tobacco and Snuff will be ſold reaſonable, and warranted as good as any on the continent. If not found to prove good, any part of it may be returned, if not damaged.
N. B. Proper allowance will be made to thoſe that purchaſe a quantity.   May 27—1m.

Dated May 27, 1789, this is the oldest known adver-tisement of the P. Lorillard Company, which began as a New York house. The list of products reflects the eighteenth century's emphasis on pipe smoking and snuff. There is also a reference to the cigar.

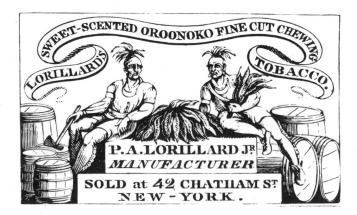

Trade card of same company in early 1800s dropped references to snuff and pipe tobacco, concentrated on its new line leader, fine cut chewing tobacco. During the nineteenth century Americans—includ-ing New Yorkers—took to sweet chew in a big way. Chewing became a distinctly American custom.

190

memorial was struck off in Washington fifty years after Clinton's Ditch was opened. In 1876 his image was selected for the new Federal tobacco tax stamp, and was part of every package of cigarettes during the next eighty-two years.

Along with its dominance of Atlantic trade came New York's leadership as a cultural entrepôt; even in the early 1800s, country folk journeyed to the Big Town for a once-in-a-lifetime fling. Restaurants, theaters, good hotels were logical by-products of the swelling commercial stream. In their tobacco habits, Gothamites were "urban" from the first: cigars are almost as prominent in accounts of New York life during the Era of Good Feeling as chew, although the constant salivation induced by the latter did not escape comment by foreign visitors to the city. Even in the theater, noted Mrs. Frances Trollope — first of a long line of English critics of American manners — men kept their hats on during the performance and expectorated frequently.

In 1839 a London writer described Americans and tobacco as follows, putting the cigar on a par with chewing tobaccos:

The Americans, who pride themselves on being the fastest-going people on the "versal globe" — who build steamers that can out-paddle the sea-serpent and breed horses that can trot faster than an ostrich can run — are, undoubtedly, entitled to take precedence of all nations as consumers of the weed. The sedentary Turk, who smokes from morn to night, does not, on an average, get through so much tobacco per annum, as a right slick, active, go-ahead Yankee, who thinks nothing, "upon his own relation," of felling a wagon-load of timber before breakfast, or of cutting down a couple of acres corn before dinner. The Americans, it is to be observed, generally smoke cigars; and tobacco in this form burns very fast in the open air, more especially when the consumer is rapidly locomo-tive, whether upon his own legs, the back of a horse, the top of a coach, the deck of a steamboat, or in an open railway carriage. The habit of chew-ing tobacco is also prevalent in "the States," nor is it, as in Great Britain and Ireland, almost en-tirely confined to the poorer classes. Members of the House of Representatives and of the Senate, doctors, judges, barristers, and attorneys chew tobacco almost as generally as the laboring classes in the old country. Even in a court of justice, more especially in the Western States, it is no unusual thing to see judge, jury, and the gentlemen of the bar, all chewing and spitting as liberally as the crew of a homeward-bound West Indiaman. It

COURTESIES OF THE WEED.

Even before Mexican and Civil Wars, cigar-smoking was a common custom among all classes of New York residents. Philadelphia still produced more cigars.

Philadelphia ad addressed gents and ladies of taste, emphasized Havana segars, Lynchburg smoking tobacco and Turkish, mentioned no brand names.

must indeed be confessed that Brother Jonathan loves tobacco "not wisely but too well," and that the habits which are induced by his manner of using it are far from "elegant." The truth is, he neither smokes nor chews like a gentleman; he lives in a land of liberty, and takes his tobacco when and where he pleases . . .

Manufacture maximized

Cosmopolitan in its tobacco manufacture as in everything else, New York was quick to take its cue from General Israel Putnam after his return to Connecticut with Havana cigars in 1762. Three years afterward cigars (but not Havana cigars) were made for sale in the city. Early in the nineteenth century, a brisk import traffic in cigars made of Dutch and German leaf sprang up; the market for these were seamen and the European immigrants who were beginning to trickle into the port. The obvious inadequacy of these rank tobacco sticks no doubt stimulated New Yorkers to get into

cigar-rolling, using the conveniently-situated and better leaf from Connecticut Valley farms. The early rivalry with Philadelphia in snuff was replaced by a more frenzied competition in cigars, both cities using immigrant labor to advantage as the rolling-rooms multiplied. Skilled German cigar-makers were prominent among the new arrivals during the "Era of Good Feeling." By the outbreak of Civil War, Philadelphia was still the leading cigar city with a slight advantage over New York in value of output, $1,240,000 as against $1,100,000. New York's cigar output alone in 1860 was almost exactly equal in dollar value to all the manufactured tobacco made in North Carolina. And the extent of the cigar craze is shown by the dispersal of manufacture into any town with capital to support an establishment holding three or four rollers and their workbenches. In 1860 $9 million worth of cigars were made throughout the nation, as against $21 million worth of chewing and smoking tobacco. Forty years later,

Lilienthal factory in lower Manhattan was typical tobacco plant of the pre-Civil War era. Trademarks were conspicuously absent from both the plant and its trade card, although the firm turned out many types of tobacco product. Under "Tobacco" at left, the main emphasis was placed on chewing mixtures.

cigars were grossing more than $160 million a year and manufactured tobacco about $90 million. Although these amounts included over $50 million in federal excise taxes, which were not in effect in 1860, the increase even without taxes was staggering.

Despite its prominence in all types of tobaccomaking, New York's principal contribution to the industry was its selling enterprise. Its factors received half of the tobacco goods made in Virginia and North Carolina, re-distributing them to wholesalers throughout the nation. Southern dependence on these factors, with their "fancy stocks, fine houses and fast teams," was keenly resented in Richmond and other Bright manufacturing cities,

but the fact remained that New York was the country's distribution headquarters for tobacco and most everything else.

Port of export

The War Between the States gave New York an extra impetus as a tobacco town by closing the port of New Orleans to western growers. European buyers shifted their locus of operations from that city to New York, which for a while became the principal port of exit for western tobacco shipped by rail from Louisville and Cincinnati. In the years following the war, more than 80,000 hogsheads of the western crop alone were annually shipped to New York.

P. Lorillard

The biggest single factor in the metropolitan area's massive tobacco output — and the oldest as well — was the Lorillard firm. Begun in Manhattan in 1760, Lorillard was one of the only two pre-revolutionary snuff mills in the colonies to survive British opposition to colonial manufacture. During the release of manufacturing activity which followed the Treaty of Paris, Pierre Lorillard built a new snuff mill on the banks of the Bronx River. Over the years this installation was expanded to include workmen's cottages, a warehouse, facilities for packing smoking tobacco, and the Lorillard family mansion. The latter was surrounded by riding trails and set in an "Acre of Roses," some of which were used to perfume the family's snuff brands. The original wooden mill was replaced in 1840 by a granite structure, still standing in the Bronx Botanical Gardens.

Changes in the national taste were mirrored by Lorillard's changing product mix. As snuff was superseded by the national stampede to "eatin' tobacco," Lorillard's emphasis shifted from the Bronx River mill to a new giant factory across the Hudson, and from snuff-and-smokum to sweet plug. In this respect, Lorillard's evolution paralleled that of the four Virginia plug towns of the antebellum years — from all-purpose tobacco or bulk chew to molded lumps and thence to flat plug.

With its ideal Jersey City location, Lorillard had a head start into the era of mass-produced national brands, which got under way after the Civil War. During the late 1870s the huge Jersey City plant accounted for nearly 10% of all manufactured tobacco made in the U. S. — nearly as much plug as Richmond's total, three times as much as New York's. Lorillard's plug grades were identified as the *Climax, Bullion, Sailors' Delight, Mechanics' Delight, Catawba, Red Cross, Green Turtle, Army & Navy* brands, each plug "branded" with a colored and printed tin tag pronged into it.

In 1885 "Leslie's Weekly" told its readers that the Lorillard Jersey City factories covered five acres and included a 15,000-volume library and 350-child schoolrooom "for the free use of the army of about four thousand persons employed in their immense tobacco establishment." The payroll was a large one: the census of 1880 had counted the total number of tobacco "hands" in the U. S. — men,

After Civil War, brand names counted. Lorillard, whose Jersey City plant made 10% of manufactured tobacco in U.S., branded its plug with tin tags.

women and children — at 86,000 (32,700 in manufactured tobacco, 53,300 in cigars and cigarettes).

During the postbellum years, Lorillard's line reflected the trend to smoking tobaccos as well as the headlong increase in tin tag plug. By 1890 only the enormous Liggett & Myers plug factory in St. Louis outproduced Lorillard in total poundage. But Lorillard even then was turning out more smokings than plug, and was one of the five U. S. companies to exceed a million pounds a year in snuff. In addition the company was participating in the upsurge of cigar production under such brand names as *Sweet Moments, Old Virginia Cheroots, Lillian Russell* and, later, *Muriel* and *Van Bibber.*

By 1906 Lorillard production was in the 25,000,-

Peter Lorillard, son of Pierre, built this stone snuff-mill in 1840 to replace a wooden structure erected in the 1780s. Still standing, the mill got waterpower from the Bronx River to turn its wheels.

000-pounds-a-year class — about equal to the total output of Winston or Durham, but still outpaced by the massive plug poundage of St. Louis or Louisville. The total included about 8,000,000 pounds of navy plug, 14,000,000 pounds of smoking tobaccos, *Union Leader* and *Sensation* being its principal brands, and nearly 3,000,000 pounds of fine-cut chewing, including the *Tiger* and *Century* brands.

Between 1898 and 1911, Lorillard was part of the tobacco combination. When this was dissolved, the company would emerge without its snuff brands, but with about the same volume of navy plug and fine-cut chewing, an increased smoking tobacco business of 40,000,000 pounds a year

(25% of national output), plus the cigarette brands of the Anargyros plant in New York City. These brands, including *Egyptian Deities*, *Mogul*, *Murad*, *Helmar*, and *Turkish Trophies*, represented about 20% of U. S. production in 1913. With later cigarette brands, they would enable Lorillard to reflect, in every era, the 200-year evolution of American tobacco manufacturing.

Top tobacco town

If the postbellum revival of manufacturing was satisfactory in Virginia, rapid in North Carolina, and steady in the western states, it was phenomenal in New York. By 1880 the big town was producing four times as many cigars as its erstwhile rival, Philadelphia; one out of every three brown rolls were made in New York, a huge proportion for a hand-labor industry. In terms of total poundage, more than a fifth of all American tobacco products were processed in the metropolitan area, including the plug tobacco factories across the Hudson in Jersey City. (Richmond's manufacturing share was one tenth, virtually all of it plug.)

If there was any single reason for New York's unlikely emergence as the nation's top tobacco town, it was the place's pre-eminence in selling. Here the arts of persuasion and communication (perhaps two words for the same thing) were developed as nowhere else. With thousands of hogsheads of leaf entering the city, it was inevitable

Around the century's turn, product mix ran to more smoking than chewing tobacco — a national trend.

194

that those with capital to invest should put two and two together to get a return of five. Leaf tobacco and manufacturing capital were both available in quantity; joined with energetic salesmen and willing pieceworkers, also available, four dollars' outlay would bring in five. Although Southern factory towns were nearer the source of supply, they were short in two of the four terms in the big business equation — able salesmen and cash. Furthermore tobacco consumption, while still on the rise, was in a state of flux: cigars were on the gallop, smoking was resuming its old primacy (aided by the invention of the friction match) while the Southern mainstay, plug, was fighting a losing battle—beset by the cigar surge on the one hand, and by the growth of western plug towns on the other. (In 1880 St. Louis ranked behind Richmond but ahead of Lynchburg, Petersburg and Danville in the production of quid; Louisville ranked behind Lynchburg and Petersburg but ahead of Danville; Alton, Illinois and Middletown, Ohio were close behind.)

For New York, the new

Perhaps the most revealing statistics among the postbellum figures were not in total poundage of New York production but in its breakdown. Always interested in the new, in growth potential, the New York manufacturers of 1880 were almost completely uninterested in plug — virtually all their production was in straight smoking tobacco or "fine-cut chewing" suitable for either mouth or pipe. (Most of the metropolitan area's considerable chewing tobacco output was made in Jersey City.) Cigarettes were not yet important enough to rate a separate classification as to leaf poundage used; yet New York City alone was turning out 60% of the little white rolls. The term "manufacturer" could hardly be applied in connection with cigars, which were made in hundreds of small shops rather than in a few large factories.

One of the most important New York manufacturers was D. H. McAlpin, founded well before the Civil War. Like most early tobaccomen in the city,

Selling rather than manufacturing was New York's forte. The arts of communication were quickly put to commercial use, as exemplified by the Currier and Ives trade card lithographed in the "classic" manner for Champion cigars. New York sold not only its own products but also tobacco made in Richmond.

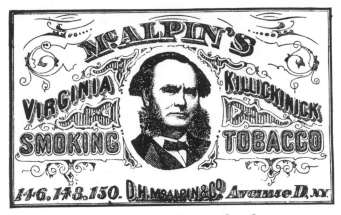

D. H. McAlpin of New York capitalized on new taste for "long cut" both for chewing and pipe smoking. Two time-tested words made successful brand name of big seller: "Virginia," an old synonym for the best tobacco, and "Killickinick," from the generic Indian term kinnikinnick, signifying tobacco blend.

THE PLEASURES OF TOBACCO,

To which young and promising TOM SMUDGER abandons himself. He wasteth the midnight oil, quantities of Killikinick, and himself simultaneously.

McAlpin started out as a retailer-manufacturer and had a shop, complete with cigar store Indian, on Catherine Street. In the flowering of manufactured tobacco brands that followed Appomattox, McAlpin did not join the plug stampede but concentrated on two specialties — a fine-cut chewing tobacco trademarked *Virgin Leaf*, and a line of smoking tobaccos including a *Virginia Killickinick* brand. These names were not particularly original but they were shrewdly selected. "Virginia" was a standard synonym for fine tobacco (in Europe it remains so although the word "Bright" has more or less replaced it in this country). *Killickinick* had found wide acceptance as the romantic Indian word for a pipe mixture and as the brand name of Maurice Moore's Lynchburg smokum. On a modest scale

McAlpin's choice of products and choice of words was quite successful, the firm attaining a volume of more than 2,000,000 pounds a year by the Gay Nineties — this poundage being comparable to that of important Richmond firms like Mayo and Patterson.

Cigarmaking was more specific to New York than manufactured tobacco production: the census of 1880 credited the city with $4,320,972 worth of manufactured tobacco produced, a modest 8% of the national total. In "cigars and cigarettes" — the latter, then hand-rolled, being a negligible number —New York turned out $18,347,108 worth of product, nearly 30% of the national output. Furthermore, New York City listed only 17 manufactured tobacco establishments as against 761 cigarmakers.

Nevertheless, cigarmaking was still distinctly small business while tobacco manufacture was big enterprise. In value of product the smoking and chewing factories averaged $2,700 per employee in 1880; the average cigar worker turned out only $1,200 worth of goods during the same year.

It is worth noting, from the standpoint of pure business efficiency, that New York City produced 8% of the total U. S. dollar value of manufactured tobacco even though it boasted only 3% of the nation's smoking, chewing and snuff factories and only 5% of the nation's employees in those categories. No such efficiency was reflected in the statistics for cigars: New York's dollar output was no greater as a percentage of the U. S. total than either its share of persons employed in cigarmaking or its share of cigar shops—a little less than 30% in each case.

One of the reason's for the higher quality of the Big Town's operations in the manufactured tobacco field was the fact, already mentioned, that its turnout of higher-priced fine-cut chews and smokings was relatively heavy and its production of cheap plug relatively light. By the same token, the statistics indicate that New York's cigar products did not command higher-than-average prices. The average cigar made in New York in 1880 was worth about 3c—about the same as the general U. S. average.

In making a new product go, part of the motive power is consumer pull — demand — and part of it is manufacturer's push — selling. That New York somehow attracted the best selling talent, the Southern manufacturers had conceded long before Sumter. This became even more evident in the upward rush of production and consumption during the Gilded Age. As a shipping and manufacturing center, New York was well placed to supply the salesman — particularly the cigar and cigarette salesman — with quantities of the cheap brummagems which were useful not only as premiums but also as conversation pieces: pictures, running to sports figures and "leg art"; wall lighters; cigar cutters; razors; flags; and matches (which are still used). It should be noted that the most valuable of these premiums did not go to the consumer but to the wholesale and retail trade as rewards for stocking the manufacturer's brand. The consumer's usual reward for buying the brand was a lithographed picture card (which did double duty as a stiffener for the flimsy slide-and-shell box). This was supplemented by silk flags, and by picture albums and catalogued premiums exchanged for box-fronts or enclosed coupons. The role of the florid-faced, extroverted backslapper — the city slicker — in breaking down preferences for local brands within the trade was indispensable in building national brands. This in turn was the indispensable prelude to mass production which, with its attendant improvement in quality and reduction of price, is the classic American formula for improvement in living standards.

New York's chief contribution to the tobacco industry was in wholesaling, now called distribution. It was, to be sure, a key manufacturing town between 1780 and 1930, during the successive eras of snuff, cigars, mass-produced plug, smoking tobacco and cigarettes. But except in size, it did not differ as a making center from any of the hundred-odd cities which jumped on the cigar bandwagon, or from quid and smokum centers like Detroit and Chicago, or early cigarette towns like Rochester and San Francisco. Like other sizable cities, New York represented a compact market as well as a labor pool and its retail tobacco trade was a highly visible indication of this.

The urban environment itself has always been accompanied by a heightened demand for tobacco. Cities are characterized by a fast pace of living, by tensions, artificiality and a lack of the earthy, the natural, the primitive. Tobacco seems to supply part of this missing element, and the trade sensed this. The London apothecaries did their part in the

The cigar had a prominent place in New York City's "stream of consciousness." Above, one of the many humorous allusions to President Grant's customary preoccupation, captioned: "The General's resource at any emergency—smoke." Below, a prophetic sign from the Presidential campaign of 1880. As poster predicted, Americans did indeed see Garfield win.

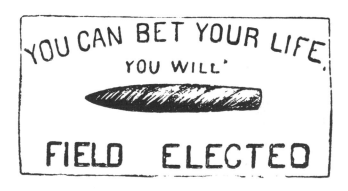

early 1600s to romanticize the mysterious "heathen wound plant." So did the wholesalers and retailers of New York; in the 1870s and 1880s many of them adorned their invoice forms with the "Great Spirit" woodcut reproduced on page 26. By that time the Indian was being hunted down in the West and a nostalgic image of him and his ways (assumed to be vanishing forever) grew up in the eastern cities. Tobacco, of course, had long been associated with the noble savage and it was merely good sales psychology to keep the association alive.

Sidewalks of New York

The most prominent manifestations of this commercialized *mystique* were the wooden Indians stationed outside the tobacco shops. At one time the

U. S. population of pine redmen — perhaps 100,000 — was nearly one-half that of living Amerinds. In New York during the postbellum years, the wooden Indian was a symbol as standard as barbers' poles and decidedly more numerous.

The story of the tobacco trade can almost be told in the evolution of the cigar store Indian. The first known wooden Indians were those of London, which appeared shortly after Rolfe's first commercial shipment of leaf. They were not American Indians at all but black men in feather headdresses and girdles of tobacco leaves, confusing the earliest purveyors of tobacco — the African slaves brought by the Spaniards to Santo Domingo — with the native Indians of Virginia. During the next century, as the Scotch entered the tobacco trade and built their reputation as snuffmakers, the tobacconist identified his place of business with a statue of a kilted Highlander. The turbaned Turk appeared with the vogue for aromatic Middle East leaf, first in London and later in New York. The true likeness of the American Indian became common in cities east of the Mississippi around 1840, by which time most of the redskins were being deported west of that river into Indian Territory. In every age most tobacco store figures were exotic ones foreign to everyday life, symbolizing the enchantment of faraway lands and so connoting the mystery and enchantment of tobacco.

These silent salesmen were not entirely symbolic. Most of them held out one or more tobacco products to catch the eye of the passersby. The early English tobacco boys—"Pomfreys," they were nicknamed—grasped a bunch of tobacco leaves in one hand and a pipe in the other. The next figure in historical sequence was a wooden Scotsman with tam-o'-shanter, kilt and bare knees, often holding a wooden snuff box. The great majority of cigar store Indians carved in the U. S. between 1840 and 1890 proferred a bunch of wooden cigars. Now and then art prevailed over commercial display and the cigars were omitted where they seemed inappropriate: in the hands of the wooden baseball player, a bat replaced the cigars. Some statues were made to hold a dagger, tomahawk or musket, holes having been carved in their fists to provide for the insertion of such weapons.

The wholesale multiplication of brands that followed the Civil War was accompanied by a widened variety of shop statues, although nine out of every ten were still Indians. In addition to the throngs of Pocahontases and peering braves there were buckskinned pioneers and trappers, cavaliers, ladies of fashion, sailors, baseball players, minstrel characters, historical figures like Raleigh or Washington, and even famous clergymen. One of the most popular types in New York was a beckoning Punch with

Typical New York tobacconist of early 1900s was a combination retailer and manufacturer. Indian was mounted on wheels, whisked inside at closing time.

a fat paunch and leer to match. Most show figures were carved in white pine; often they were made from lengths of discarded ship spars and masts by ship carvers who turned from figureheads to trade signs as steam replaced sail. As might be imagined, they were highly prized not only by the shopkeepers who owned them but by passing lovers of folk art who sometimes swept the silent wooden figures off their feet in an irresistible frenzy of kleptomania. Those not kidnapped outright usually lost to passing admirers their noses or the tomahawks doweled into their wooden fists. Tobacconists in large cities took to chaining their cigar-bearing sentinels to the outside wall, or mounting them on rollers to be wheeled indoors at nightfall.

After the Civil War cigar store Indians began to

Sidewalks of New York were populated with wooden cavaliers and turbaned Turks, though nine of ten figures were Indians. Metal brave (right) was cast in New York; a heavier figure was harder to steal, but arrow was missing from right hand hole. This model was said to have been Longfellow's favorite.

199

be cast in metal. There were three reasons for this. First, a metal Indian was harder to carry off — heavier than wood, and more readily anchored in the concrete sidewalk outside the shop. Second, cast iron was a characteristic material of the early Industrial Era, not only for utilitarian machinery but also for decorations of many kinds, from lawn urns to ornamental fretwork. And third, the upsurge in manufactured tobacco products and in retail shops to sell them increased the demand for figures beyond the capacity of the limited supply of woodcarvers. The Demuth firm of New York City specialized in "show figures," both wooden and cast metal, and tried by means of advertising to extend their use from tobacconists to druggists, notion stores, theaters and even banks. Operating on the new principles of mass production, Demuth espe-

cially pushed his metal figures, many of which could be formed with the same mold. His most famous product was the so-called "Longfellow Indian," a noble brave with bear-claw necklace, strap-iron bow in one hand and a separate metal arrow inserted into a hole in the other. One of these stood guard before a cigar establishment on the Boston-Cambridge road and was said to be greatly admired by Henry Wadsworth Longfellow, who had written "Hiawatha" in 1855. But even Longfellow's iron redman was not vandal-proof, for most surviving specimens have been relieved of bow, arrow, or both.

The same urbanization which created a mass market for cast metal Indians thickened street traffic and thereby halted the increase in the metal-Indian tribe almost as soon as it began. City ordinances made him an outlaw, a sidewalk obstruction. Like his living prototype, the cigar store Indian was crowded out by the white men.

Between 1840 and 1910 or so, the stolid cigar store Indian did not signify retailing exclusively. Many a small shop retailed well-known brands of chew, smoking tobacco and cigarettes up front and rolled its own brand of cigar in the backroom. These shops (see cut, page 198) were a transitional stage between the era of farm manufacture and the era of national brands. Cigar-making made possible the existence of these retail outlets in vast numbers, not only in New York but in other cities, for the cigar was the last form to be mass-produced by machine and thus the last to enter the national brand phase.

The boys in the backroom

Not that the exuberant release of free enterprise was a pure picnic: before the happy plateau of brand land was achieved, many a vale of tears had to be crossed. One of these was the crowding of the underpaid backroom bunchers in the cigar shops— "sweatshops" as they (and other piecework establishments) were called. The cigar workers who plied their trade at home — most were not skilled rollers but turned out "molded" cigars—were in an even worse plight. Often the landlord who rented them tenement quarters, and the factory-owner who paid them barely enough for rent and subsistence, were one and the same person. In fact, by distributing the work to the cigar rollers in their own

Figure of Punch was a special favorite in New York.

Cleaner than the average turn-of-the-century cigar establishment was this dingy New York loft. There were 20,000 such workrooms throughout the nation.

Of every dollar spent on tobacco, cigars accounted for 60c. Brand names were many and magnificent but did not carry any assurance of consistent quality.

Worse off than backroom bunchers were home cigar workers. Families like this one worked each day as long as light permitted. Boy at right uses curved blade to slice wrapper from tobacco leaf; worker at left does not literally roll cigars but shapes them in mold, a cheap, relatively unskilled method.

"homes," the shrewd operator was able to avoid much of the heat, light, floor space and other costs of a legitimate manufacturing business. The New York cigar-makers went on strike for higher wages in 1864; however, it was not the employees of sizable factories but the piece-workers at home who needed help. Their workweek extended during all the daylight hours, every day, for which week many rollers earned $8.00 or even less. Into this unfortunate situation in 1863 came a young immigrant cigar-maker named Samuel Gompers; stung to action by what he found, Gompers managed to interest a New York assemblyman, Theodore Roosevelt, in remedial legislation. Laws were passed, and later thrown out by the courts; but Gompers, who went on to found the American Federation of Labor, is credited with making a progressive out of the well-born Theodore Roosevelt.

Even this dingy phase in the history of cigar-making contributed in its way to the history of human freedom. From 1880 through 1895, New York was the headquarters of José Martí, guiding genius of the Cuban revolution against Spain. Like any self-respecting Cuban, Martí was in love with cigars; to him a tobacco plant was a "delicate lady" to be protected and cared for, the cigar a companion of loneliness. But the cigar rollers played a more practical part in his revolutionary planning. The reading-tables of workrooms not only in Havana but also in Tampa, Key West and New York, were "pulpits of liberty." From refugee cigar workers in these American cities Martí received not only

Samuel Gompers, an immigrant cigar roller, headed drive for better working conditions in the trade, finally founded the American Federation of Labor.

Theodore Roosevelt, a New York state assemblyman, was sympathetic to Gompers' movement, introduced legislation to eliminate sweated tenement labor.

moral support but ten percent of their weekly earnings. When the plans for revolution were completed in 1895, the order to rebel was sent from Key West to Havana rolled in a cigar.

Cigarette city

All this had a foreign flavor to it; and whatever might be said on the Fourth of July about "the melting pot," each successive wave of immigrants tended to be despised and ignored by the previous one. Yet it was this very foreign flavor that made New York first the test market, then the manufacturing center, and finally the financial capitol of the industry based on the most universal tobacco form of all: the American cigarette.

A distinctive American cigarette was not to emerge until 1913, but the groundwork was laid by New Yorkers who, more than most Americans, were sensitive to foreign influences. Originally a Central American custom, cigarette smoking was observed in New Mexico by the rugged trappers and traders who opened the Santa Fe trail, early in the nineteenth century. But the cigarette was to arrive in New York by a more devious route. The starting point can be placed in Seville, the world's first tobacco manufacturing capitol. In that ancient "clear Havana" town, cigarettes were a poor man's by-product of the lordly cigar — scraps of discarded cigar butt wrapped in a scrap of paper. So it appears that the first use of paper to wrap a cigarette (instead of cornhusk or hollow reed in the Aztec mode) was a pure expedient: paper was at that time a city

Cuban rollers were "cigartists," differed from the unskilled molders of New York City. They hired a workroom reader (center, elevated) to keep them up on politics. Dedicated to freedom, many emigrated to the factories of New York and Tampa, used their wages to finance Cuba's revolution against Spain.

Exotic origin and aromatic flavor of Turkish leaf gave the cigarette its first appeal for Americans. British soldiers "discovered" Turkish cigarettes dur- *ing Crimean War of 1854-56, set up a demand for them in London. Leaf was (and still is) lightered in small boats to ships anchored off Turkish coast.*

item, and the cigarette also remained a city item until the twentieth century. During most of the seventeenth and eighteenth centuries the Sevillian *papalete* was a beggar's smoke, ascending the social ladder sometime before 1800 and moving to Portugal, Italy and South Russia. In Brazil it was called *papelito;* in Spain, *papalete* or *cigarillo;* in Italy, where the product was larger than we know it, a paper cigar. The French monopoly, or *Regie,* began its manufacture in 1843 and the word "cigarette" is of French origin. Drawings of French cigarette girls and French "ordering" or conditioning cylinders for tobacco were published in New York weeklies before the American cigarette industry itself became the subject of the engraver's art. It may have been known in England shortly thereafter, for in an 1854 letter to a British friend Charles Dickens asked for

cigarettes (although he might have meant small cigars). It was certainly known in New York around that year, for in 1854 one Dr. R. T. Trall observed that

> some of the *ladies* of this refined and fashion-forming metropolis are aping the silly ways of some pseudo-accomplished foreigners, in smoking Tobacco through a weaker and more *feminine* article, which has been most delicately denominated cigarette.

The taste for Turkish

The new mode did not catch on as quickly as the alarmed Dr. Trall appeared to fear: America was still in the throes of its fascination with the cigar, still had its mouth full of quid. But it made some headway in England after the Crimean War of 1854-56. There the French and Turkish used them,

Tiny leaves of Turkish tobacco—grown in Balkans, Greece and Turkey—are cured in the sun, threaded or "manipulated" tediously onto strings by hand.

small-leaved and extremely aromatic. At first it was the pungent flavor of this unique tobacco, redolent of the mysterious Orient, that gave the cigarette or *papalete* its appeal. In 1854, a veteran of Crimea named Robert Gloag experimented with a cigarette mixture poked into pre-formed paper tubes in the French manner. He is credited with opening the first full-fledged British cigarette factory in 1856, his early product bearing the cryptic name *Sweet Threes*. In the late 1850s a London tobacco merchant named Philip Morris — whose business had been established in the early part of the decade — went into the manufacturing of hand-made cigarettes to order. Later, when production techniques permitted, the Philip Morris firm introduced a cork tip. Both Gloag's and Morris' cigarettes were distinguished by the use of Latakia, a smoke-cured variety of Turkish tobacco. Intrigued by this exotic incense of the Middle East, both Bond Street and Fifth Avenue took up the cigarette as a novelty.

Even with the fashionable example set by the British, and even with the exotic appeal of the words "Turkish" and "Egyptian", the cigarette probably would not have registered with the New York market except for the unusual fragrance of the Turkish leaf. New York had been exposed to cigarettes before the French or British took them up, in the course of its heavy cigar trade with Cuba. On that island, *cigarillos* wrapped with cotton paper had been in use for nearly two hundred years. But the strong cigar leaf used in "Spanish whiffs" did not yield the light smoke that the form seems to require (in Cuba today, as in many countries, dark cigar leaf is still used in cigarettes out of necessity: light American cigarette grades will not grow in Cuban soil and imported American brands, though preferred, are too expensive for the average man after duty is added).

probably rolling their own, while the Russian enemy smoked cigarettes made in a St. Petersburg factory. There seem to be two reasons why British officers took up the cigarette: (1) pipes did not stand up under the rigors of the campaign and cigars were not to be had; and (2) the tobacco available to both sides was the Turkish leaf, mild,

Foreign flavor of the New York market showed in demand for cigarettes like the straight Turkish Mogul and for cigars like El Principe de Gales, a   *clear Havana. Although New York was a quantity producer of snuff, plug and smoking tobacco, its big specialty was cigar and cigarette production.*

Bright idea

Revenue statistics show confusing variations in cigarette manufacture during the years immediately after the Civil War. The rather high figure for 1865 — nearly 20,000,000 — which was the first reported may indicate that substantial production began during the war years. At any rate, the earliest manufacturing of any consequence was done by hand in New York shops operated by Greek and Turkish immigrants (Greece and Turkey being the chief sources of "Turkish" tobacco). One such shop, run by the Bedrossian brothers, first used American Bright tobacco in cigarettes sometime before 1870. The innovation did not escape notice by the alert New Yorkers one of whom, F. S. Kinney, imported European rollers in 1869 to teach his factory people how to make cigarettes. In the same year Kinney began cigarette production in Richmond; the large factory he built there in 1886 is still standing, having been renovated in 1930 for use as a stemmery by one of today's largest cigarette manufacturers. Like most of the other early cigarettemen, Kinney blended the expensive Turkish leaf with Bright tobacco, which at that time was less costly. The idea of such a blend of East and West was not entirely original: Seville at one time turned out a *cigarillo* of Virginia tobacco wrapped in a Havana leaf.

The straight Virginia cigarette

Consumption of cigarettes climbed, being unchecked even by the panic of 1873. Though still a "novelty business" in the United States, cigarettes were growing to some importance abroad, and doubtless the first manufacturers had an eye peeled

New York imported Russian and Polish hand rollers to satisfy demand for straight Turkish cigarettes after Civil War. First cigarettes made in New York were for the "carriage trade" and carried premium prices. Today's blends still contain some Turkish tobacco—10% or less—as a "seasoning ingredient."

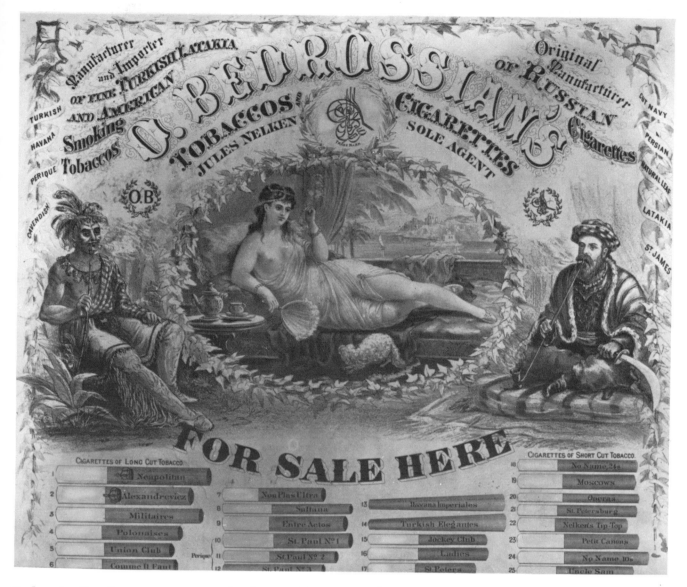

Bedrossian brothers were among the first to blend Virginia leaf with Turkish in cigarettes, sometime before 1870. They managed to cram all the romantic words in the tobacco lexicon onto their trade card. Great variety of cigarette shapes, most with fancy names, was intended strictly for big-city markets.

for the foreign market. Kinney's chief New York City competitor was Goodwin & Company, which also employed Russian immigrants who had experience in the London cigarette factories. Another important firm, W. S. Kimball & Company, manufactured in Rochester, New York. In Richmond, Allen and Ginter (the latter a transplanted New Yorker) began making cigarettes in 1875; among that firm's earliest brands was a Havana brand of the type smoked in Cuba. A little later the Richmond firm departed completely from the foreign-tobacco idea with *Richmond Straight Cut No. 1,* containing only "the brightest, most delicate flavored and highest cost Gold Leaf Tobacco grown in Virginia." It was this "Virginia cigarette" that went farthest at the start; by 1883 Allen and Ginter had a branch factory operating in London (England still favors the straight Virginia cigarette) and were selling in France, Germany, Switzerland, Belgium and Australia.

All in all, this was an auspicious beginning. The popularity of straight Turkish cigarettes was largely limited to New York with its big foreign-born population, but Allen and Ginter's experiment showed that a Bright tobacco cigarette had a fairly universal appeal. And for those who fancied Turkish-type cigarettes but did not take to the fancy price, the blend of Turkish and Virginia put out by Kinney

Turkish cigarettes had a long vogue in New York. In 1900 Turkish Trophies took fashionable glamor from the Florodora girl, then toast of the town.

One of the earliest "national" cigarette brands of the hand-rolling era was Vanity Fair, which was on sale as far west as Chicago during the early 1880s.

seemed satisfactory. By 1880, cigarette sales in units amounted to more than 400,000,000 which bore some sort of comparison with that year's unit sales of cigars, 2,400,000,000, although the leaf poundage consumed in cigar form was of course much greater, unit for unit.

However, the cigarette was by no stretch of the statistics a national form of tobacco consumption in the sense that the cigar was. There were no fewer than 94 cities turning out 2,000,000 cigars a year or more; but there were only a dozen centers with any cigarette production at all. Of these only four (New York-Jersey City, Rochester, Baltimore and Richmond) accounted for 75% of the 1880 national total; none of the others, including such mighty tobacco towns as St. Louis and Durham, had as much as 2%. At this stage the cigarette was clearly a specialty item meant for big-city markets.

This much was clear not only from the urban locus of manufacture but from the brand names themselves. Unlike the rowdy handles used with eatin' tobacco and the uninhibited words and phrases used with smokings, cigarette trademarks had a certain hauteur. Kimball's Peerless Tobacco Works in Rochester, which had a good sixth of the U. S. market, advertised half a dozen important brands in 1885: *Vanity Fair, Fragrant Vanity Fair, Cloth of Gold, Three Kings, Old Gold,* and *Orientals (Turkish).* Allen and Ginter of Richmond listed such fancy trademarks as *Bon Ton, Napoleons, Dubec, The Pet,* and *Opera Puffs,* in addition to its international *Richmond Straight Cut No. 1.*

Indicative of Baltimore's zest for manufacture was the "early foot" shown in the cigarette race by Marburg and Felgner, the versatile makers of smoking tobacco blends. Their cigarette output was slightly greater than Richmond's. They too aimed at the carriage trade, Marburg numbering *Estrella, High Life, Melrose* and *Golden Age* among its cigarettes and Felgner offering *Sublime, Principal, Perfect* and *Herbe de la Reine.*

New York had only two cigarette makers with national aspirations, Kinney and Goodwin. Kinney's seven trademarks were very easy to identify since they formed a related sequence of names: *Kinney's Straight Cut, Kinney's Straight Cut (Full Dress), Full Dress, Caporals — Halves, Caporals — Wholes* (referring to the packings, not the cigarettes themselves), *Sportsman's Caporal,* and *Sweet Caporal.* The word "caporal," French for corporal, was intended to suggest that the tobacco was a cut above common leaf, as a corporal was a cut above a common soldier.

Goodwin's names were the folksiest: *Canvas Back, Old Judge* and *Welcome.* Not that the others ignored the common-man market completely — Allen and Ginter had *Old Rip,* Marburg *Lone Fisherman, Our Boys* and *Acme* and Felgner *Our Little Pilot.*

The six big firms—Kimball in Rochester, Allen & Ginter in Richmond, Marburg and Felgner in Baltimore, Kinney and Goodwin in New York—among them had 44 of the 94 "important" brands of the day, if importance is defined as being in some demand as far west as Chicago. There was a good deal of "keeping up with the Joneses" in cigarette competition then, as there is now. Three firms had "Old" brands — *Old Judge, Old Rip, Old Gold.* Three had "Our" brands — *Our Boys, Our Little Pilot, Our Little Beauties.* Allen & Ginter opposed its *Perfection* brand against Felgner's *Perfect.* Marburg had a *Lone Fisherman,* inspired no doubt by the old Lynchburg brand, *Lone Jack,* which was made as a cigarette along with the antebellum smoking mixture of that name.

The *Lone Jack* cigarette was one of several links between tumblings and white rolls. Kimball's *Three Kings* was an offshoot of a smoking mixture of Turkish, Perique and Virginia, and his *Vanity Fair* and *Old Gold* cigarettes developed from flake cut pipe tobaccos of those names. However, only "high-toned" smoking tobacco names were suitable for use in the cigarette trade; it was not until the mad multiplication of 1900 or so that almost every brand name with a following was registered for smoking mixture, plug, cigarette and sometimes cigar use as well. Eminently qualified by this standard was the *Duke of Durham* smoking tobacco brand, offered in cigarette form in 1881. Less suitable, perhaps, was the name *Blackwell's Durham* for a cigarette made by the Dukes' crosstown competitor and intended to borrow a little market muscle from its sacked smokum, *Bull Durham.*

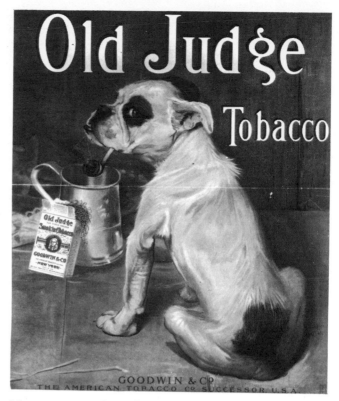

Many cigarette brands used brand names of smoking tobaccos. Old Judge, made in New York, was such a product. As a national rather than a metropolitan brand, its trademark was more folksy than elegant.

209

Before the U. S. had cigarette factories, New York weeklies carried pictures of French manufacturing.

This was an "ordering" cylinder in which tobacco arriving at a cigarette plant was reconditioned.

Two-way trade

The cigarette trade had a split personality, an echo of which is present to this day. On the one hand there were the "big city" brands with no pretensions to high volume but with very definite intentions of high profit. Most of these were aimed at the New York City market, and most had oriental names—*Bafrah, Cairo Superior, Persian, Egyptian, Levant, Monopole (Cairo), Moscow (Russian), Smyrna, Khedive,* and the like. They came high: *Egyptian* retailed at 50c for 20, and *Huppmann Imperiales* at $1.20 for 20. Most of them were layered in paper-hinged, foil-lined boxes — like many current big-city, small-volume brands which sell at premium prices. The tobacco in these brands was straight Turkish, the designation "straight Turkish" having the same significance for nineteenth-century cigarette smokers as "clear Havana" for cigar fanciers. To carry out the "custom trade" idea, most could be furnished with or without mouthpiece and in mild, medium or strong types. For those who had the yen but not the money, there were semi-premium brands with fancy packages and Oriental names but with Virginia-Turkish blends; these sold for 10c to 20c a box. Apparently the foreign foofaraw and jacked-up prices did the trick, for these Turkish and pseudo-Turkish cigarettes represented a good proportion of total sales. As late as 1903 they accounted for about 25% of the national market.

210

Not many of these exotic Middle East creations crossed the Hudson River; of the 94 brands important enough to be listed for the Chicago trade in 1885, only a couple had Oriental names. The "all-America" brands—representing the simpler side of the split cigarette personality—were priced to retail in nickel multiples, the standard being 5c for a box of ten and 10c for a box of twenty. Some brands retailed for an even nickel more. A typical price to the trade was $2.25 per 1,000 cigarettes. This figure included 50c for Federal tax and perhaps 30c for leaf, leaving $1.45 for labor, packaging, selling and profit.

The corresponding 1958 price was $8.28 per 1,000 at wholesale, of which $4.00 was for Federal tax and about $1.75 for leaf, leaving $2.53 for manufacturing, selling cost and profit. Since the 1958 dollar was worth about 25c in terms of 1885 purchasing power, big volume and mechanization have actually reduced manufacturing costs from $1.45 to the 1958 equivalent of 63c, or more than half. Over the same period leaf costs, which have not been reduced by the principle of mass production, have moved upwards from 30c to the 1958 equivalent of 43c.

Maids, morals and machines

There was, however, a built-in limit to cigarette production during the early 1880s. It required as much skill to roll a delicate "tailor-made" cigarette as to fashion a robust, perfecto-shaped cigar. The French cigarette girl of the 50s worked with a pre-formed tube into which she poked the tobacco; but London cigarettes were rolled from flat paper rectangles by dextrous Poles or Russians, and the American mode followed the English. After rolling the shredded leaf and paper slip into a reasonably compact cylinder, the seam was sealed with a touch of flour and water. Even after a cigarette girl was well-trained she could scarcely exceed four per minute at top speed. It was a difficult and expensive process. This relative sluggishness of hand production would have defeated itself eventually from a lack of skilled personnel, if not from a lack of high-paying puffers: running at their 1958 rate, the six largest cigarette companies turn out the entire production of the year 1880 in two hours. Even with the skimpy production of the day, work forces

French cigarette girl of 1850s poked tobacco into a pre-formed hollow tube. In Spain, the cigarette was a beggar's smoke; in France, a novel fashion.

Cork Tipped Cigarettes are a luxury to the lips

PATENTEES & SOLE MANUFACTURERS.
PHILIP MORRIS & C?
41 & 42, POLAND STREET. LONDON. W.

But until the twentieth century, cigarettes were to remain a specialty. In 1889, the Philip Morris firm of London advertised a cork tip in daring fashion.

211

were getting unwieldy: Allen & Ginter required 500 girls in 1883, 900 in 1886.

There was nothing about these young ladies reminiscent of Carmen, Bizet's violent and multi-lovered cigarette girl. A New York visitor observed:

> One of the most surprising features is the intelligent and comely appearance of the girls. This is accounted for by the fact that an applicant for admission into the factory must go through a most thorough examination as to character and habits, and none are admitted who, after careful examination, are discovered wanting in good moral character.

Comely, moral and dextrous as they might be, however, their very numbers presented staggering problems in supervision alone. The solution came very shortly as mechanized production was perfected by J. B. Duke in Durham. Like his larger competitors, "Buck" Duke had started by bringing 125 European immigrants from New York to do his hand-rolling and in his first year, 1881, turned out 9,800,000 cigarettes—about 1.5% of the industry total. Bonsack, the machine inventor, had been in touch with the big four companies, who turned down his contraption on two grounds: (1) it was not reliable in operation, and (2) consumers would resent machine-made cigarettes. Duke brushed aside the second objection, and set his own mechanics to work correcting the first. In 1888, his fifth year of machine operation, he turned out 744,000,000 cigarettes—more than the national output in his "tooling-up year," 1883—and had nearly 40% of the nation's cigarette business. For once, the South had gotten the jump on the New York city slickers.

Durham to New York

Unlike most of his fellow-manufacturers in Virginia and North Carolina, Duke was not content with a modest country operation. He realized from the first that the cigarettes were an urban smoke. Of course, he had to learn the game of selling in the best school for it—New York. As soon as the bugs were ironed out of his production lines and his price competitive—5c for a box of 10, against the previously standard 10c — he sent his salesmen throughout the country (one went "on the road" through Europe, Africa, India, Australia and New Zealand and wrote so many orders he didn't return for two years) and in 1884 moved to New York. He got the feel of the budding market by canvassing retailers himself, arranged for billboards and newspaper advertisements, and swelled New York's production totals by setting up a branch factory in a loft on Rivington Street. In addition to his original cigarette brand, *Duke of Durham*, young Duke manufactured *Cyclone, Cameo, Cross Cut* and *Duke's Best,* the last four introduced in cigarette form when he invaded New York.

CAPT. PAUL BOYTON
SWAM THE STRAITS OF GIBRALTAR MAR. 20, 1878.

W. G. GEORGE
RUNNER
I MILE. 4 MIN - 12¾ SEC.

H. W. SLOCUM, JR.
LAWN TENNIS CHAMPION OF NEW ENGLAND 1887/88.

JAMES RYAN.
CENTRE FIELDER - CHICAGO.

Cigarette cards helped stiffen package as well as providing inducement to buy. Pictures of athletes were popular fillings for the "cigarette sandwich" as were miniature blankets and flags. Only in 80s were sports fans impressed by blazered tennis champions and tailcoated center fielders. However Mr. W. G. George's time for the mile run—4 minutes 12.8 seconds—was not far below today's standards.

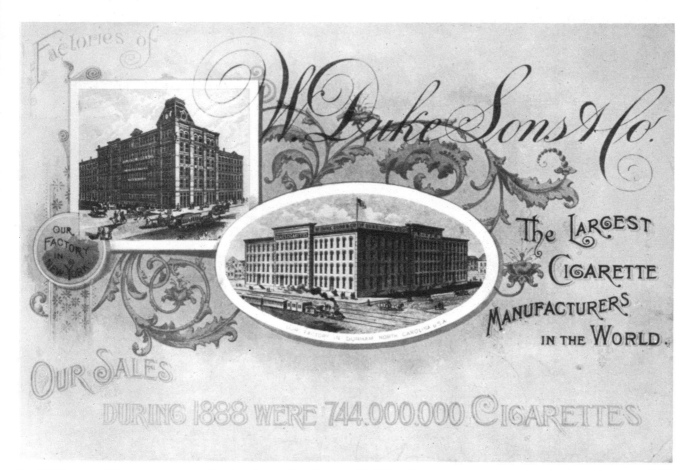

In 1888, *its fifth year of mechanized production, the Duke firm of Durham and New York had achieved 39% of all cigarette sales. By emulating the* Bull Durham *pattern of national advertising and direct selling to the trade, Duke transformed cigarettes from an expensive novelty to a common man's smoke.*

The American Tobacco Company

The arts of promotion which Duke polished in New York were designed, not to increase the use of tobacco as such—history had already demonstrated that would take care of itself—but to funnel as much of it as possible into cigarettes and into his particular brands. Having begun as a "commercial traveler" at the age of eight, Duke was well equipped to train the drummers who blanketed his market—in this case, the entire world. The tools of their trade were of New York origin: "photo-arto-types" or picture cards, sometimes called "Russell cards" after their principal subject, actress Lillian Russell, although cards picturing baseball players, boxers, and other notables helped fill the "cigarette sandwich." Coupons redeemable for "mantelpiece clocks" and the like were widely used. Duke's Cross Cut Polo Team advertised the cigarette and smoking tobacco of that name as it rolled across the country to meet all comers (it played on roller skates, not on horses). Where the local situation

permitted, attractive women salesmen were employed, in itself an attention-getting device. His advertising, not only via newspapers and billboards but on his own cigarette packages, was direct and to the point. While his competitors shrank from machinery, fearful that smokers would resent anything but a handmade cigarette, Duke labeled his *Pin Head* brand: "These cigarettes are manufactured on the Bonsack Cigarette Machine." His package itself was new and different — the "slide and shell" box now used for more expensive brands —and was described, in the jargon of the day, as "a perfect scream." His object was to learn how the leading manufacturers played the game, and then beat them at it—by plowing back most of his profits into advertising, for example. In 1889 he poured $800,000 into promotion, a staggering sum for a small business.

In 1890, it was obvious to the big four that they couldn't lick Duke, so they joined him. The new corporation was named The American Tobacco

Toward the end of the nineteenth century, even in New York, cigarette smoking was an act of daring for a lady. This very sensational photograph bore the breathtaking caption: "She's going to smoke!"

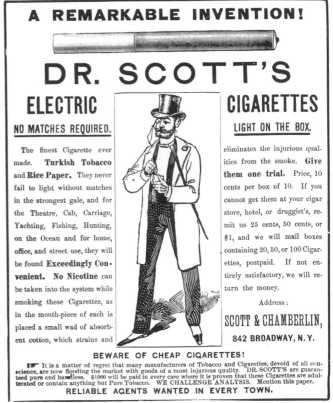

Every conceivable variant of the new form had its tryout in New York. This "electric cigarette" was actually a match-ended smoke, with "anti-nicotine" filter tip of cotton thrown in at no extra charge.

Company. As a spindly boy of eight, Duke had received a "payment" of one bag of brown sugar for his first business trip—the 1865 mule-and-wagon ride with his penniless father to sell a few sacks of flailed Bright leaf on the road to Raleigh. Twenty-five years later, at the age of thirty-three, he was president of a $25 million company.

The skyrocket career of J. B. Duke was based on the fact that he patterned his cigarette business after the first tobacco product to become a "big business" if that term is understood to include (1) mechanization, leading to (2) uniformity of product, permitting (3) national brands supported by (4) a national distribution system and (5) national advertising. Duke's model was, of course, the Blackwell company and its mighty *Bull Durham.*

Puff huff

But while *Bull Durham* fitted into the long-accepted custom of pipe smoking, the cigarette had to create its own acceptance and this led to a controversy quite as turbulent as that precipitated by

James I of England. The foreign origin of the white roll made it suspect: in 1884 the New York Times ventured into the field of international sociology by editorializing that

> The decadence of Spain began when the Spaniards adopted cigarettes and if this pernicious practice obtains among adult Americans the ruin of the Republic is close at hand . . .

The vogue for Turkish cigarettes accelerated in 1895 and accounted for a full fourth of cigarette sales between 1898 and 1903. During this time the energetic Lucy Gaston—a tobacco tintype of Carrie Nation—organized a campaign against the white roll, with headquarters in Chicago, arousing the Midwest against the new form. The growth of Turkish smokes almost exclusively in foreign-flavored New York was probably the root cause of this crusade, which resulted in the prohibition of cigarette sales in twelve states. The Federal excise tax on cigarettes was raised in 1897 from 1c to 2c and again to 3c in 1898 to raise funds for the Spanish-American War, and this tripled tax burden drove unit sales down. Even in foreign-flavored New York a 1908 ordinance banned smoking in public by women, but this was not taken seriously either by lady puffers or by the authorities themselves. There is no way to gauge the effect of this legislative flurry on sales, which began to rise again in 1901, when the tax was lowered to 1.08c per pack. In 1909, when the last of the state laws against cigarettes was enacted, national sales were double the figure of five years before.

It was an odd feature of the "little white slaver" movement that the use of quid or pipe tobacco drew no objection. Pipes and cigars were not affected by the state laws against cigarettes. Although the main disadvantage of the cigarette, as expounded by Miss Gaston, was that it drove its devotees into insane asylums, what made the pub-

lic receptive to her campaign was a feeling that cigarettes were effeminate while chaw and pipes were virile. The controversy was taken up in the sporting world: Gentleman Jim Corbett smoked cigarettes, while John L. Sullivan scorned the new item and was not reluctant to be quoted on the subject.

Nevertheless, from 1885 to 1902 the cigarette had made the kind of progress that cannot be wholly measured by statistics. Its volume had tripled; but more important was the fact that the new form had gained rather wide popular acceptance as distinct from the novelty "big city" acceptance won by *Opera Puffs* and *Huppmann Imperiales*. There were now 2,100 "cigarettes, cigarros and cheroots" listed in Connorton's Directory, along with 9,000 plugs and twists, 3,600 fine cuts, 7,000 smoking to-

Controversy on the manliness of cigarette smoking was widespread during the Gay Nineties. Champion heavyweight John L. Sullivan publicly deprecated

the new smoke; challenger "Gentleman Jim" Corbett espoused it. Corbett's 1892 knockout of the Boston Strong Boy did not end the cigarette controversy.

215

baccos and 3,600 snuff brands. Some of the new cigarette names were quite as vernacular as the earlier plug and pipe tobacco trademarks: *Bear Facts, Corn Husk, Jim Dumps, Driving the First*

Stake (!), *General Hobo, Gloomy Gus, Misfits, Pigs Foot, Rocket, Fire Cracker, Scrape-Goat, Coal Smoke, Total Eclipse, Strawboard*. The cigar was more pre-eminent than ever as an aristocratic or pseudo-aristocratic article. Most of the clear Havanas carried regal designations — *El Principe de Gales* and the like—but even "nickel goods" carried such tony trademarks as *Swell Set* and *Hoffman House*, the latter being a cosmopolitan hotel on Fifth Avenue into whose bar everybody who was anybody came to see and be seen.

The decade of the 90s, gay and troubled by turns, was a kind of "shakedown" period not only for the tobacco business but for the nation itself. The last battle between U. S. Cavalry and western Indians did not take place until 1890, at Wounded Knee Creek in Dakota; the last Washington powwow with an Indian war chief took place in 1891. The fight for Cuban liberty was in the forefront of national consciousness toward the end of the century, and like most wars the Spanish-American war had the effect of widening American horizons, of heightening interest in the new and the different. The Prince of Wales, son of the long-reigning Queen Victoria, visited the United States and was warmly received.

"You may smoke"

In 1901, on Victoria's death, the Prince ascended the throne as Edward VII. At his first royal dinner as king, the distinguished visitors were apprehensive, for Victoria had forbidden the use of tobacco at her court. Not so Edward: to the unasked question he replied loftily, "Gentlemen, you may smoke." The gracious remark might well have been directed to Americans; for while the custom of chewing had ceased to increase, smoking was growing. Between 1900 and 1910, pipe and cigarette smoking on a per capita basis made impressive gains; cigar consumption per capita reached its all-time U. S. peak—86—in 1907. Leaf tobacco used in manufacturing increased 45% between 1900 and 1910, as compared with a 14% increase during the 90s and gains of 18% and 22% in the 1910-20 and 1920-30 periods.

Nor was the spread of the smoking custom an uncritical one. The unbounded enthusiasm for straight granulated Bright was tempered by the appearance of blended smoking tobaccos and pipe

Smoking of pipes and cigars as well as cigarettes gained impetus during 1900-1910. King Edward VII set the style with famous remark after his ·first royal dinner as king: "Gentlemen, you may smoke!"

Edwardian era in New York City was characterized by elegant nomenclature even for five-cent cigars. Hoffman House was a fashionable Fifth Avenue hotel whose bar was peopled by celebrities eager to see

and be seen. Vicarious enjoyment of this splendor cost five cents, the price of Hoffman House cigar. Peak of cigar consumption, most aristocratic form of smoking, was attained in 1907: 86 per capita.

fanciers at large—not merely connoisseurs—turned to the new blends and even used them in roll-your-own cigarettes. The welter of cheap cigar brands had gone about as far as it could go by 1907; no longer was the average smoker willing to part with his nickel for any harsh rope that looked like a cigar. After that year the volume of stogie and cheroot business fell away and the consumption of brown rolls, though not so great in point of units sold, thereafter centered in the medium quality grades. The principal reason for the disappearance of vile cigars was, of course, the adoption of cigarette smoking which was not only milder and sweeter than the crude stogie but actually less expensive, puff for puff.

There was, however, more to it than that. The "citification" of America which had occupied the last 35 years of the nineteenth century was now substantially accomplished. The felt replaced the dignified topper; the automobile came in and the stately carriage went out; the leisurely noon meal yielded to the quick-lunch counter. Urban hurry had been institutionalized, and in this fast-moving context the deliberate and prolonged pleasure of pipe and cigar was a little out of place. The briar went with slippers and the evening newspaper; the brown roll was "saved for after dinner." The cigarette could be snuffed out instantly if need be. It was easier to pocket than pipe or cigar. It required less thought, less attention, and did not interfere with conversation as much. Above all, it was a quick smoke.

Big business

During the 90s, the commercial climate held out two lessons for tobaccomen. First, if a little big business was good, a bigger big business would be better. Second, if cigarettes faced a hostile reception in the Midwest diversification of the product mix would be prudent and profitable. James B. Duke, who already dominated the cigarette business, began to take a keener interest in quid, in snuff, in domestic cigars and even in Havana *tabacos*. The "plug war" of 1895-1898 was not so much a price-cutting epidemic as a duel between two "combinations." These combines or trusts were being built in most basic businesses including oil, steel, lead, sugar, copper, cotton oil, linseed oil, distilling and cordage.

On one side, Duke began by acquiring the National Tobacco Works of Louisville, the Marburg and Gail & Ax firms of Baltimore; later the Butler, Drummond and Brown companies of St. Louis were added and the plug businesses combined under a new corporation, Continental Tobacco Company. On the other side, a group of powerful New York financiers including Thomas Fortune Ryan, Anthony N. Brady, and P. A. B. Widener organized the Union Tobacco Company. Union bought the National Cigarette and Tobacco Company, Blackwell's Durham, and an option on a controlling interest in the biggest plugmaker, Liggett & Myers. In 1899 the two combines became one, bringing together the best of the tobacco managements and the most influential (and moneyed) financiers of the day.

Within a few years, most of the nation's prominent tobacco firms had entered the combination: Lorillard and McAlpin of New York; Mayo, Wright and Patterson of Richmond; Reynolds, Hanes and Brown of Winston; Beck of Chicago; Scotten of Detroit; Bollman of San Francisco; Sorg of Middletown; Finzer of Louisville, and others. By 1910 the group consolidated 86% of national output in cigarettes, 85% in plug, 76% in smoking tobacco, 97% in snuff, and 14% in cigars. The last-cited percentage indicates that cigars — after a full century of brand-name manufacture—still did not lend themselves to mass production and volume economies.

They were still being tediously rolled by hand in more than 20,000 small shops and plants throughout the country.

Big stick

Beside the controversy generated by the formation of trusts, the anti-cigarette movement paled to the significance of a high school debate. The nation suffered through two wrenching depressions, in 1893 and 1907; farmers and city people alike blamed their misfortunes on "big business." A school of anti-business literature—the "muckrakers" —arose to paint in lurid language every hardship and inconvenience inherent in large-scale production. Into the White House came Teddy Roosevelt with his "Big Stick," his zeal for reform and, no doubt, his memories of the sweatshops run by the small cigar makers of New York. Between 1901 and

The accelerating pace of city life, symbolized by the quick-lunch counter of late nineteenth-century New York, was perhaps the principal reason for the

218

1909, the Trustbuster brought suit against forty-four trusts and combinations, among them the tobacco combine.

The original action was begun in 1907, and in its verdict of 1908 the U. S. Circuit Court of New York stated:

> The record . . . does not indicate that there has been any increase in the price of tobacco products to the consumer. There is an absence of persuasive evidence that by unfair competition or improper practices independent dealers have been dragooned into . . . selling out . . . the price of leaf tobacco . . . has steadily increased until it has nearly doubled, while at the same time 150,000 additional acres have been devoted to tobacco crops . . . new markets have been opened in India, China and elsewhere.

Nevertheless, the combination was judged to have restrained competition in violation of the Sherman Anti-Trust Act, and following Supreme Court confirmation of the decision in 1911, it was redivided into its component companies. The four principal manufacturers to emerge were American, Reynolds, Liggett & Myers, and Lorillard. The effect of dissolution on the tobacco business was, however, slight. Retail prices did not change, factory costs remained as they were, and leaf prices varied no more than usual. However, the restoration of competition vastly increased the cost of selling and advertising, from $18.1 million in 1910 to $32.4 million in 1913.

As corporate blending ceased, the blending of tobacco increased. The straight Bright cigarette, the straight Maryland pipe tobacco, and the straight Burley plug gave way to a new kind of "combination." This—the blended American cigarette—was destined to receive a favorable verdict.

replacement of the cigar by the cigarette. Cigars became luxury items to be saved for "after dinner"; they were somewhat out of place during the hours of work. Cigarettes fitted better into the urban routine: they were easier to snuff out quickly if need be, easier to talk through, easier to carry.

In the twentieth century all major strains of U.S. leaf were blended into the American cigarette, and regional tobacco products all but disappeared. Both planting and processing had been greatly improved; the American blended cigarette became the tobacco standard in the U.S. and around the world as well.

THE AMERICAN BLEND

THE rivalries that make up the story of Americans and tobacco during their first three centuries were finally resolved in the American cigarette. Tobacco, focus of struggles between colonist and king, Kentuckian and Spaniard, East and Midwest, North and South, was finally blended into a national product. Competition was no longer between regions, but between manufacturers.

It took exactly three hundred years for Rolfe's first commercial shipment of dark air-cured in 1613 to evolve into the American blended cigarette of 1913. This latest step in tobacco evolution corresponds with the latest stage in the development of Americans themselves. "Tobacco use," observed a scientist in 1956, "and particularly cigarette smoking, has become widespread throughout the world, especially in the more highly developed countries."

The cigarette, light, mild, quick, was "tailor-made" for an urban civilization perpetually in motion and perpetually in need of relaxation.

If the development of the American cigarette was slow and even devious, it was because the development of the American way of life, American manners, American taste was itself a gradual process. Cigarettes were a prominent feature of sophisticated Aztec life. They passed over into the worldly Spanish culture, which carried them as far north as the City of the Holy Faith, screened from the plains savages by the Mountains of the Blood of Christ: Santa Fe. They were common in nearby Cuba while the Atlantic ports were throwing out lines of commerce. As early as 1850, the American cigarette was foreshadowed in St. Petersburg, where the La Ferme factory is said to have blended Turkish leaf with American Burley and Maryland for the Russian trade. So the early acceptance of

the cigarette in the United States, traced from its use by British, French and Russian soldiers in the Crimean War of 1854, was perhaps initiated by a blend somewhat like our present one. At any rate, it was not merely a matter of cigarettes growing up to meet the market; it was also a matter of Americans growing into the cigarette.

Like snuff to the colonials, cigarettes to the postbellum Americans were at first a foreign luxury. Their appeal was cosmopolitan, combining the exotic lure of the Middle East—*Egyptienne Straights, Fatima, Omar, Helmar, Hassan, Mecca, Zubelda*—with the social self-assurance of London—*Pall Mall, Piccadilly, Lord Salisbury.* American taste declared its independence of European fashion long before the American vocabulary did. The popular article at the century's turn was a blended Turkish cigarette, and it has been observed that the "Turkish"

was more prominent on the cigarette package, festooned with minarets, pyramids and palm trees, than it was in the cigarette.

Although this oriental symbolism persisted, and although today's cigarettes still use a small percentage of aromatic Turkish leaf, the American cigarette as we know it did not evolve from the straight Turkish product or even from the Turkish-Virginia blend. The blend which finally won out was derived from smoking tobacco via the "roll-your-own" cigarette. First flue-cured Bright, then sweetened Burley, then a mixture of both captured the taste buds of American pipe smokers. As the cigarette form became more popular, two things happened: manufacturers brought out cigarettes with the brand marks of their more successful smoking tobaccos, and smokers who disdained the tailormade tube — a goodly number — began to roll their own cigarettes from Burley, Bright, or Burley-and-Bright pipe mixtures. Some smoking tobaccos had long been sold with cigarette papers attached, the best known of these being the nonblended Bright *Bull Durham*. Even while his straight Turkish cigarettes were gaining headway in the city market, during the early 1900s, J. B. Duke was advertising *Dukes Mixture* not only "for pipes" but also "for cigarettes." In the year 1907, which marked New York City's transition from the horsedrawn Fifth Avenue coach to the motorbus, both kinds of vehicles carried the two-way car cards for *Dukes Mixture*.

This was more than a coincidence: the pipe as such was making its exit with the horse-and-buggy era, and the cigarette—a different form which used essentially the same tobacco blends — was on the threshold of national acceptance. But apart from the luxury-conscious and novelty-conscious in the urban markets, this acceptance did not come until the American blend was developed to supplant the straight or blended oriental cigarette.

Bright, Burley, Maryland, Turkish

The three brands which were to revolutionize world tobacco consumption were all introduced before our entry into World War I; two of them evolved directly from smoking tobaccos. In her definitive study of the Bright-tobacco industry, Tilley states that in 1907 "R. J. Reynolds used a Burley blend for his *Prince Albert* smoking tobacco and in so doing marked a turning point in his business career by laying the foundation for his famous domestic blend to come six years later in the *Camel* cigarette."

Lucky Strike, chief competitor to the *Camel* brand, was developed in New York, still an important tobacco manufacturing center, by The American Tobacco Company. The name *Lucky Strike* had been synonymous with Burley since R. A. Patterson had used it for his plug tobacco in pre-Civil War Richmond. Later *Lucky Strike* was sold as sliced plug for pipe smoking. The first *Lucky Strike* cigarette ads proudly called attention to the Burley component, which presented something of

a manufacturing problem. Burley leaf shredded to cigarette strips quickly loses its aroma, so the Burley part of the blend had to be separately "cased" (flavored) and then "bulked" (allowed to absorb the casing overnight) before being shredded into the final mixture. Since the New York factories were not equipped to handle Burley in this way, it had to be prepared in Richmond and shipped to New York for blending and manufacturing. First marketed in 1916, the brand's initial progress was halted by World War I, but it moved into the first rank of competition during the 1920s and alternated with *Camel* as the No. 1 brand between 1930 and 1950.

A third important cigarette was Liggett and Myers' *Chesterfield*, a 1912 brand which was shifted in 1915 from a slide-and-shell box into a tight paper-and-foil wrap, like that used by *Camel* and *Lucky Strike*. *Chesterfield* was the third of the "standard" brands which were to become, as *Bull Durham* had once become, the standard of America and eventually the standard of the world. *Chester-*

field was labeled "a balanced blend of the finest aromatic Turkish tobacco and the choicest of several American varieties." *Lucky Strike* was labeled "A blend of Burley and Turkish tobacco (based on the original Lucky Strike Tobacco formula)" and *Camel* "Turkish & Domestic Blend." The emphasis on Turkish indicates, in retrospect, the initial importance of straight Turkish and blended Turkish formulas in the cigarette market. *Chesterfield* ads in 1917 carried this paragraph in small type: "The *Chesterfield* blend contains the most famous Turkish tobaccos — Samsoun for richness, Cavalla for aroma, Smyrna for sweetness, Xanthi for fragrance, combined with the best domestic leaf."

R. J. Reynolds

It was something of a paradox that Richard Joshua Reynolds, the unyielding defender of flat Bright plug, should revolutionize the cigarette field with the Burley-blended *Camel*. When the tobacco trust was dissolved, Reynolds reverted to its status as a manufactured tobacco firm and was awarded

As late as 1912, tailormade cigarettes featured straight Turkish tobacco content and were sold mainly in New York City and other urban markets. Big billboard at Broadway and Seventy Second St. (left) advertised Egyptian Straights. In tobacco content the brand was not Egyptian but Turkish.

American pipe mixtures rather than Turkish leaf foreshadowed content of big cigarette brands. The changeover from pipe and plug to cigarette smoking coincided roughly with the change from horse-and-buggy to automobiles. In 1907 (right) motor busses supplanted the horsedrawn carriage along New York's Fifth Avenue, and Dukes Mixture began to be promoted on coach and car cards not only for pipe smoking but also for cigarette use.

Camel cigarette took its brand image from "Old Joe," a circus dromedary which passed through Winston with Barnum & Bailey. In 1913 cigarettes empha- *sized Turkish leaf content; labels were festooned with oriental decorations. Camel package followed this trend although cigarette blend was American.*

no cigarette brand. For this reason, and motivated by a long-standing animus toward the cigarette king, "Buck" Duke, Reynolds launched several cigarettes of his own. He tried *Reyno,* a nickel brand; he tried *Osman,* a Turkish blend; and he tried *Camel.*

Reynolds' success in marketing flat Bright plug against the Burley trend, beginning in 1875, did not close his mind to innovation. He entered the smoking tobacco field in 1895 and introduced a Burley pipe mixture, *Prince Albert,* in 1907. So the new *Camel* was no half-hearted compromise with the burgeoning taste for Burley: it was then, and remains, one of the burliest of the Burley blends, emphatically flavored. Because it contained less of the imported Turkish leaf, *Camel* undersold the

typical Turkish brand, 10c per pack of twenty as against 15c. And because it gave smokers what they were looking for, *Camel* took the lead among cigarette brands, a position it held in thirty-one of the next forty-six years. As with many tobacco innovations, circumstances lent a helping hand: the World War I shortage of Turkish leaf hobbled the oriental blends just as *Camel* was hitting its stride.

Though a Southerner — he was a 15-year-old boy on a Critz, Virginia tobacco farm when Lee surrendered to Grant at Appomatox, 115 miles away — Reynolds had a Yankee's thrift and a Yankee's sharp pencil. As a manufacturer, he quickly got the hang of mass production: R. J. Reynolds Tobacco Co. is still unique in that all its manufacturing is concentrated in one cluster of factories in Winston.

As a salesman he had learned to go after business himself (on horseback, in his twenties) and rejected the leisurely old consignment system. As a businessman, he was quick to adapt his flat plug to the national sweet tooth, quick to ride the Burley bandwagon, quick to try the Burley blend in cigarette form just as the white roll was catching on. Stubborn enough to resist J. B. Duke even while Duke had financial control of his firm, he was not too stubborn to abandon tobacco traditions at the right time. In this respect he was the opposite of his cantankerous Winston neighbor, Bill Taylor.

In retrospect the great moves in tobacco-making seem logical, orderly, indicated. Granulating sweet Bright tobacco for easy pouring, as in *Bull Durham;* blending Burley and Bright in cut plug; blending Burley and Bright for cigarettes, as in *Camel* — these, with the aid of hindsight, seem evolutionary rather than revolutionary. So do the more recent moves which have produced dramatic growth curves like that of the 1913 *Camel:* the lengthening of the cigarette to king-size in 1939, which gave rise to the brand that is now *Camel's* closest challenger, *Pall Mall;* the combination of menthol flavoring and a filter tip — neither in itself novel — in the 1956 *Salem,* the latter a modern Reynolds "invention." The capacity for such invention, sometimes miscalled intuition, is the essence of the successful business mind. It enabled the bearded Dick Reynolds to achieve 40% of the nation's cigarette business and 20% of its chew and smokum volume by the time of his death in 1918.

Concentration of production in Winston-Salem has characterized Reynolds Tobacco since its founding.

Winston plants, research laboratory, headquarters building are within walking distance of each other.

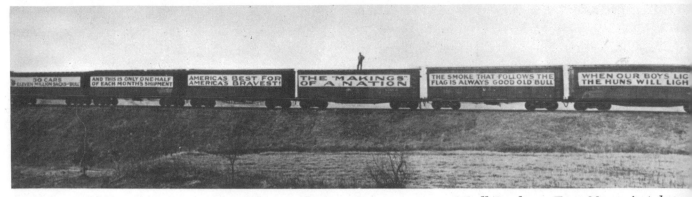

During World War I, the U. S. insured the supply of tobacco for overseas troops by commandeering full factory output of Bull Durham. Two 30-car freight trains a month carried the sacked tobacco to port

In many ways, this switch from foreign or pseudo-foreign cigarettes to "domestic blends" was similar to the change from foreign snuff to good old American quid a century before. It reflected, in a subtle way, a new stage of maturity, a change from imitation to self-realization. No doubt the exhilarating experience of the 1917 war had a good deal to do with this.

The use of tobacco, especially new forms of it, is almost always enhanced in one way or another by war, and World War I was no exception. General John J. Pershing, commanding the American Ex-

General Pershing commanded American Expeditionary Force in France, said: "You ask me what we need to win this war. I answer tobacco as much as bullets."

One of Pershing's officers had been photographed in 1911 with his corncob pipe. Douglas MacArthur became great general, pipe became his trademark.

from Durham. This string of freight cars held more than 11,000,000 sacks—enough to make 400,000,000 cigarettes on a "roll-your-own" basis, 33 per bag. Doughboys were exhorted to "smoke out the Kaiser."

peditionary Force, made his requirements clear: "You ask me what we need to win this war. I answer tobacco as much as bullets." Past military experience had indicated the value of tobacco to morale, and the Federal Government commandeered manufactured products for its troops. (The entire production of the *Bull Durham* factory, still in Durham, was requisitioned for overseas shipment in 1918.) In addition, such private agencies as the Y.M.C.A. and the Our Boys in France Tobacco Fund sent tobacco by the ton to be sold at cost or given to the doughboys. Turkish tobacco, which had played so important a role several wars previously, was this time cut off from its western customers. This permanently cooled the rage for Turkish among American smokers, who went over in a body to domestic blends. The dwarfed Turkish leaf remained an important "seasoning" ingredient, but by now the blend was the thing; even the redoubtable *Bull Durham*, straight Bright in a sack, was no longer sufficient unto itself for pipe smoking. Advertisements recommended its use "mixed with your favorite pipe tobacco, like sugar in your coffee."

Although the typical American cigarette was known in the industry as a "Burley blend," more than half of the mixture was Bright tobacco. The amount of Burley varied between a fifth and two-fifths, with lesser proportions of Turkish and Maryland leaf. In 1919, only half a dozen years after this formula evolved, the smoking market was a three-way proposition with cigarettes, cigars and pipe tobacco each consumed to the tune of one-and-a-half pounds per American per year. Ten years later cigarettes were twice as important, by weight, as either of the two rival smokes; twenty years later, four times as weighty; thirty-five years later, the mythical average American smoked seven pounds of cigarettes a year, one pound of cigars, and half a pound of pipe tobacco.

Loose-leaved auctions

Although this steady rise in tobacco consumption (about 3% a year) would seem to be ideal from the standpoint of planters, the story of the leaf growers is punctuated with violence and discontent. Like the tidewater tobaccomen, who literally outgrew the rising European demand and suffered low prices from their over-production, modern farmers have been handicapped by surpluses generated by zeal for volume in their cash crop. Although this problem has never been completely overcome, farm unrest seems to have reached a climax with the change-over from hogshead to loose-leaf selling. Loose-leaf selling pinned prices to quality of leaf more exactly than had ever been done before: nesting inferior leaf inside good, and "sanding" hands of tobacco to add weight, were largely eliminated. Resentment was first evidenced in Danville, Virginia during the 1870s, and the target was the warehouseman, who was held to be responsible for low prices. A Granger movement arose, then dissolved when prices went up again.

As loose-leaf auctions became general in the Bright country, the suspicion grew that warehousemen were parasites, and that too much of the sale price was absorbed by clerks, weighmen, auctioneers and others in the warehousing business. A Farmers' Alliance attempted to cut down on the cost of marketing and even set up its own ware-

Tobacco crop is begun in early spring, seedlings being planted in a special patch of fresh ground which has first been burned over, then hoed, then *raked. During weeks of first growth, plant bed is bordered with logs, covered over with cheesecloth. When six inches high, seedlings are transplanted.*

houses. This did not result in any lowering of commissions, but it led to a related effort, the tobacco pool. By 1907 the Tobacco Growers' Protective Association was redrying its own flue-cured leaf and storing it for direct bulk sale to the manufacturer. Bulk sale of leaf "in dry prizery" was not only advantageous in bargaining, but overcame farmers' objections to the speed of auction sales. Although most markets limited the chanting auctioneers to 300 baskets an hour, growers felt that twelve seconds was too short a time for either seller or buyer to do justice to the leaf's true quality. Warehousemen in the Bright country, of course, bitterly opposed the pool idea during the six years it lasted. But the pools did not bring in the best prices for their redried leaf, and farmers began to drift back to the auctions.

Still, the notion of dispensing with the middleman was a long way from being squashed. A new group, the Farmers' Union, reminded planters that "men go into the warehouse business as poor as a church mouse, and strut out as big as a king." Plants for redrying and storage were built in a score of localities, including Wilson and Reidsville, North Carolina; these were operated successfully, although they did not handle more than a small fraction of the flue-cured crop.

The Black Patch

Pooling in the Burley area had a parallel history but a more violent one, beginning in the 1900s. The most troubled area was the so-called Black Patch of western Kentucky and Tennessee, this dark tobacco area being the last to go over to loose-leaf

Flue-cure is a touchy process requiring all-night vigil against the risk of fire. Barn must be heat-tight so that temperature can be controlled. Near *end of cure a hot barn with its very dry, spaced-out tobacco leaves is a virtual tinder box. Lemon coloring requires great heat for 48 hours or more.*

selling. The local protective association built a force of "Possum Hunters" or "Night Riders" which eventually numbered around 10,000 men. Their object was to persuade all tobacco planters to join, using physical force if necessary. The association started up its own storages, and by 1907 sold virtually all the Black Patch crop. Farmers who held aloof or spoke out against the association—known as Hill Billies—were given tangible cause to regret it, and many fled north across the Ohio. Violence bred more violence: destruction of plant beds and barns was followed by the burning of factories and warehouses; murder was committed by both sides. The local courts took no action, but one of the "Night Rider Refugees," Robert Hollowell, sued a group of his former tormentors in the federal courts. He was awarded damages. Other suits fol-

lowed, and the military speedily moved in to slap a rein on night riding.

Again, farmers drifted back to the loose-leaf auctions by choice after the pool had failed to yield any price advantage.

No sooner had peace broken out in the two great tobacco regions than war broke out in Europe. Average prices on the Old Belt, which had run around 13c between 1911 and 1915, shot to 35c during the next four years. A similar price bonanza visited the rest of the Bright country and the Burley region as well. Pooling was forgotten—until the years of reckoning, 1920 and 1921. All over the nation wartime prosperity collapsed with a dull thud, and tobacco was no exception. Old Belt price averages declined from a dizzying 53.9c in 1919 to 22c in the two years following. Leaf growers' associations again formed, this time in a more businesslike than bitter mood. There were three new groups, one for Burley, one for Bright, one for dark tobacco in the Black Patch (Maryland, always an island unto itself, had kept its own growers association unchanged for some years). Farmers in every region signed into the pools by the tens of thousands, and in 1923 nearly half the nation's crop was marketed through the "co-ops."

Pools and prices

The brief success of pooling was founded on the thirty years of pro and con propaganda which had conditioned the farmer to doubt the fairness of independent auction selling. But no sooner had the pools swung into volume operation than the farmer began to doubt the fairness — and sometimes the integrity — of the co-op officials to whom he had committed his financial future. No tangible proof of gain was forthcoming; prices in most areas

hovered around the 1921 level. Again, farmers thought their chances might be better if they took their own leaf to market, and after three or four years of pooling, most of them returned to the auction sales. A possibly higher price was more desirable than a certainly average one.

An interesting sidelight on the pooling rush of the mid-20s was that the buyers for European concerns — among them the dominant British firm, Imperial Tobacco—were said to regard the co-ops as a kind of farmers' trust and therefore hesitated to lend support by purchasing from them. However, the pools counted substantial customers among American manufacturers and even received encouragement from them, so the European attitude was not vital to their survival. In the last analysis, it was the individual farmer who decided whether to play pool or not. And his answer—given this time without the rosy influence of rising prices—was again negative.

There is no better term to describe this aversion

Black Patch area of western Kentucky was last to adopt auction system. In 1900s planters organized a selling pool and Night Riders used violence to

force all tobacco growers to join. To protect the "Hill Billies" from Night Riders the military was called in (above). But pools did not raise prices.

Auction sale is highly-organized method of selling millions of pounds of leaf in small lots. Tobacco buyers (right) walk single file alongside row of *baskets, auctioneer and warehouse clerks on other side facing them. Buyers judge leaf with look and touch, signal their bids by wink or raised finger.*

to collective action than "rugged individualism," a trait which persists even in the present age of farm subsidies.

Crop control

The market averages kept to a plateau during the 20s, slightly under the 20c level. By now the puzzle of leaf surpluses, which had defied solution ever since the Jamestowners rushed to duplicate John Rolfe's garden, had been mulled over in a tentative way by the Federal Government. As early as 1924 a bill was proposed in Congress to set up an export corporation with government funds, buy the oversupply of leaf from the domestic market and sell it abroad. This idea was defeated in Washington four times. When the Great Depression of 1930 struck, dropping leaf to 8c, tobacco was not

overlooked in the flurry of remedial legislation. It was one of the seven basic commodities to come under the Agricultural Adjustment Act of 1933; at that time the "adjustment" took the form of acreage restrictions and loans against surplus production. Five years later the national economy, including leaf prices, plummeted again and a second control was added — marketing quotas (not production quotas, but acreage limits) subject to a validating vote by two-thirds of the farmers themselves. Pools of a new kind were established to receive farmers' leaf. However, these were not obliged to resell the surplus tobacco they accumulated, for the capital for their operation was furnished on an indefinite loan basis by the U. S. Government, and the farmers received cash on the hogshead.

From 1938 onward it was an unusual year that

did not set a new price record for flue-cured or Burley tobacco or both. In that year, tobacco was the most valuable farm crop grown in North America, next to grain. Demand might push up the price —as in 1956-57, when Burley averaged 63.3 cents, up 8% from the crop year before—but the "parity payment" system of loans prevented the price from collapsing. Any farmer with gradable tobacco could turn it over to the government, if he chose, for a price equal to 90% of parity, the latter computed by the Department of Agriculture to equate the price of farm produce with a constant amount of purchasing power.

Supported prices and restricted acreage did not outmode the rural equivalent of business enterprise. In the Bright region a saying goes, "Every time they take an acreage cut, they build another barn." The added barns were to handle the extra yield. By closer spacing of plants, intensified fertilizing and the planting of high-yield strains, poundage per acre zoomed between 1929-33 and 1956, yield increasing from 777 to 1,591 pounds per Burley acre, from 707 to 1,609 per Bright.

The combination of price support and acreage restrictions had its disadvantages. One obvious way to get around these confinements was to space the tobacco plants very close together. Also there was widespread adoption of new varieties notable for disease resistance, high yield, thinness and lack of flavor; it was "pale and slick" in the circuit rider's language, "low to lacking in flavor and aroma, generally of light body, and/or currently with poor acceptance in the trade," in Department of Agriculture phraseology. There had accumulated by 1956 in the government-financed pool some 200,000,000 pounds of such unsalable leaf; one manufacturer suggested that it ought to be burned, but not in pipes or cigarettes. With loans against surplus farm commodities pressing toward the legal dollar limit and foreign buyers reducing their purchases, the Secretary of Agriculture announced that these varieties would be supported at only half the support price of comparable grades. A month later he was moved to add:

> We are not restricting the right of tobacco farmers to grow these varieties if they wish. We are merely saying that public funds will not be used to encourage production of tobacco varieties judged by the trade to be inferior. This principle has been previously applied to wheat. It is a part of our general policy of maintaining and expanding markets through encouraging, where possible, the production of quality products.

There were difficulties, too, with some of the chemicals marketed to farmers in the years that followed World War II. The excessive use of fertilizer, for instance, could and did affect the chemical composition of *Nicotiana tabacum* — in particular, the all-important nicotine content. Not only chemical composition but physical properties were affected by a growth inhibitor sold in the tobacco country. This substance ended mitosis, or cell division, in the developing plant but permitted the existing cellular structure to enlarge. Growers were almost as enthusiastic about this chemical as its manufacturer, for it not only spared them the tedious hand labor of removing the suckers (side sprouts) but increased yield as well. Cigarette makers were not so enthusiastic, however, for the resulting tobacco leaf tended to be coarse, slick and small — a step backward from the light, fluffy leaf developed over many decades.

With price support levels not only firm but inching higher, it became more difficult to maintain leaf quality in the face of the understandable quest for quantity. But the upward spiral posed a new problem, threatening to price American farmers and American tobacco out of their traditional export market. In 1958, exports of unmanufactured leaf were actually below the average of the pre-

A tablespoonful of tobacco seed sows six acres.

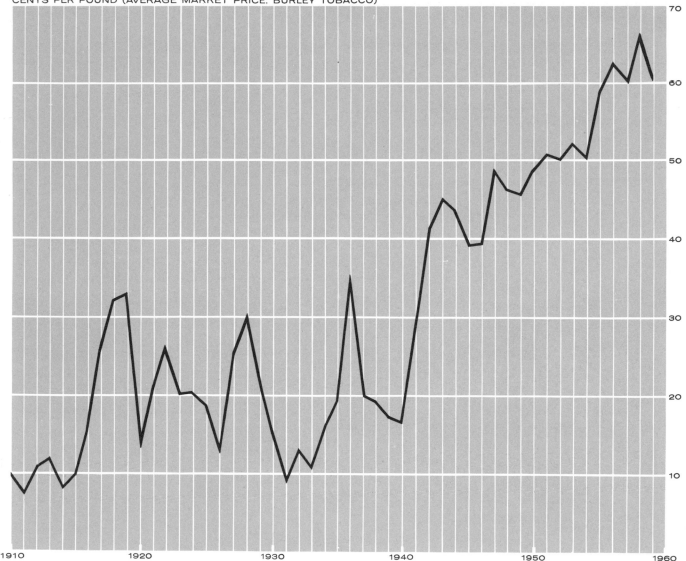

70

60

50

40

30

20

10

1910   1920   1930   1940   1950   1960

Average price per pound paid farmers for Burley leaf (above) shows fluctuations similar to those for Bright. Postwar and depression lows occurred *in 1920, 1931, 1940, 1945. However, 1945 drop was slight, checked by price support system. Average market price has quadrupled in last sixteen years.*

vious ten years. And this average, in turn, was a scant 5% higher than that for the 30s, when the depression and agricultural adjustment made their appearance in quick succession.

"Roll your own and save your roll"

"Little tube of mighty power" the cigarette may be, but its status has been shaken at times. As its early nickname of "tailor-mades" suggests, the manufactured cigarette is really a convenience article, by no means the least expensive way of satisfying the taste for tobacco. A nickel sack of *Bull Durham* (carrying a tax of ½c) can be rolled into about 33 "handmades." A pound tin of pipe to-

bacco contains the equivalent of 18 packs of cigarettes at a third of the cost (the tax differential, again, being a large factor). Since the cigarette blend is related more closely to the pipe mixture than to any other form, one might expect some degree of interchangeability between the two. There is—and it makes itself felt when the money pinch is on. Part of the cigarette's growth in good times has represented pipe smokers converted to the white roll, and in bad times vice versa.

This two-way convertibility was first noticed after the panic in 1907. The expensive cigar fell off abruptly; the fast-rising cigarette curve flattened; but per capita pipefuls went up. Again, as the postwar depression of 1920-21 curtailed the purchase of

233

Depression after 1929 revived demand for smoking tobaccos granulated to "pour" into roll-your-own cigarettes. Bull Durham emerged from its pen for one last fling. In 1932 the sales of factory-made cigarettes dropped 10,000,000,000; sale of papers for rolling your own increased by the same number.

silk shirts and imported Havanas, smoking tobacco sales took an upward turn and the upward surge of the cigarette was slowed. Between 1929 and 1933, more brothers could spare a dime for smoking tobacco, fewer could lay out 15c for cigarettes.

The obvious answer to this was a ten-cent pack of cigarettes, made possible by the drop of leaf tobacco on the markets from 20c to 8c. To rescue their own trademarks from the "ten-centers" the established manufacturers had to meet the dime price. At the same time, to rescue the farmers, they promised President Herbert Hoover to purchase stipulated poundages of Burley and Bright at average prices of 12c and 17c respectively. Old Man

"Roll-your-own" cigarettes are becoming a lost art. First step is pouring tobacco into a folded paper— a crease is recommended for beginners. Second step is making a hollow in the tobacco to distribute it. Third step, start of roll, is done with horizontal thumbs, as cigarette rests on the middle fingers.

Depression proved harder to chase away than the upstart ten-cent brands, and while the money squeeze was on, *Bull Durham* and the other "roll your own" tobaccos snorted back for one last fling.

The gain in *Bull Durham* alone between 1930 and 1932 was 9,000,000 pounds — enough to roll three and a half billion "do-it-yourself" cigarettes. As measured by increased sales of cigarette papers, some ten billion cigarettes were rolled by hand (or on little machines sold by smoking tobacco manufacturers) in 1932. At the same time, and not by coincidence, the sales of "tailor-mades" dropped by ten billion. Despite the severity of the Great Depression, per capita consumption of tobacco in all forms showed a relatively slight dip — from 7.18 pounds in 1929 to a little over six pounds in 1932 and back to 7.16 pounds by 1936. These figures, of course, reflect only tax-paid withdrawals; no one knows how much leaf was consumed by farmers short of cash as "long green" or "hillside navy."

Clipped cigars

While the decline in cigarette output between 1929 and 1932 was substantial—about 12% in terms of leaf used in manufacture—in cigar smoking, even more sensitive to income changes, it was a drastic 50%. But even before the depression struck, cigar sales had been gently declining.

Cigar-making machinery, rendered practical by 1917, came too late to stem the brown roll's gradual volume loss. In 1924, only about a tenth of all cigars were machine made; in 1929, little more than a third. Cigarette machinery had a head start of 34 years, and the cigarette industry was a kind of big business in miniature, organized and efficient, by 1890, while the more massive cigar business was literally a multiplication of tiny shops — 20,000 in 1900, 22,000 as late as 1910. Furthermore a single "domestic cigar" of standard quality had to retail at 10c or more after World War II. In share of market this class — led by the *El Roi-Tan, Phillies* and *White Owl* brands—became the most important. Bonded clear Havanas or imported Cuban cigars of top quality in corona size (about 6" long, ½" in diameter) can scarcely sell for less than 35c apiece. With cigarettes available in 1,500,000 outlets at 25c or so for 20—and almost everywhere in a fresher state than cigars, an important consideration for a perishable product — the cigar has abdicated its everyday place even in New England, and has been kicked upstairs to the luxury class.

The five-cent cigar

This fact of economics had been immortalized in wistful fashion by Thomas R. Marshall, Vice President of the U. S. under Woodrow Wilson. A Democrat, Marshall listened to a Republican Senator ramble on at length about the country's needs and reacted with: "What this country needs is a really good five cent cigar!" Nothing else Marshall ever said was quite so well put; certainly, he is remembered for nothing else—proof, perhaps, of the place held by cigars in the story of Americans and their tobacco.

Marshall's remark contained the germ of economic truth; manufacturers realized that only a five-cent cigar could even begin to compete in the mass market with cigarettes costing three-quarters of a cent apiece (the pack of 20 generally sold around 15c during the 20s and 30s). As machines were perfected it appeared to some tobaccomen that, given automation plus national promotion, the brown roll could give the white one a run for the smoker's money. The attempt was made;

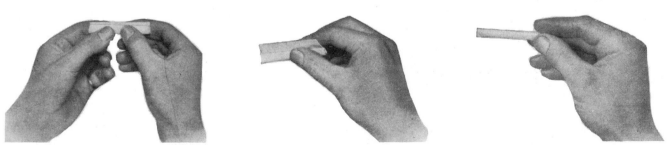

As roll is finished, the hands are gradually drawn apart. If near flap of paper is properly tucked in, cigarette will hold shape when one hand is removed.

Final step is to moisten and seal the farther flap (result, right). One of the ends—the end to light — is pinched or twisted sufficiently to close it.

Thomas R. Marshall is remembered for his classic remark: "What this country needs is a really good five cent cigar!" He was also U. S. Vice President.

Pipe smoking was second only to cigarettes on per capita basis between 1930 and 1945. Among its most noted exponents was Charles G. Dawes, who was Vice President under Coolidge. Most satisfactory wood is hard, even-grained French heath root, bruyere.

machine-made cigars accounted for nearly half the market in 1930, more than half in 1931, 80% by 1933. The small shop disappeared: there were 10,800 cigar factories in 1925, 1,200 in 1955. Meanwhile a massive advertising campaign was mounted for *Cremo*, dramatizing the hygienic nature of mechanized production: "Spit is a horrid word. But it is worse on the end of your cigar . . . Why run the risk of cigars made by dirty, yellowed fingers and tipped in spit? Remember, more than half of all cigars made in this country are still made *by hand*, and therefore subject to the risk of spit!"

True enough, the typical cigar shop had been a most unsavory-looking den (as the picture on page 201 indicates·) but it turned out that the absence of saliva was not an effective selling point. Nickel cigar sales rose, but not enough to justify advertising budgets of cigarette proportions.

During 1931 and 1932 it was difficult to sell even apples for a nickel, and the mighty effort to fulfill Marshall's desire was abandoned. Since then cigar consumption per capita has just about held its own; the cigar remains a specialty rather than a truly national branded product. Vast differences in brand rankings prevail from one region to another, and advertising is still as much regional as it is national. One prominent cigarette man called it a "cloak-and-suit" business, referring to the constant changes of cigar shapes going in and out of fashion. It is perhaps more accurate to call it a luxury hangover from the Gilded Age, for the number of those who can afford to like fine Havanas (at 25c or more apiece) is not legion.

Exit pipe, pinch and plug

Even though smoking tobacco and cigars were on the rise in 1890, that year saw the use of "eatin' tobacco" reach its per capita peak — nearly three pounds of plug, twist, or fine-cut being chewed for every man, woman and child. The "new" vogue for pipe-smoking reached its per capita peak (1.75 pounds per American) in 1910, although by that time the cigarette was on the way up in popular esteem. Because population grew so quickly, the amount of leaf converted to chewing and smoking products increased apace: in 1917 this total reached a high of 446,000,000 pounds for both forms. Since then it has dwindled consistently, the present production of 150,000,000 pounds a year being equal

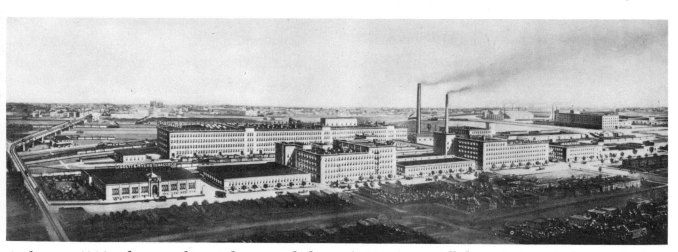

As late as 1921, plug, smoking tobacco and the cigarette were about equal on a poundage basis. In that year the huge St. Louis plant of Liggett & Myers was still the mainstay of plug production. Sculptured hedges on its broad lawns identified the company's bellwether chewing tobacco — "Star."

to somewhat less than half a pound of chaw per person and about the same amount of "smokum." Whether or not it has any significance, it is interesting that scrap tobacco was included with smoking tobacco figures by the Internal Revenue Bureau until 1930, while after that year it was lumped with chewing. Assuming scrap to be half smoked and half chewed, the use of pipe tobacco passed the chewing habit sometime in 1921 or 1922.

The death knell of cud was rung on September 14, 1955 by this memorandum to all Directors, Officers, Department Heads and "Others Concerned" in the headquarters of The American Tobacco Company:

> It has become impossible to hire persons in the New York area to clean and maintain cuspidors. Since the cuspidors presently on hand in the New York Office can no longer be serviced, it will be necessary to remove them promptly from the premises. Removal will take place this week end. Your cooperation in doing without this former convenience is solicited.

Snuff, strangely, has hung on grimly for the last fifty years, varying very little from a per capita consumption of a quarter pound per annum during that time. In amount consumed snuff is now about even with scrap—the two forms being the cheapest modes of tobacco use. The taking of snuff, however, is today far removed from the lordly sniffing of Regency *beaux*. Nine out of ten snuffers do not consume it as nose dust but place the powdered leaf in the mouth between gum and cheek. Thus

The bulging cheek, once characteristic of most American men, is now seldom seen. Only men whose work precludes smoking — like this baseballer — chew tobacco. Others who can't smoke on the job suck snuff, now really a form of "eatin' tobacco."

Consumer advertising during the 20s was dominated by three big blended cigarettes. "I'd Walk a Mile for a Camel" was signature of Reynolds campaigns.

Chesterfield, Liggett & Myers' brand, identified itself with slogan, "They Satisfy." Association of brand and given idea is a costly, long-term effort.

snuff is at present a variant of chewing tobacco except that it is sucked or tasted, not chewed.

The pipe, too—classic smoking medium of North America and Europe—continued to lose in favor. It is one form of smoking which requires a degree of skill. The tobacco must not be too dry, lest it bite, nor too moist, lest it fail to hold fire; the pipe must be caked, so as not to yield a raw taste, yet not soggy, so as not to impede the draw. Its maintenance requires copious pockets and large supplies of patience, matches, and leisure — qualifications met mainly by the college set, the retired set, and fishermen. In a desperate effort to revive the flagging art, a large pipemaker advertised in 1957: "Do Pipe Smokers Live Longer?" To which the wits were quick to reply: "No, it only seems longer." That smoking tobacco had seen its best days was underlined in the same year when the proprietors of *Bull Durham* moved the diminishing production of that once-lordly brand from Durham to Richmond. It was just one year less than a full century before, that Bull production, which was to revolutionize America's smoking tradition and to put

Durham on the map, had begun in that town. But the move caused scarcely a ripple, inside or outside Durham.

To the men who manage tobacco companies, the decline of snoose, smokestack, stogie and chaw was a highly predictable phenomenon even before World War I. By 1921—on a per capita poundage basis—the cigarette had pulled even with pipe and cigar; after 1922 (see chart, page 244) it was no contest. In any market as nearly universal as the smoking public — which now approximates 65,000,000 persons in the U.S. alone—the momentum of change is slow in gathering, but once under way is inexorable. The dropoff of pipe-smoking and chewing did not occur because the large companies diverted their advertising from these forms; rather, the reverse is true.

Advertising

The strategy of profitable promotion was expressed by George Washington Hill, who advertised *Lucky Strike* Cigarettes to brand leadership, as follows: "I believe in merchandising in the flow of the stream . . . I don't like to sell horse shoes and buggy whips, I like to sell what is growing; then it is more easy for me to get my share of what is growing." In 1957 Hill's dictum was confirmed by a proponent of the mathematical technique known as operations research. Advertising, claimed Dr. Marcello Vidale of the Arthur D. Little research organization, is highly effective in attracting new buyers of a product, but ad dollars spent to retain old customers accomplish considerably less.

Although twentieth-century changes in smoking fashions have stimulated massive advertising campaigns as each company scrambled to get its "share of what is growing," the precise role of advertising in the tobacco industry is not well understood. Advertising did not provide the impetus for the American smoking tradition, nor has it played a major role in effecting changes in tobacco usages. National consumption did not jump suddenly upward from 1910 to 1913, when tobacco advertising nearly doubled following the dissolution of the tobacco combination. And cigarette consumption actually experienced its sharpest increase during World War II, when all advertising was curtailed and the promotional budgets for some fairly large brands completely disappeared. Advertising is intended to win for a specific brand a larger share of the market, or to defend a specific brand against competitive products.

Except for the introduction of new brands, the expense of advertising tobacco products is surprisingly low on a unit-cost basis. Referring to his 1952 operations, the president of one of the largest companies told his stockholders that advertising expenses amounted to about one-third of a cent per package of twenty cigarettes. On the company's 1952 volume of 141,000,000,000 cigarettes, this translates into $24 million worth of advertising, or 17c per thousand cigarettes. By comparison, the value of the 2.8 pounds of leaf or thereabouts that go into a thousand finished cigarettes was something like $3.00, and the value of the fifty blue Federal excise stamps was exactly $4.00. In a going business comprised of big-volume brands, advertising is an indispensable expense but not an overpowering one — 2.5% of the cost of manufacture if the 8c Federal tax is included, 5% or 6% if it is not. The 17c-per-thousand figure is a minimum, applicable only to the three or four very largest brands;

Advertising and selling dominated the 20s and 30s. George Washington Hill was advertising virtuoso, pulled his Lucky Strike brand up to Camel's level.

an average for the fifteen largest brands would be perhaps twice that figure. There is, too, the reciprocal relationship between leaf and advertising layouts — some companies pay more for leaf and less for promotion, others the reverse.

Advertising plays its most critical part in the introduction of a new brand. Analysis of published statistics on unit sales, tax payments, and costs of sales for the large cigarette companies in 1957 places the factory cost of 1,000 cigarettes of standard size in the $6.50-$7.00 range. Against the wholesale price of $8.28 this yields a "spread" between $1.25 and $1.75, out of which must come freight, selling-administrative overhead, and advertising. The breakeven point on a typical brand thus assumes an expenditure of no more than $1 or so per thousand on advertising.

The minimum or "threshold" figure for a year's national advertising, according to trade magazine estimates, is hardly less than $3 or $4 million — which means that an actively promoted new brand cannot contribute to profits until its volume exceeds three or four billion units per year. If the brand

"YOU WOULDN'T TURN A DOG OUT ON A NIGHT LIKE THIS!" wailed NELL

"But father, with his slick city ways and perfumed hair, he turned my head . . ."

"Out ye go!" roared the irascible old yeoman . . : "any gal of mine that gives away the last of my smoother and better OLD GOLDS suffers the consequences. Down to the corner store with ye, and bring back a fresh carton or never darken my doorstep again!"

OLD GOLD

FASTEST GROWING CIGARETTE IN HISTORY . . . NOT A COUGH IN A CARLOAD

Listen in . . . OLD GOLD—PAUL WHITEMAN HOUR, every Tuesday, 9 P. M., Eastern Time

Old Gold brand was advertised on a large scale beginning in 1926. John Held woodcuts were among many themes and approaches used in the brand's promotion. By 1937 Old Gold had 5% of the market.

does not win this kind of volume within a year or two, advertising support is usually withdrawn. At least half of the 16 new brands introduced by the large manufacturers between 1950 and 1956—most of them king size or filter tip cigarettes—were "two-year rockets" in this category. Each represented an advertising investment of substantial proportions— $7 million, $8 million, $10 million, as Amos 'n Andy would have put it. In effect, the manufacturer must spend that much to introduce his product to the public before he can discover whether it is acceptable. The cost of making a new product known, of "buying" the general public reaction, is

a necessary cost of doing business. But the expenditure itself is no guarantee of success.

Selling, selling, selling

By the 1920s tobacco manufacturing had completed its long transition from a leisurely country craft to a competitive war waged on a national battlefield. In this war advertising was the heavy artillery. But the big cigarette brands had their infantry too—the foot-slogging sales forces which carried the competitive fight all the way to the smallest retail outlet, the "Mom and Pop" store.

The main job of these sales forces was not taking orders, but reinforcing the advertising for their brands. This they did in several ways: by placing point-of-purchase display materials at or near the retail counters; by helping retailer and wholesaler rotate tobacco stocks properly, so as to keep a regulated flow of fresh merchandise going to the consumer; and by "maintaining distribution," that is, inducing the storekeeper to carry their brands or tiding him over if he should be temporarily out of stock. This activity was quite as competitive, if not so spectacular, as the advertising barrages. And it grew more intense and more expensive as the number of retail outlets for tobacco multiplied.

The tobacco salesman—now more properly called a brand missionary—was a breed distinctly different from the nineteenth-century drummer. Reliance on premiums as a means of wheedling cooperation from retailers was passé, along with consumer premiums like the silk flags, cigarette cards and prize coupons of the prewar period. The manufacturer's missionary man had no brummagems or special discounts to sell. Rather, his stock in trade was massive volume, rapid turnover—generated by the great weight of advertising directed at the consumer. Thus mass production was inevitably followed by mass retailing and the disappearance of the thousand-odd miscellaneous brands which divided the market at the century's turn.

Old Gold

Advertising and selling dominated the 20s and 30s, and these were by no means limited to the three-cornered battle waged by *Camel, Lucky Strike* and *Chesterfield.* P. Lorillard, which had concentrated its cigarette efforts on Turkish brands since 1911, entered the battle of the blends in 1926

240

Philip Morris brand, introduced as domestic blend during the 1930s, rounded out the so-called Big Five cigarettes. The brand's advertising featured little Johnny's clarion "call for Philip Morris."

with *Old Gold*. Among its advertising techniques was the "Blindfold Test" (involving *Old Gold* and three "unidentified" brands); print ads featuring John Held flappers, Petty girls, and Ripley's "Believe It or Not"; radio; comic strips; and prize contests. Using every medium at its disposal, the brand fought its way into sizable volume and by 1937 accounted for 5% of the U. S. cigarette sales total.

Philip Morris Inc.

In 1933, this achievement was duplicated by another new brand whose name dated back to the London tobacconist of the 1850s: *Philip Morris.*

By now, the London firm had become Philip Morris & Co., Ltd., Inc., an American publicly-owned tobacco manufacturer.

The new brand was introduced in the midst of the depression and in the face of strong competition from the well-established Big Four. *Philip Morris English Blend*, in a distinctive brown package, was priced to wholesale at 12c and retail at 15c, as against 10.5c and 12.5c on the average for the established brands. This gave the trade an extra penny of profit during the new brand's formative years, and this incentive served *Philip Morris* well. Early advertising was not on a massive scale, although it was memorable for the hiring, in March of 1933, of a diminutive page boy from the Hotel New Yorker, Johnny. He became, in effect, a living trade mark for the brand and his clarion "Call for Philip Morris!" was widely heard. The principal emphasis of the brand's growth, however, was in selling as distinct from advertising.

By 1940 the *Philip Morris* brand achieved a penetration of 7% of national cigarette sales, and in 1950 reached a peak of 40,000,000,000 units, or 11% of the U. S. total.

The success of *Philip Morris* traced not only to concentration on personal selling, but also to the aristocratic aura with which the brand was surrounded. The company's older brands — including *English Ovals, Marlboro, Philip Morris Oxford Blues* and *Philip Morris Cambridge* — were expensive products. Thus *Philip Morris English Blend*, the full name under which the domestic cigarette was introduced, traded on the prestige of the costly Turkish brands already produced by the firm. It was this intangible advantage, along with its unusual tobacco-brown packing and somewhat different aroma, which enabled *Philip Morris* to command a higher retail price for a time. By World War II, when the brand had reached the No. 4 position, the price was made competitive with that of other domestic blends.

In common with its rivals, the Philip Morris company in recent years has turned to what has been called a "department store" line of products — different brands for different tastes. It has been especially active in the repackaging of its major brands, beginning with the filter tip *Marlboro* in 1955, followed by new package designs for *Philip Morris, Parliament,* and *Spud.*

World War II

Partly as a result of the depressions of 1932 and 1938, partly as the result of war production from 1940 on, the expansion of city populations was accelerated. This showed up clearly in the statistics of cigarette consumption, which made their greatest percentage gains during the rapid urbanization of 1940-1946.

In 1945, some 267 billion cigarettes were sold on the domestic market, an increase of 12% over 1944, 48% over 1940, 124% over 1930. Yet demand was literally insatiable. Long lines formed outside tobacco shops; the "offbrands," thrown together with any and all leaf available on the markets, had a sales picnic.

Leaf tobacco production on the farms was not the only bottleneck; there were shortages in packaging materials, in sugar, in glycerin, in transportation space.

In terms of total production there was no short-age: but some 18% of the cigarette output during 1941-45, or 222.6 billion cigarettes, was sent overseas. Tobacco was classed by President Franklin D. Roosevelt as an essential crop; draft boards were directed to defer tobacco farmers to insure maximum output. Employees of Wright Aeronautical put up a fund of $10,000 for the war effort, wired General Douglas MacArthur to ask what his troops needed most. His reply was an echo of the one given by his old commanding officer, Black Jack Pershing, twenty-five years before. "The entire amount," he answered, "should be used to purchase American cigarettes which, of all personal comforts, are the most difficult to obtain here."

Although they were intended for the personal use of the troops, cigarettes were widely put to use overseas as barter goods. Troops in France, for example, were paid in francs at 50 to the dollar. But it took 400 francs to buy a dollar's worth of merchandise where most desirable merchandise

Although cigarette production increased 48% during the five years of World War II, 18% of total output was shipped overseas to servicemen. This created a shortage on the domestic market, and patient queues formed outside tobacco establishments. This store, in downtown New York City, sold cigarettes between the hours of 11-12 and 3-4 daily. In January, 1945, the proprietor served coffee to waiting customers.

As in previous wars, field commanders called for tobacco for the troops and got it. In addition to satisfying their smoking desires, troops utilized American cigarettes as barter goods. For two years after V-E Day, cigarettes remained the most stable currency in the retail marts of European countries.

changed hands — in the black market. The same situation obtained throughout Europe, where currencies all but evaporated. It was inevitable that the grumbling American doughfaces should use their cigarettes and chocolate bars to buy what their pay could not. And they were encouraged by shopkeepers, who ran after strolling G.I.'s on the streets to bargain for American cigarettes. For two years after V-E Day, cigarettes remained the only stable currency in the retail marts of Germany, Italy and France.

King size

The changes that come in the wake of war usually include tobacco changes, and War II was no exception. Along with ranch houses, foam rubber mattresses and plastic toys, modern design influenced the cigarette. The king size, 85 millimeters in length versus the "regular" 70 millimeters, took long steps toward the 25% of the market it was to capture by 1953. There was, as always, an underlying consideration of taste, for the attenuated cigarette meant a milder smoke (the physical dimensions of a cigarette, like those of a cigar, greatly influence the characteristics of the delivered smoke).

The coming of the kings was not, actually, a sudden break in the direction of mildness. Gradually, in the two decades before Pearl Harbor, cigarette grades of leaf were becoming less strong as farmers refined growing practices. Less strong meant, in effect, lower in nicotine content; virtually all the standard-size brands had become milder in this sense — although the adjective "milder" was so overworked in advertising that it nearly lost its meaning. The kings simply fitted into this trend. Those that succeeded owed their success not to fashionable length, but to the fact that they delivered the "Burley-blend" taste in a somewhat filtered degree.

The "modern design" of the king-sized cigarette marked an important change in the tobacco business. From the multitude of brands on the market in 1903 (12,600 chews, 7,000 smoking tobaccos,

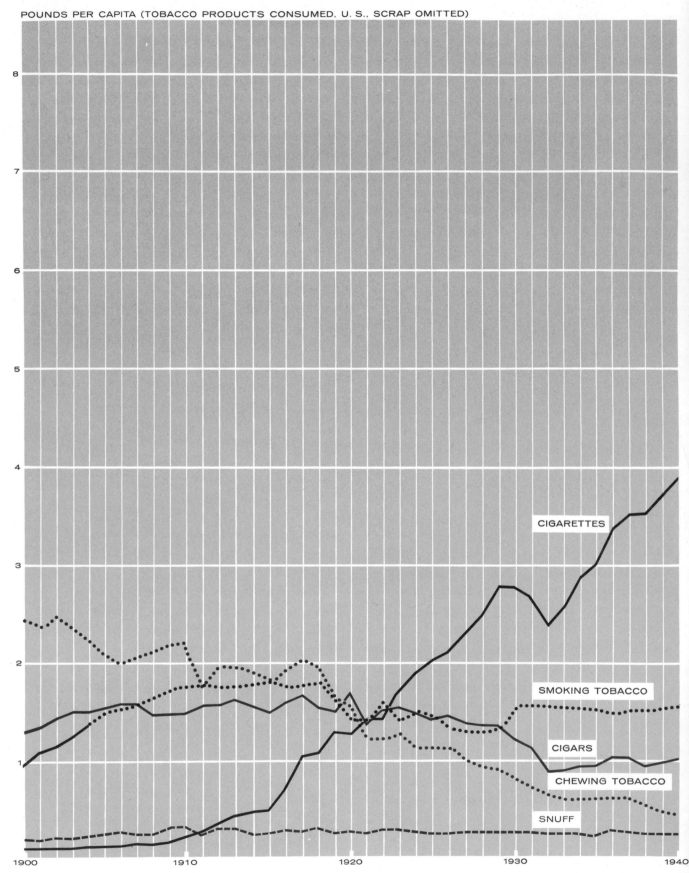

POUNDS PER CAPITA (TOBACCO PRODUCTS CONSUMED, U. S., SCRAP OMITTED)

CIGARETTES

SMOKING TOBACCO

CIGARS

CHEWING TOBACCO

SNUFF

8

7

6

5

4

3

2

1

1900   1910   1920   1930   1940

Per capita consumption of cigarettes by Americans (red line) is now seven pounds a year. Smoking of cigars (black line) has held close to a pound per *year since the 30s, while pipe smoking (dotted red line), chewing (dotted black line) and snuff usage (broken black line) together account for a pound a*

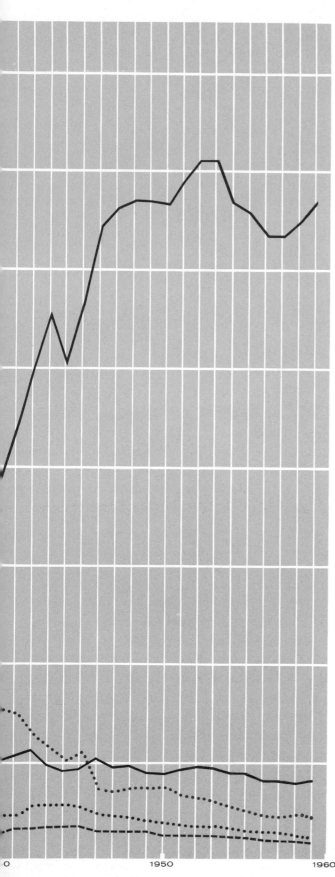

year per American. Recent cigarette consumption is understated by leaf-poundage comparison, since the filter cigarette gives equal puffs with less leaf.

2,100 cigarettes and cigars) there had emerged the battle of the big brands. Although many of the turn-of-the-century products coasted along on small volume (and still do), the bulk of each company's business soon narrowed into one big brand. Almost the full weight of a company's advertising resources was placed behind a single cigarette. For a while, there were three big brands selling between 90% and 95% of the nation's cigarettes (*Camel, Lucky Strike, Chesterfield*). In 1926, P. Lorillard advertised its *Old Gold* brand into contention, and in the 1930s the *Philip Morris* brand rounded out the so-called "Big Five."

There were five big brands, and five big tobacco companies. Within a company, minor cigarette brands were not allowed to get in the way of the big one; quite a number of lesser brand names were sold off or farmed out.

In 1939 George Washington Hill, whose advertising ability had brought *Lucky Strike* into perennial competition with *Camel* for the No. 1 spot, broke away from the one-big-brand idea with a king-size cigarette, *Pall Mall*. The new cigarette competed against all five standard brands, including Hill's own *Lucky Strike*. *Pall Mall* was given to a separate subsidiary company, American Cigarette and Cigar, and made to stand or fall "on its own bottom."

The new corporate setup was analogous to General Motors' splitting of its automobile brands into five divisions, competition thereafter taking place within the company as well as between companies. Chevrolet, Pontiac, Oldsmobile, Buick and Cadillac battled each other in the market place, in addition to their existing rivalry with Ford and Chrysler lines.

Something of the same sort occurred in all cigarette companies. By 1951 each large manufacturer had a king-size brand alongside its regular. By 1956, each of the six major cigarette makers was actively promoting a regular, a king, and two filter brands. After five years of serious advertising, the filter brands included regular and king sizes as well as mentholated smokes. The old stiff cardboard box was revived in the form of the crushproof or "flip-top" box introduced by the *Marlboro* filter brand in 1954. This packing brought with it "long size" cigarettes, 80 millimeters long. During this fast shuffle, new brands zoomed to major status and old

Franklin D. Roosevelt smoked a pipe as Secretary of the Navy, was a cigarette smoker as President. Long holder foreshadowed the king size cigarette.

Starting in 1939, king size cigarettes (85 mm. as against 70 mm. for regulars) climbed steadily. In 1956 55% of cigarettes were kings or 80 mm. "longs."

ones faded to insignificance in the space of a year or two, putting a premium on quick-minded management. In an age of mass advertising and mass distribution, national magazines and network television, any return to the old thousand-brand days seems doubtful; on the other hand, a return to a "standard" cigarette, with five brands holding 80% or 90% of the market, seems equally unlikely. The total demand for tobacco is, in the jargon of the economists, "relatively inelastic"; but the forms in which it is consumed, and the brand names attached to those forms, are seldom static for very long.

In 1959, the brands actively promoted by the six large cigarette manufacturers numbered twenty-seven, marketed in some forty-four sizes and packings.

Reynolds offered *Camel* (70 mm.), *Cavalier* (80 mm.), *Winston* (filter tip, 80 mm. and 85 mm.) and *Salem* (filter tip mentholated, 85 mm.).

American Tobacco offered *Lucky Strike* (70 mm.), *Pall Mall* (85 mm.), *Herbert Tareyton* (85 mm.), *Hit Parade* (filter tip, 80 mm. and 85 mm.), *Riviera* (filter tip mentholated, 85 mm.) and *Dual Filter Tareyton* (filter tip, 85 mm.).

Liggett & Myers offered *Chesterfield* (70 mm.), *Chesterfield* king (85 mm.), *L & M* (filter tip, 70 mm., 80 mm. and 85 mm.), *Duke* (filter tip, 85 mm.) and *Oasis* (filter tip mentholated, 85 mm.).

Lorillard offered *Old Gold* (70 mm.), *Old Gold* king (85 mm.), *Old Gold* Filter King (85 mm.), *Kent* (filter tip, 70 mm., 80 mm. and 85 mm.), *Spring* (filter tip mentholated, 85 mm.) and *Newport* (filter tip mentholated, 80 mm. and 85 mm.).

Philip Morris offered *Philip Morris* (70 mm.), *Philip Morris* long (80 mm.), *Marlboro* (filter tip, 80 mm. and 85 mm.), *Parliament* (filter tip, 80 mm. and 85 mm.), *Alpine* (filter tip mentholated, 85 mm.) and *Spud* (filter tip mentholated, 80 mm.).

Brown & Williamson offered *Viceroy* (filter tip,

80 mm. and 85 mm.), *Kool* (mentholated, 70 mm.), *Kool* (filter tip mentholated, 85 mm.), *Belair* (filter tip mentholated, 85 mm.), *Life* (filter tip, 85 mm.), *Raleigh* (85 mm.) and *Raleigh* (filter tip, 85 mm.).

Brown & Williamson

Among the large cigarette makers, the exception to the "one big brand" philosophy was Brown & Williamson. Originally a small snuff firm in Winston-Salem, Brown & Williamson was purchased in 1927 by British-American Tobacco Company (which had been severed from The American Tobacco Company in 1911).

From the first, Brown & Williamson attempted to build its cigarette volume not by meeting the big brands head on, but by offering "specialty brands" appealing to limited segments of the market. It experimented with cork tips, filter tips, premium coupons, wetproof paper, menthol—in short, with all the features the giant brands did not offer.

Appropriately enough for a British-owned firm, B & W named its first cigarette for Sir Walter Raleigh, the legendary British tobacco promoter. *Raleigh* was made up with a blend similar to that of *Camel*, packed in a "saddlebag" box and priced at 20c in 1929, when cigarettes were selling two packs for 25c. Forced by depression into price competition, B & W swung to the other extreme with *Target,* a 10c roll-your-own tobacco with a steel-and-rubber rolling gadget, designed to yield fifty cigarettes for a dime. Price-consciousness among the public plus the low price of leaf tobacco led to *Wings* and *Avalon,* the so-called "ten centers." And the low cost of merchandise generally inspired B & W to revive premium coupons, which had died out after *Camel* emerged in 1913 with the legend on its pack "Don't look for premiums or coupons." Coupons were offered with a repackaged, popular-priced *Raleigh,* with the mentholated *Kool,* and with the filter tipped *Viceroy.*

Following World War II B & W offered *Life* cigarettes with wetproof paper in the 80 millimeter "long" size. This length, five millimeters short of full king size, was to become popular ten years later in the flip-top box, but in the soft "cup" package it did not catch on. Brown & Williamson's filter brand, *Viceroy,* represented less than 8% of its cigarette volume as late as 1952, sixteen years after its original introduction. But it was this brand

which lifted the company from the marginal category during the 1950s. By 1956 *Viceroy* reached a volume of 25,000,000,000 units; first on the filter scene at a popular price, *Viceroy* was the leading filter brand through 1954.

Specialty markets, specialty makers

Although cigarettes made up seven-eighths of U. S. tobacco purchases in 1958, the remaining eighth represented a retail volume of some $832 million. About $250 million of this was spent for

Appropriately, British-owned Brown & Williamson used Raleigh brand name for its first venture into cigarette field. Originally a high-priced product, Raleigh became a coupon brand during depressed 30s. Shop figure of Sir Walter Raleigh, English tobacco promoter, stands in Louisville headquarters.

"manufactured tobacco"—smoking tobaccos, chewing tobacco, and snuff.

Five of the six large cigarette firms originated in this "manufactured tobacco" field, and they retain many of the important pipe, plug or snuff brands. Other companies specialize in one or another of these categories; in snuff, U. S. Tobacco, American Snuff, George W. Helme Co.; in smoking tobacco, Larus & Brother, Bloch Brothers. There is still a "specialty cigarette" field, which includes Stephano Brothers and G. A. Georgopulo, among others. Many of their brands fall into the premium-priced category by virtue of special packing, tinted paper, or unusual (i.e., limited-demand) blends.

Mechanization or no, there are still about 600 cigar factories in the U. S., which in 1958 produced nearly $600 million worth of the brown rolls. Not all are small: the largest cigar firms (Consolidated, American Tobacco, General, Bayuk, D.W.G.) account for roughly half of dollar cigar sales. Only in relation to the well-nigh-universal cigarette custom (56% of American men, 30% of the ladies are regular cigarette smokers) can the cigar business be called a "specialty." The custom which it serves is both long-standing (300 years) and widespread (one of every six American men occasionally, one out of twenty regularly). So it is not surprising that the changing shape of cigarettes and their market should find a parallel in cigars.

Thinned cigars

Longer, thinner cigarettes after World War II were reflected in the static-volume cigar business.

Where fat perfectos and "banker" sizes had once ruled the glassed counters, slim panetelas and palmas moved to the front row. Cigarillos, a short-filler cross between cigar and all-tobacco cigarette, gained some headway as a "thin" smoke. In addition to their "youthful" slenderness and 4c or 5c price, they were helped by redesigned boxes and five-packings and for a time their makers thought they saw a bright, brown vision of the long-sought nickel cigar coming into its own. But the brown roll's turn-of-the-century dominance was not to return: per capita consumption in 1957 was almost identical with the 1932 figure.

The constant research efforts of the cigar-men did give rise to an unexpected development during the 1950s — a development which, ironically, promised greater advantage to cigarette manufacture than to cigar making. This was the development of reconstituted binder leaf, also known as HTL (homogenized tobacco leaf). As it comes from the field, the natural binder leaf yields four pieces suitable for use in cigars plus a 30% remainder that is sold as scrap. By pulverizing the entire leaf and reconstituting it into a paper-like sheet, the wastage is eliminated. In September, 1955, the Department of Agriculture was moved to observe that "the development of a binder sheet is attracting considerable attention and appears to have possibilities of extending the mechanization of the industry and reducing the labor in the production of cigars . . . One 5-cent brand of cigars and one brand of cigarillos containing Homogenized Tobacco Leaf have been on the market for more than 1 year, and very

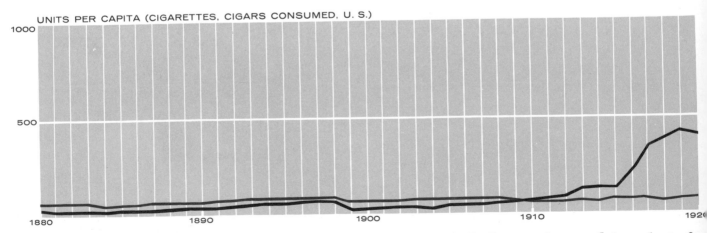

UNITS PER CAPITA (CIGARETTES, CIGARS CONSUMED, U. S.)

Between 1880 and 1910 cigarettes (red line) were a big-city luxury comparable to cigars (black line). Late in the 1890s unit cigarette sales approached *the cigar totals, but tax increased from 1c to 2c per pack of 20 in 1897 and to 3c in 1898. Volume dropped off sharply. In 1902 tax reverted to 1.08c per*

good consumer acceptance has been reported for these products."

Acceptance of HTL by tobacco growers could not, however, be described as "very good." Something of an editorial storm arose in protest, not only in the Connecticut Valley but also in Virginia, the Carolinas, Kentucky and Tennessee. Cigarette manufacturers had also seen the possibilities in the new process, and a Senate investigation the following spring revealed that several of the big brands were using varying proportions of reconstituted leaf. Although the hearings produced talk of "junk smokes" and "synthetic leaf," no evidence was adduced to indicate that adulterants were being used — the leaf was simply taken apart and reprocessed in its own extracts. Even while the hearings were fresh in mind, however, some of the editorials took a calmer tone. Said one in a Raleigh, North Carolina daily: "The trouble is that science apparently has made the synthetic tobacco leaf so good that people like it . . . What bothers us is the hand-sized cloud on the horizon which betokens a future struggle to throw a net of restrictions around homogenized tobacco leaf . . . We hope tobacco doesn't do it . . .

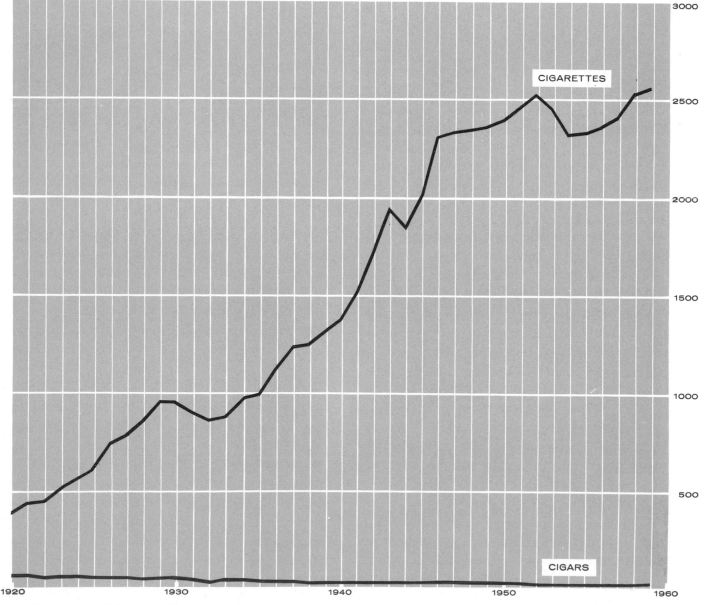

pack of 20, and white rolls resumed increase. First dramatic growth impetus was supplied by the first world war, during which American doughboys took to cigarettes. Growth was checked in 1930-32, when "roll your own" cigarettes cut into "tailor-mades." Korean War peak, 1952, was topped in 1958 and 1959.

"Cigarette girls" of several eras depict story of the white roll. Carmen, the Spanish cigarette girl of Bizet's opera, was the archtype of recklessness.

Flapper of 1920s may have smoked cigarettes out of sheer affectation, but symbolized the emancipation of women and made cigarette a truly national usage.

Those whose livelihoods are involved in tobacco could profit from experience, and think up some other way of marching with the times."

The HTL argument passed almost unnoticed outside the tobacco states; it was a brushfire rather than a full-fledged controversy. But the cigarette itself was once again to be the subject of flaming headlines and incendiary allegations.

Trial of the cigarette

The figures for cigarette consumption from 1913 to 1929 do not suggest controversy, for the curve (page 248) is smooth and upward. But the wowsers were not yet finished. Passage of the Eighteenth Amendment, prohibiting *spiritus frumenti*, encouraged a revival of the anti-tobacco movement. No less a root-and-branch man than Billy Sunday himself declared: "Prohibition is won; now for tobacco."

The original attacks on tobacco were based on guilt by association; tobacco was discovered being used by the New World barbarians, ergo, tobacco was bad. This was the initial reaction of the educated Spaniard, and it was echoed in 1604 by James

I of England who asked: "What humour or policie can move us to imitate the barbarous and beastly manners of the wilde, godlesse, and slavish Indians, especially in so vile and stinking a custome?"

Like many who followed him, James tried to "document" his essentially moral objection by imputing harmful effects to smoking. "A custome," he wrote, "loathsome to the eye, hatefull to the nose, harmefull to the braine, dangerous to the lungs," and so forth. Echoes of his "Counterblaste to Tobacco" have recurred in many forms. In 1689, the Medical School of Paris officially sponsored the view that tobacco smoking shortened life. In 1798, Dr. Benjamin Rush blamed smoking and chewing tobacco for exciting a desire for strong drinks, "and these when taken between meals soon lead to intemperance and drunkenness." Strong drink had taken the place of the savage Indian in Rush's theory of guilt by association.

Guilt by association was the basis of the 1854 assault against cigarette smoking; in that year the white roll was denounced as effeminate. But the charges against tobacco itself had not been dropped, although the tobacco-smoking custom was well into its fourth century. *The Lancet,* an English medical journal, featured "The Great Tobacco Question" during 1856-1857. One Dr. Hodgkin associated tobacco with the increase of crime. A Dr. Solly associated tobacco with nervous paralysis and loss of intellectual capacity. And a Dr. Schneider wrote, without documentation, that "So frequently is vision impaired by the constant use of tobacco, that spectacles may be said to be a part and parcel of a German, as a hat is to an Englishman. In America, likewise, where my practise has been extended, I have noted the same pernicious effects, and it is a well attested fact that the Americans wear themselves out by the use of tobacco." These charges, based on superficial observation or no evidence at all, are remembered for their quaint romantic interest. But it is easy to forget that they did not still the voice of reason. *The Lancet* itself noted at the time that "the use of tobacco is widely spread, more widely than any one custom, form of worship, or religious belief, and that therefore it must have some good or at least pleasurable effects; that, if its evil effects were so dreadful as stated the human race would have ceased to exist."

But the formula of guilt by association was used in almost every conceivable variation. Between 1895 and 1909, cigarettes were accused of inducing moustaches on ladies' lips and increasing the population of insane asylums. In 1912 a Dr. Tidswell opined that "the most common cause of female sterility is the abuse of tobacco by males . . . those countries which use most tobacco have the largest number of stillbirths." Anti-tobacco campaigners demanded censorship of the nursery rhyme about Old King Cole because his majesty "called for his pipe." During the first World War one intemperate temperance leader cried that cigarettes were being doped to produce addiction and insure a steady flow of sales.

Infancy of cigarette industry was marked by pretty Richmond hand-roller of the 1880s. No Carmen, she was highly trained, highly moral, painfully slow.

Modern cigarette girl is called a "catcher." She monitors the output of high-speed machinery so as to catch imperfect cigarettes before packing stage.

After the 1918 Armistice, these somewhat far-fetched objections were supplemented by less specific ones. The 1854 charge was turned around: cigarettes were not effeminate but unladylike. The poor etiquette practiced by many ash-droppers and public puffers was cited in support of this. The redoubtable Lucy Page Gaston announced in 1920 she would run for President on the no-tobacco issue. Some males, annoyed at feminist pretensions in general, affected horror at the idea of public puffing by their womanfolk and went along with Miss Gaston. Others, annoyed at the rising tide of "sticky-beaking," formed smokers' leagues to defend the right to light. Miss Gaston did not run for President, although she continued to campaign. Meanwhile the nation's ladies took to cigarette smoking in large numbers; the steep climb of cigarette sales, a distinct departure from the gradual change that had characterized previous shifts in tobacco fashion, was generally credited to the fair sex.

With the passing of Miss Gaston, her successors ranged the realm of medicine as well as the realm of manners. Tobacco was a poison, some charged, although the lengthening span of human life hardly bore out this contention. Opposition to tobacco during the 20s also continued to be based on social objections, with the short-skirted, cigarette-brandishing "flapper" as the symbolic target. Some men of medicine, made newly aware of the importance of psychological elements in human well-being, came to the defense of the tobacco tradition — in moderation, of course. The American Tobacco Company added this line to its *Lucky Strike* adver-

tisements: "Be moderate — be moderate in all things, even in smoking." The clamor faded, and the anti-tobacco states one by one dropped their no-smoking-in-public statutes from the books.

There was little time or inclination to carry on the debate during the grim 1930s. Tobacco was one of the few creature comforts that could be enjoyed by those in financial straits, even though some were obliged to abandon cigarettes for pipes or hand-made cigarettes. With the advent of War II, the need of G. I. Joe for fags and lucifers — and the need of home-fronters for solace — again came into focus.

But the tendency to associate tobacco with ailments of unknown cause continued. As recently as 1943 one anti-cigarette author wrote: "There is little doubt that smoking leads to consumption or tuberculosis. A study of the period 1930-1950 will be most interesting and will doubtless show a marked increase in tuberculosis of the female population." (In 1956 the U. S. Public Health Service reported that the tuberculosis death rate for females had decreased from 68.2 in 1930 to 14.7 in 1950, 7.0 in 1953, and was still on the decrease.)

The tuberculosis association was dropped as the infectious nature of that ailment became known. Medical attention shifted to increasing death rates from cancer, and especially lung cancer (although the lung cancer death rate did not rise as much as the tuberculosis death rate decreased). It was inevitable that someone should attempt to associate tobacco with this new — or, rather, previously rarely-diagnosed — ailment.

Newest cigarette factory is this Lorillard plant at Greensboro, North Carolina. The Old North state *now manufactures 56% of the nation's cigarettes, 38% of its smoking tobacco, and 82% of its plug.*

Tobacco tradition remains strong along the banks of the James River where it began. Richmond makes one-fourth of the nation's cigarettes and also a quarter of the country's smoking tobacco poundage.

"Tobacco Row," above, includes factories of Philip Morris, Larus & Brother (Edgeworth smoking tobacco) and The American Tobacco Company. Not visible in picture is Liggett & Myers plant.

The attempt to associate smoking with respiratory cancer was touched off in 1953 by a researcher who painted mice with concentrated tobacco extract and thereby induced skin cancers. Thousands of the little creatures were sacrificed in scientific efforts to duplicate these results, most of them unsuccessful. No lung cancer was induced in any experimental animal by the administration of tobacco smoke. Yet this was glossed over by the anticigarette crusaders: statistics were produced to show correlations between smoking and respiratory death rates. The lengthening span of life, the vanquishing of infectious diseases, and the resultant increase in neoplastic ailments whetted interest in the unknown cause of cell growth run wild. Newspapers converted their reporters into science writers who outdid one another in grisly interpretations of death rates.

It was in Washington, before a Congressional hearing in July 1957, that the "Great Tobacco Question" got its most complete examination. A number of reputable scientists testified that there was no sound basis for the cigarette cancer theory. The chief medical statistician of the Mayo Clinic observed that the statistical studies alleging association were rendered suspect by the lack of any

pathological or biological evidence. A Yale pathologist testified he had found it impossible to induce cancer in sensitive embryonic lung tissue with tobacco derivatives, although he had done so with coal tar. An American Medical Association cancer research committee chairman testified that, even accepting the mouse skin cancer experiment as valid, a human would have to smoke 100,000 cigarettes daily to get an equivalent exposure. A New York professor of medicine pointed out that the relative percentage of female lung cancers was decreasing, although the number of female cigarette smokers was increasing. A Texas pathologist questioned whether lung cancer was increasing, or only the diagnosis of lung cancer. Dogs, it was pointed out, showed an increase in lung cancer but no increase in cigarette smoking. Possibly prompted by the publicity attending the hearings, Dr. Charles W. Mayo, head of the famous clinic, was moved to announce: "I just don't believe smoking causes lung cancer."

Later the same year, the Southern Medical Association received proof that cigarette smoking is not necessarily associated with diminished longevity or a higher risk of lung cancer or heart disease. Studies in nine cigarette plants of The American

Tobacco Company, involving more than 115,000 person-years and extending more than ten years, documented a population which

  (1) smoked far more cigarettes than the average — double the number consumed by the U. S. urban population;

  (2) definitely lived longer than average; and

  (3) showed average or lower-than-average death rates for cancer, lung cancers, cardiovascular and coronary disease.

"The existence of such a population," the study concluded, "makes it manifest that cigarette smoking per se is not necessarily or invariably associated with a higher risk of lung cancer or heart disease or with diminished longevity." The basic research was not a cigarette company product: mortality conclusions had been published by two scientists of the U. S. Public Health Service, Dorn and Baum, and the smoking habits survey of the same general population was done by the Institute of Statistics of the University of North Carolina.

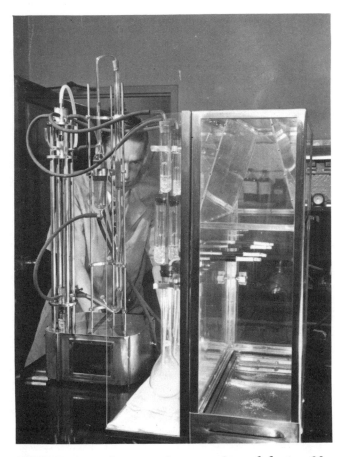

Automatic smoking machine, perfected during 30s, removes solid components of cigarette smoke under conditions which simulate normal human smoking.

The filtered fifties

The upward curve of cigarette use continued, but the "health scare" led to the revival of the old mouthpiece cigarette once favored by Russian aristocrats and novelty-keen New Yorkers. From a fringe position in 1951, with 1% of the domestic market, filter tip brands rose to 46% of sales by 1958.

What started as a health fad was undoubtedly spurred by the attenuation of American taste in general: "mildness" became a desired attribute not only in cigarette smoke but also in beer, coffee, and other comestibles. The filter-tip also contributed to the cigarette as a convenience article, eliminating loose tobacco ends and affording a firmer purchase between the lips. Since filter tips were less expensive than the tobacco they replaced, manufacturers tumbled over each other in the race to create and promote new filter brands.

The filter brands evolved from the so-called "mouthpiece" cigarette which dates from the nineteenth century. A stiff paper tube extended from the tobacco column contained a puff of cotton through which the smoke stream passed. These were hard-to-manufacture, expensive specialties (as brand names like *Tolstoi* and *Svoboda* suggest). The premium-priced *Parliament* introduced in 1932 by Benson & Hedges was such a mouthpiece cigarette.

In the popular-priced field the filter cigarette was also very much of a specialty item prior to the 1950s. The *Viceroy* brand, introduced in 1936 by Brown & Williamson, used a cylinder of folded paper rather than a hollow tube with cotton. It achieved only nominal volume until 1952, when the filter move began. In 1954 *Viceroy* changed to the tip of cellulose acetate, a material which quickly became the "normal" filter.

As filter demand rose, brands multiplied. *Kent* began in 1952 as a high-filtration brand with the tradename "Micronite" to suggest the micro-dimensional fibers in its tip. *L & M*, brought out in 1953 with the cellulose acetate tip, later added crosswise fibers to increase filtering efficiency. *Winston* was introduced in 1954, also with a cellulose acetate tip, and by 1955 became the largest-selling filter brand. *Marlboro* appeared in 1954 with a cellulose acetate filter tradenamed "Selectrate" and packed in a

"Practical" or everyday research is described by the phrase "quality control." Here cigarette shreds are magnified for accurate laboratory measurement.

hinged "flip-top" or crush-proof box. In 1956 came *Salem,* which offered menthol flavoring in addition to its filter tip. These six brands constituted the major entries in the filter field by 1958.

The market multiplied. In 1954 filter versions of the *Herbert Tareyton* and *Old Gold* brands appeared; the latter brand was now a three-way cigarette, offering a regular, a nonfilter king, and a filter, all under the same brand name. Other *"splits"* followed: *Kool* and *Raleigh* came out with filters. (*Chesterfield* and *Philip Morris* had already split into two-way nonfilter brands, each adding a king size to its standard size brand.)

Innovations in filtration continued. *Parliament* promoted high filtration and a ¼-inch recess at its mouth end. The use of cellulose acetate was abandoned in 1958 by *Hit Parade* in favor of an alpha cellulose tip, the object being higher filtration. The same year a double tip was offered by *Dual Filter*

Tareyton; this tip was designed to give high filtration of smoke vapors as well as the high filtration of smoke solids previously emphasized, and used activated charcoal in its inner filter element for this purpose.

The innovating process was greatly spurred in 1957 by a quickened public interest in high filtration. This term was generally understood to mean substantial reduction in delivered smoke solids; to achieve this, some filters were tightened, some added granular material to the bundle of cellulose acetate filaments, and some used microscopic crimping processes. High filtration — expressed in various ways — became prominent in the promotion of several filter brands, most notably *Kent, Parliament,* and *Hit Parade.* Volume increases during the half-dozen years ended with 1958 were sudden and substantial: by the end of this span *Winston* had achieved a volume of 42,300,000,000, *Kent* 36,000,000,000, *L & M* 25,900,000,000, *Viceroy* 21,000,000,000, *Marlboro* 20,700,000,000, and *Salem* 19,000,000,000. These levels compared with reported totals of 63,500,000,000, 58,000,000,000, and 47,200,000,000 for the three largest brands, the nonfilter *Camel, Pall Mall* and *Lucky Strike,* respectively.

In its rise the filter market absorbed (and enlarged) the once-limited demand for mentholated smokes. This traced to 1926, when the old Axton-Fisher company brought out its *Spud* brand. However this market, like the mouthpiece market, remained small for many years. Only Brown & Williamson's *Kool* — which offered prize coupons along with menthol flavoring during the 1930s — managed to achieve any kind of volume as a nonfilter cigarette (12,700,000,000 by 1955). In 1956, however, *Salem* combined menthol flavoring with a filter tip and began to increase. By the end of the following year the menthol-filter market included a filtered *Kool,* a filtered *Spud, Oasis* and *Newport* in addition to *Salem.* By the end of 1958 mentholated brands accounted for about one out of every six filter cigarettes smoked, one out of every twelve cigarettes of all types.

Research

Although each of the large cigarette companies now boasts an impressive research department, research in the scientific sense is relatively new to the tobacco industry. For the first quarter of the present century only the very largest firms even used the word — to mean, for all practical purposes, the kitchen craft of mixing flavoring recipes. Leaf buying was an art learned by tobacco men, not in any respect a science.

During the 20s and 30s, as individual brands grew big enough to require up to 120,000,000 pounds of good cigarette leaf in a single year, it was possible for the smartest leaf buyers to be outsmarted on the markets. Sometimes a bad-weather crop did not yield enough good leaf for all; sometimes an alert company would snap up all the low-nicotine leaf on a given market the very first day, perhaps buying two years' supply instead of one and thus forcing the competition to buy the stronger pipe grades. Brand trends were sometimes created right on the warehouse floor, since the stronger cigarette thus "created" might easily lose consumers irrespective of the influence of advertising and brand psychology.

Here was an opening for science — to define leaf characteristics (principally nicotine content) in precise chemical terms, preferably in advance of the market breaks by analyzing leaf samples gathered by scouts. This foreknowledge of the crop in various regions led to better management of buying organizations, better utilization of inventoried leaf. Analysis was extended to other tobacco constituents — sugar, essential oils, aromatics. During the 1930s, with development of the automatic smoking machine, the composition of smoke itself was investigated, and the components of smoke traced to their precursors in the leaf. Fundamental differences were found between the acid-producing Bright, the base-forming Burley and the aromatics-rich Turkish. In contrast to the flavoring formulas, always closely guarded trade secrets, much of this basic research was published in scientific journals.

As research disclosed that the dimensions of a cigarette strongly influence the composition of its smoke and therefore its taste, research was drawn

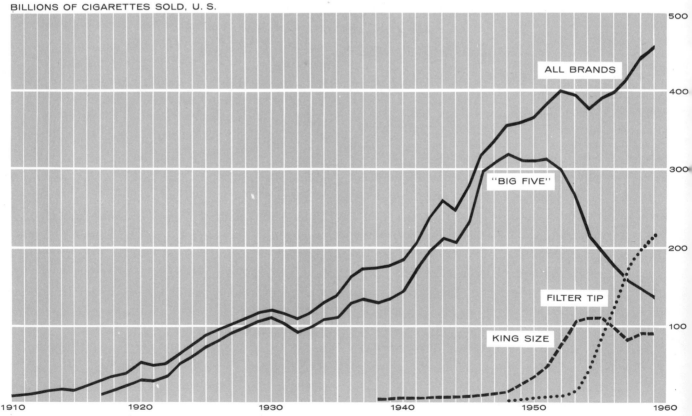

BILLIONS OF CIGARETTES SOLD, U. S.

Battle of the brands began as three-cornered fight among Camel, Lucky Strike and Chesterfield; these brands at one time accounted for 90% of cigarette sales. Entry of Old Gold in 1926 and Philip Morris in 1933 made the big brands five in number. Brand battlefield expanded as kings became big factors — Pall Mall, Herbert Tareyton, and 85mm. offshoots of Chesterfield, Philip Morris, Old Gold. In last five years filter brands have moved up—Winston, Kent, L&M, Viceroy, Marlboro, Parliament, Salem.

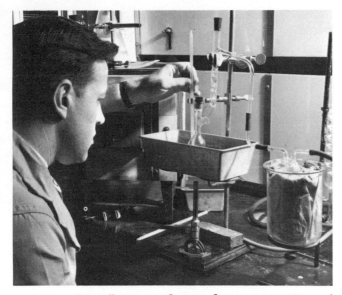

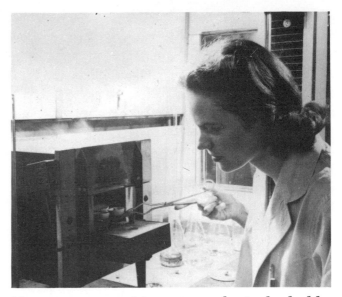

Basic or "pure" research on the composition of cigarette smoke makes no headlines but has great long-run importance in bettering product quality.

Moisture content of factory samples is checked by drying the tobacco in miniature laboratory oven. Tests of this kind are part of a regular routine.

into quality control of manufacturing. Using various tests — tests for airflow or "draw," tests for moisture content, tests for strand length, tests for loose ends, tests of cigarette paper — the laboratories made major contributions to uniformity of product.

The logical next step, developing milder and sweeter strains of tobacco, was a joint effort, shared by company researchers and the Experiment Stations of the U. S. Department of Agriculture and of the various states. This type of cooperation was begun in 1949, and by 1953 most of the large cigarette firms were participating.

The rise of the filter brands during the 50s brought research into the limelight. Findings of the "independent laboratory," confirming company research, became a prominent feature of cigarette ads. Usually such finding testified to a low level of nicotine and smoke solids (the latter inaccurately referred to as "tars"). From a scientific viewpoint, the emphasis on reduced smoke solids was anomalous, since these solids embody the taste and flavor of tobacco smoke. However, the public had been conditioned to demand reduced smoke solids, and such reduction simply responded to this demand. But different methods of smoke analysis yielded different results. As the 60s began, companies which had used nicotine and "tar" references in advertising eliminated them.

Although no amount of chemical analysis can predict what the public taste will be, research can tailor a product to what the public taste is. Variations in filter tips were manufactured in factories but conceived by white-coated Ph.D.s in the laboratories.

As in other industries, scientific maturity in tobacco was signalized by the arrival of basic research — research not aimed at an immediate or momentary competitive edge, but rather intended to surround manufacturing with a thorough knowledge of tobacco in its growing, its curing, its aging, its combustion. Beginning in 1952, radioactive tracers were used for more precise smoke analysis; one large company even purchased an interest in a nuclear reactor to further this line of inquiry. Studying an organic substance like tobacco is akin to studying the life process itself, for the constituents of leaf change constantly during aging and burning. In this sense, research on tobacco may never end. And in the practical, competitive sense research may also be endless, for every generation of consumers seems to redefine the meaning of "tobacco quality."

Pounds and dollars

There are now 600,000 farmers who grow tobacco for cash sale. The cash averages more than one billion dollars a year, and much of it goes to small farmers. In the flue-cured tobacco area allotments average about 3.4 acres; in the Burley region, about one acre.

By the time the annual billion dollars' worth of tobacco is auctioned, ordered, stemmed, aged, cut, blended, cased and packaged as cigarettes or smoking tobacco, it is worth about $1.6 billion. That value is more than doubled by the addition of Federal excise taxes, which in 1958 amounted to $1.7 billion. Costs of shipment, selling and advertising, plus the manufacturer's profit, add about $0.5 billion, lifting the value of the crop to $3.8 billion. When it is distributed to the jobbers the state taxes —about $600 million worth—are added. After allowance is made for wholesalers' and retailers' profits,

and a smidgeon of tobacco imports made from foreign crops, the retail total of tobacco products in America for 1958 was $6.5 billion. Virtually the only place where the big cigarette brands are not on sale is the bottom of the Grand Canyon.

Fresh "vegetable"

One of the problems — perhaps the most important problem — in this wide distribution of tobacco is keeping it fresh. In a country like Cuba, a natural humidor, cigars and cigarettes keep well; in the temperate zones, artificial means of moisture control are needed, and the irregularity of such care in retail outlets has prevented any wide appreciation of the flavor of fine cigars. Dried animal bladders

A beginning in automatic packaging was made with the "cup" package—layers of paper-backed foil, a paper label and, later, a glassine or cellophane

jacket. At first, laminated "cups" were preformed and cigarettes inserted by hand (above); now, the pack is machine-shaped around twenty cigarettes.

used as tobacco containers by the early Spanish sailors were equivalent to the sealed cellophane wraps introduced in 1931 for cigarettes. Tinfoil, originally used as a plug preserver, was carried over to pipe tobacco and cigarettes. Cardboard boxes, the first packing for cigarettes, were relatively durable but their contents were subject to bruising and drying-out, particularly after the first couple of cigarettes had been smoked. The foil-lined, cellophane-wrapped, flexible cup package, which minimizes this kind of damage, came into general use along with the first American blends, and most brands have used this packing since.

As important to the slender cigarette as its outer wrapping is its inner preservative or hygroscopic agent, for holding the moisture content constant. The first such agent was glycerin, which came into general use during the 1890s. Like the giant "ordering" cylinders which recondition the leaf as it comes from the markets, and the electronic moisture meters which keep tabs on the blended tobacco during its factory stages, the hygroscopic casing thwarts the rotting and withering that plagued the Tobacco Fleet shipments of colonial times.

Since the flavor of the delivered smoke is strongly influenced by the cigarette's weight, length and diameter, precision manufacture is vital to uniformity of product. Shredding machines and "making machines," both adjustable to hairline tolerances, are much the same in every factory. For exact con-

Making machine now has "cruising speed" of 1,200 cigarettes per minute, top speed over 1,500. Flow of paper and shredded tobacco is exactly regulated so that weight and dimensions of finished product will not vary. Machine prints brand name on ribbon of paper, forms, pastes, and shears tobacco tube.

259

Difficulty of preserving optimum flavor in retail outlets put the cigar at a disadvantage as against the cigarette. Latter had more protective package, *contained moisture-retaining agent lacking in the cigar. Open-box display in non-humidified showcase made for dried-out goods, especially in the North.*

trol of the weight, length and thickness of each individual cigarette, beta-ray control devices are synchronized with the makers. But along with the factory similarities there are differences. Some producers still stem the raw leaf by hand, so that after the "strip leaf" passes through the factory and its cutting knives the shreds in the finished cigarette will be long. Others use thrashing machines to separate stem from leaf, the heavier stem particles being separated out by gravity. Even the timing of stemming is varied: a "green-leaf" stemmery takes out the midrib before the strip leaf is aged in the storage sheds, while the unmodified word "stemmery" usually refers to the stemming of leaves after they have been sweated in hogshead for two or three years.

There is no universal standard for this long "to-bacco sleep," either; for some years tight storage in sealed steel-roofed sheds was the rule, but of late ventilated storage has been widely and successfully used. The most obvious variation from brand to brand is the blend formula, now as in the plug-and-licorice days the best guarded of trade secrets.

What's in a name

Thus the leaf market has been stabilized by the buying pattern of the large cigarette makers who use about 80% of each year's crop. As their brands have become national, manufacturers have been forced to buy the leaf grades that maintain consistent taste in their trademarked brands. Buying to price is not, of course, unknown. But over the years farmers came to know in a general way whose buyers went for which grades. As the "Big Five"

Vitally important is tag meter, which measures the tobacco's moisture content at every manufacturing stage. Although typical cigarette plant is itself a huge humidor, exact control of moisture level is necessary so that final product will retain flavor as long as possible through the distribution chain.

standard brands split up into king-size, filter tip and mentholated specialties during the 50s, the pattern of "buying to the trademark" was obvious not only to the leaf grower but even to the consumer. In creating new blends, a company's manufacturing department is not given to wide departures from the proven recipes which had secured its particular share of the market. Each company's various cigarette brands—even if advertised independently of each other under different trademarks — tend to comprise a recognizable "family." One maker might be geared to Burley blends in which the Burley runs to the lighter "cigarette grades" and is moderately flavored. Another's blends might run to heavy Burley, even approaching the pipe tobacco types, thickly cased. A third might keep the Burley proportion down, relying on a greater amount of Bright

for sweetness, and adding a minimum of flavoring.

Around these different formulae grew different management formulae, different approaches to the market. At one extreme, it was buying the best leaf available and spending less per 1,000 cigarettes for advertising — relying heavily on the brands' built-in ability to generate their own repeat business. At the other extreme, it was the reverse: limiting the leaf expenditure to provide a wide "factory spread" and make liberal promotional outlays possible. In launching a new brand, this posed (and still poses) a nice problem. To win business from established brands, quality of product must be maximized; on the other hand, building a new brand name, winning consumer attention against the competition of hundreds of advertisers in all media, requires a maximum of "available spread" for advertising. In the flurry of new-brand activity following World War II, the odds against new brands — even those pushed by large corporations — were amply demonstrated. More than half the new cigarettes to enter the fight for sales did not gain enough volume to justify multimillion-dollar promotion budgets, and quietly joined the ghostly limbo of minor brands two or three years after birth. Every manufacturer's price list to the trade is packed with such trademarks, once promising and now unadvertised. They hang on, maintaining a trickle of repeat business here and there, even after all promotion has ceased, for nothing is so difficult to kill outright as a tobacco brand. There are still a few smokers who want to be nonchalant and light a *Murad*, who

remember "ask Dad, he knows," and stay with *Sweet Caporal* even though neither brand has received any advertising to speak of since the 20s.

East vs. West

Tobacco has been described as filling a changeless need in a world of change. The world of change influences form and fashion; today the bulging cheek is outlandish, yesterday the cigarette was a foreign curiosity, a "paper-collar stiff." Yet the changeless need is much the same as the American Indians knew two thousand years ago. The taste of the leaf has always been of the essence, despite the contention that smoking is purely psychological, "something to keep the hands busy." The most re-

Once the standard tobacco "package" for shipping, the hogshead is now a form of storage used mainly by manufacturers. Immediately after purchase, leaf is reconditioned and factory-prized into hogsheads, each weighing about 1,000 pounds. It is then moved into storage sheds for two- or three-year "sleep."

In batteries of storage sheds outside plant towns, manufacturers maintain inventories of leaf tobacco valued at more than $2.2 billion. Proper aging of leaf requires two or more years, during which the *tobacco "sweats," undergoes chemical change. Crops from several years are kept for blending purposes. Large inventories also make it possible to average out occasional crop failures, keep blend unchanged.*

cent demonstration of this has been the filter tip fashion, which spread to nearly one-half the total cigarette market between 1951 and 1959. The leading filter brands, following the shakedown period, were those that preserved the taste of the tobacco. The same basic truth had been shown before in the failure of vegetable substitutes for tobacco to survive, and in the failure of denicotinized smokes to win more than the barest fringe of the market for tobacco products.

No doubt the precise physiological need filled by tobacco will someday be known. Up to now, its exact nature has been a puzzle to scientists. The measurable effects include an almost immediate contraction of the smaller blood vessels and a lowering of skin temperature. Professor Sidney Russ of the University of London describes this as "a slight cooling of the skin of the extremities of the body or a feeling of nervous relief." This is not, however, the whole story, for more recent research indicates that the peripheral vaso-constriction is accompanied by dilation of the larger, inner blood vessels. Thus, as Russ observes, smoking "although a stimulant, may nevertheless act as a sedative and allow the seeker after sleep to find it." Smoking as such is older than tobacco smoking; the smoking of opium (morphine) for its powerful sedative effect had become a common custom in the Far East long

Columbia postage stamp commemorates 1956 visit to U.S. by Javier Pereira, said to have been born in 1789, year Washington was inaugurated as President. Legend quotes 167-year-old Pereira's advice: Don't worry, take plenty of coffee, smoke a good cigar."

before tobacco was introduced. Hemp (marihuana) has also been smoked in various parts of the world in "reefers," or its essence taken as hashish. "If man must smoke," concludes Russ, "let it be something which in the past has left him with a good bill of health, for no such degradation of the mind or body has been attributed to smoking tobacco as can be abundantly proved among the addicts of opium and hemp."

A half-serious, half-comic echo of Russ' viewpoint arrived in New York City in 1956, in the person of the one Javier Pereira, an ancient citizen of Colombia, South America. Less than five feet in height, toothless but scrappy, Señor Pereira was alleged to be 167 years old. Although public interest in his long life was a transitory, newspaper-nourished phenomenon, Pereira managed to communicate his secret for longevity before being whisked back to his native South America village: "Don't worry; take plenty of coffee; and smoke a good cigar." It was appropriate advice from a descendant of the jungle Indians who may have rolled the first cigars from *Nicotiana tabacum.*

The use of incense to produce fragrant smoke is as old as civilization; among the gifts brought by the Three Wise Men to Bethlehem were frankincense and myrrh. In ancient Greece, long before "Turkish" tobacco was grown there, the smoke of burning laurel enveloped the prophetess of Delphi, and the smoke of coltsfoot was used as a medicine. (In Britain, centuries afterward, coltsfoot was used for this purpose and also as an adulterant of pipe tobacco). Herodotus wrote of the scattering of hemp-seeds on hot stones to produce an intoxicating smoke which was especially appreciated after dinner. It seems probable that smoking for pleasure was more characteristic of the older East, while smoke as a medicine more typical of the "scientific" civilizations of the West. This cultural characteristic was illustrated by the sixteenth-century European emphasis on tobacco as a cure-all when it was first introduced from the New World.

One world

If any proof of the universality of smoking were needed, it was given in 1954 when ashtrays were set around the tables of the Security Council in the United Nations building. "Apparently," interpreted the New York Times, "United Nations officialdom could no longer hold out against delegates who felt that ambassadorial rank should at least carry with it the right to put match to cigarette." More significant than this concession to the *herbe de l'ambassadeur* was the recognition that the common man's right to a good cigarette transcends ideological differences. Later the same year this roundup of Communist newspaper items was dispatched from Vienna:

> Government-operated tobacco plants in Poland, Hungary, Bulgaria and Rumania have come under official fire for marketing smokes adulterated with straw, dirt, stones and worse.
>
> Polish cigarettes are often so dry and loosely packed that they flare up like a fuse and scorch the smoker's lips, Warsaw newspapers reported.
>
> The Bulgarian Communist publication Narona Tribuna said that workers in many districts were sold cigarettes coated with mold. Budapest's Magyar Nemzet said that one irate customer went to a state tobacco factory and forced the director to smoke one of his cigarettes. The director "turned green" and suffered a choking spell, the newspaper added.

In their taste for tobacco, free men and slaves are not far apart; in manufacture, the two have been worlds apart, as the experience of Americans themselves suggests.

In point of distance, it is only 19 miles from Jamestown to Yorktown. And in point of tobacco progress, it was not far from the Jamestown settlement to the Yorktown surrender even though 175 years separated the two events. Tobacco cultivation did not advance; rather, it was extended. No manufacture arose, no significant improvements were made in the quality of leaf. Nor did America as a whole develop greatly during the colonial years — it merely enlarged, mile by mile, village by village, farm by farm.

But the next 175 years were quite different. The spark of independence set off chain reactions in manufacturing, agriculture, manners and tastes. Ultimately, it fired America to the greatest productive power and the highest standard of living known to mankind. The emergence of the world's leading tobacco industry is only a part of that transformation. But so precisely does it parallel the emergence of the United States that the story of Americans and tobacco is more than an industrial chronicle. It is a lesson in social science, in economics, in history; it is, in its own way, a testament of freedom.

Evolution of the American Cigarette

1492 Columbus reaches West Indies, finds natives smoking tobacco rolls.

1518 Juan de Grijalva lands in Yucatan, observes cigarette smoking by natives.

1519 Cortez conquers Aztec capitol, finds Mexican natives smoking perfumed reed cigarettes.

1530 Bernardino de Sahagún, missionary in Mexico, distinguishes between sweet commercial tobacco (*Nicotiana tabacum*) and coarse *Nicotiana rustica*.

1534 "Tall tobacco" — sweet, broadleaved *Nicotiana tabacum* — transplanted from Central American mainland to Cuba and Santo Domingo.

1548 Portuguese cultivate tobacco in Brazil for commercial export.

1556 Thevet transplants *Nicotiana tabacum* from Brazil to France, describes tobacco as a creature comfort.

1560 Jean Nicot sends *Nicotiana rustica* plants from Lisbon to Paris court, describes tobacco as panacea.

1564 Sir John Hawkins and/or his crew probably introduce pipe smoking into England.

1612 John Rolfe tries Latin American seed at Jamestown, raises first commerical crop of "tall tobacco" (*Nicotiana tabacum*) in what is now the U. S.

1614 Spain channels all tobacco exports from her New World colonies to Seville; Virginia colony enters world tobacco market under English protection.

1633 Connecticut settled; tobacco crop raised at Windsor shortly thereafter.

1634 Maryland settled by Calverts under land grant for the "planting of tobacco."

1639 Governor Kieft bans smoking in New Amsterdam (New York); citizens ignore edict.

1676 Heavy taxes levied in tobacco by Virginia Governor Berkeley lead to Bacon's Rebellion, a foretaste of American Revolution.

1713 Inspection regulations passed to keep up standards of Virginia leaf exports (not effective until 1730).

1730 First American tobacco factories begun in Virginia — small snuff mills.

1750 Gilbert Stuart builds snuff mill in Rhode Island, ships his products in dried animal bladders.

1762 Colonel Israel Putnam returns to New England from Cuban campaign with three donkey-loads of Havana cigars.

1780 "Tobacco War" waged by Lord Cornwallis in
-81 Virginia to destroy basis of America's credit abroad.

1781 Thomas Jefferson suggests tobacco cultivation in the "western country on the Mississippi."

1788 Spanish New Orleans opened for export of tobacco by Americans in Mississippi valley.

1794 Congress levies tax on snuff but leaves smoking and chewing tobacco untaxed.

1805 Lewis and Clark explore Northwest, using gifts of tobacco as "life insurance."

1810 Cuban cigar-roller brought to Suffield, Connecticut to train local workers.

1820 American traders open the Santa Fe trail, find ladies of that city smoking "seegaritos."

1832 Tuck patents curing method for Virginia leaf.

1839 Slade "yallercure" in North Carolina — presages flue-cured Bright tobacco.

1843 French monopoly begins manufacture of cigarettes, previously a beggar's smoke in Spain.

1854 Cigarettes with Turkish tobacco used in Crimea
-56 by Russian, Turkish, French and British troops. Soldiers bring vogue back to London.

1864 White Burley first cultivated in Ohio Valley; highly absorbent new leaf proves ideal for sweetened chewing tobacco.

1865 Soldiers of Union and Confederate armies sample granulated flue-cured Bright tobacco at Durham's Station, North Carolina. National demand for bagged Bright tobacco grows; pipe smoking increases.

1865 Demand for exotic Turkish cigarettes grows in
-70 New York City; skilled European rollers imported by New York tobacco shops.

1883 Bonsack cigarette machine perfected in Durham.

1890 Peak of chewing tobacco consumption in U. S., three pounds per capita.

1907 Peak of cigar consumption in U.S., 86 per capita.

1910 Peak of smoking tobacco consumption in U.S., 1.75 pounds per capita. Sweetened Burley as well as Bright, Maryland and Turkish tobacco used in pipe blends.

1913 American blended cigarette evolved from pipe blends.

1921 Cigarette becomes leading form of tobacco consumption.

1939 Introduction of 85 millimeter "king size" cigarette marks first significant change from the regular or 70 millimeter size.

1952 Filter tip cigarettes begin to increase in popularity.

1955 Reconstituted tobacco leaf recognized as a technological improvement by Department of Agriculture. Used first in cigar binder, then in cigarette blends.

1958 Sales of tobacco products approximate $6.5 billion, of which cigarettes account for seven-eighths. Retail total includes about $2.5 billion in federal, state and municipal taxes.

References

Although many "histories of smoking" have been published over the years, the number of well-documented sources is small. Most of these concentrate on a special aspect of the tobacco story:

Discovery of tobacco in the western hemisphere — Dickson, S. A., "Panacea or Precious Bane," The New York Public Library, New York, N. Y., 1954

Development of the continental market — Mac-Innes, C. M., "The Early English Tobacco Trade," Kegan Paul, Trench, Trubner & Co., Ltd., London, 1926

Emergence of the American manufacturing industry before the War Between the States — Robert, J. C., "The Tobacco Kingdom," Duke University Press, Durham, North Carolina, 1938

Rise of Bright Tobacco in Virginia and North Carolina after the War Between the States — Tilley, N. M., "The Bright-Tobacco Industry," University of North Carolina Press, Chapel Hill, North Carolina, 1948

Rise of the cigarette industry — Tennant, R. A., "The American Cigarette Industry," Yale University Press, New Haven, Conn., 1950

For a complete summary of current statistics covering most phases of the industry, the "Annual Report on Tobacco Statistics" is published each spring by the Agricultural Marketing Service, U. S. Department of Agriculture, Washington, D. C. This agency also issues a quarterly review entitled "The Tobacco Situation."

The best comprehensive histories of tobacco are:

Brooks, J. E., "The Mighty Leaf," Little, Brown and Company, Boston, 1952

Robert, J. C., "The Story of Tobacco in America," Alfred A. Knopf, New York, N. Y., 1949

The best-known collection of tobacco materials has been annotated in Brooks, J. E., "Tobacco, Its History Illustrated by the Books, Manuscripts and Engravings in the Library of George Arents, Jr.," Rosenbach, New York, N. Y., 1937-1943.

An individual company history was published in 1954 by The American Tobacco Company, New York, N. Y., entitled "Sold American!"

For the student desirous of tracing the year-by-year progress of a particular cigarette brand or company, the best factual source is the series of annual industry surveys published each December by Printers Ink Magazine, New York. This series began in 1941, and includes estimates of unit sales by brand.

Selected bibliography:

Anderson, P. J., "Growing Tobacco in Connecticut," Bulletin 564, Connecticut Agricultural Experiment Station, New Haven, Conn., 1953.

Apperson, G. L., "The Social History of Smoking," Putnam, New York, N. Y., 1916

Billings, E. R., "Tobacco, its Culture, Manufacture and Use," American Publishing Company, Hartford, Conn., 1875

Boyd, W. K., "The Story of Durham," Duke University Press, Durham, N. C., 1927

Connorton, J. W., "Tobacco Brand Directory of the United States," Chicago, Ill., 1885, 1886-87, 1903

Corti, E., "A History of Smoking" (trans. Paul England), Harcourt, Brace, New York, N. Y., 1932

Cox, R., "Competition in the American Tobacco Industry, 1911-1932," Columbia University Press, New York, N. Y., 1933

DeVoto, B. (ed.), "The Journals of Lewis and Clark," Houghton Mifflin Company, Boston, 1953

Dodge, J. R., "Statistics of Manufactures of Tobacco and of its Commercial Distribution, Exportation, and Prices," Tenth Census, 1880, III, 881-950

Dowdey, C., "The Great Plantation," Rinehart, New York, N. Y., 1957

Fisher, R. L., "The Odyssey of Tobacco," The Prospect Press, Litchfield, Conn., 1939

Gage, C. E., "American Tobacco Types, Uses, and Markets," Circular No. 249, U. S. Department of Agriculture, Washington, D. C., 1942

Gage, C. E., "Historical Factors Affecting American Tobacco Types and Uses and the Evolution of the Auction Market," Agricultural History 11:43-57 (January, 1937)

Gottsegen, J. J., "Tobacco," Pitman, New York, N. Y., 1940

Hamilton, A. E., "This Smoking World," Century, New York, N. Y., 1927

Horgan, P., "The Centuries of Santa Fe," E. P. Dutton, New York, N. Y., 1956

Jenkins, J. W., "James B. Duke," George H. Doran Co., New York, N. Y., 1927

Killebrew, J. B., "Report on the Culture and Curing of Tobacco in the United States," Tenth Census, 1880, III, 583-880

Lavender, D., "Bent's Fort," Doubleday, Garden City, N. Y., 1954

McDonald, A. F., "The History of Tobacco Production in Connecticut," Yale University Press, 1936

Middleton, A. P., "Tobacco Coast," The Mariners Museum, Newport News, Va., 1953

Morton, L., "Robert Carter of Nomini Hall," Colonial Williamsburg, Inc., Williamsburg, Va., 1945

Nicholls, W. H., "Price Policies in the Cigarette Industry," The Vanderbilt University Press, Nashville, 1951

Northrop, E., "Science Looks at Smoking," Coward-McCann, New York, N. Y., 1957

Nussbaum, F. L., "American Tobacco and French Politics, 1783-1789," Political Science Quarterly, Vol. XI No. 4 (December, 1925)

Ortiz, F., "Cuban Counterpoint: Tobacco and Sugar," Alfred A. Knopf, New York, N. Y., 1947

Penn, W. A., "The Soverane Herb," Grant Richards, London, 1901

Ross A., "The Fur Hunters of the Far West," University of Oklahoma Press, Norman, Okla., 1956

Russ, S., "Smoking and Its Effects," Hutchinson's, London, 1955

Spinden, H. J., "Tobacco is American," The New York Public Library, New York, N. Y., 1950

Stoughton, J. A., "A Corner Stone of Colonial Commerce," Little Brown and Company, Boston, 1911

Werner, C. A., "Tobaccoland," The Tobacco Leaf Publishing Company, New York, 1922

Willison, G. F., "Behold Virginia!" Harcourt, Brace, New York, N. Y., 1952

Winkler, J. K., "Tobacco Tycoon," Random House, New York, N. Y., 1942

Wroth, L. C., "Tobacco or Codfish," The New York Public Library, New York, N. Y., 1954

Young, W. W., "The Story of the Cigarette," Appleton, New York, N. Y., 1916

Picture credits

The American Tobacco Company — 8 top, 41, 98(4), 99(4), 13, 131 left, 145, 153 right, 162, 163, 164, 165 bottom, 177, 185, 196 top, 204, 206, 212(4), 213, 221, 226-227 top, 228, 232, 234(4), 235(3), 239, 251 right, 254, 255, 257(2), 259, 261, 262, 263.

Arents Collection, New York Public Library — 9, 10, 11(2), 12, 13, 14, 15, 18, 19(4), 20(2), 23, 24 bottom, 27, 28, 30, 31, 32-33, 35(2), 37 left, 38, 39, 43, 46, 53, 54(2), 55, 62(2), 79, 87, 105, 118, 124, 216.

Bella Landauer Collection, New York Historical Society — 96, 97, 106, 107(2), 131 right, 133, 147, 149, 157, 168, 170, 171, 172, 174, 176(2), 183, 191(2), 192, 193, 207, 208(2), 209(2), 217.

Bettman Archive — 16 right, 34, 37 right, 39, 51 bottom, 61, 63, 65 bottom, 66, 75, 120, 121, 148, 189, 195, 199 center, 205 top, 210, 211 top, 250 right.

Brown Brothers — 17 bottom, 26, 29, 47, 48, 51 top, 60, 64 left, 82, 109, 110, 115, 122(2), 136, 144, 165 top, 180, 198, 199 left, 199 right, 201 bottom, 202 right, 203, 205 bottom, 214 left, 215(2), 230, 246 left, 258, 260.

Brown & Williamson Tobacco Company — 247.

Culver Service — 7, 8 bottom, 16 left, 17 top, 24 top, 25, 36, 49, 52, 65 top, 68, 69, 73, 74, 77, 78, 81, 83, 86, 90(2), 91, 94, 103, 108, 114(2), 116, 119, 125, 130, 143, 159, 160(2), 161, 169, 173, 182, 184 center, 187, 196 bottom, 197 top, 200, 201 top, 202 left, 214 right, 226 bottom (2), 236(2), 242, 246 right, 250 left, 251 left.

Jamestown-Williamsburg-Yorktown National Celebration Commission — 45.

Liggett & Myers Tobacco Company — 140, 237 top.

National Park Service — 50.

P. Lorillard Company — 190 top, 194(3), 252.

Philip Morris, Inc. — 211 bottom, 241.

R. J. Reynolds Tobacco Company — 184 right, 224, 225.

Sol Lesser Productions — 21.

Standard Oil Company (New Jersey) — 5, 111, 181, 231, 265.

Underwood — 222.

Virginia State Chamber of Commerce — 44, 70, 71, 76, 229, 253.

Wide World Photos — 64 right, 237 bottom, 243.

Index